MW00862147

THE SOCIAL
MEANINGS
OF MONEY
AND PROPERTY

To MacKenzie Richardson Doyle

KENNETH O. DOYLE

THE SOCIAL MEANINGS OF MONEY AND PROPERTY

In Search of a Talisman

SAGE Publications
International Educational and Professional Publisher
Thousand Oaks   London   New Delhi

Copyright © 1999 by Sage Publications, Inc.

All rights reserved. No part of this book may be reproduced or utilized in any form or by any means, electronic or mechanical, including photocopying, recording, or by any information storage and retrieval system, without permission in writing from the publisher.

For information:

SAGE Publications, Inc.
2455 Teller Road
Thousand Oaks, California 91320
E-mail: order@sagepub.com

SAGE Publications Ltd.
6 Bonhill Street
London EC2A 4PU
United Kingdom

SAGE Publications India Pvt. Ltd.
M-32 Market
Greater Kailash I
New Delhi 110 048 India

Printed in the United States of America

Library of Congress Cataloging-in-Publication Data

Doyle, Kenneth O.
    The social meanings of money and property: In search of a
talisman / by Kenneth O. Doyle.
        p.   cm.
    Includes bibliographical references and index.
    ISBN 0-7619-0208-2 (acid-free paper)
    ISBN 0-7619-0209-0 (pbk.: acid-free paper)
    1. Money—Psychological aspects.   2. Property—Psychological
aspects.   I. Title.
    HG222.3 .D69   1998
    332.4′01′9—dc21   98-40185

99 00 01 02 03 04 05 7 6 5 4 3 2 1

Acquiring Editor:	Peter Labella
Editorial Assistant:	Renée Piernot
Production Editor:	Diana E. Axelsen
Editorial Assistant:	Nevair Kabakian
Designer/Typesetter:	Rose Tylak/Lynn Miyata
Cover Designer:	Ravi Balasuriya

Contents

List of Tables and Figures

Preface

Writing a book is like going to confession: Nearly every chapter reveals some intimate feature of the author's life. Here, the chapter on law is surely the result of my having grown up in a family of Irish lawyers and judges, listening, long before television, to my father's nearly nightly declamations on jurisprudence, learning from those an abiding respect for the science (if not always the practice) of law. The chapters on philosophy and religion come directly from my experiences as a young monk, especially at the Gregorian University in Rome. In particular, Professor Filippo Selvaggi's dialectical study of the history of ideas and Professor Bernard Lonergan's principle of transculturality excited my interest in similarities and differences between and within cultures. This curiosity about patterns of culture was strengthened by additional experiences as diverse as following (at different times!) the monastic life and married life; living in the suburbs and in the inner city; working on an Indian reservation; practicing financial planning with urban, suburban, and rural families and business owners; writing for and consulting with the American Institute of Certified Public Accountants, the International Association of Financial Planners, and other financial advising and counseling organizations; and collaborating with academic colleagues in various parts of Europe and Asia, most recently, the Republic of Georgia and the People's Republic of China.

My interest in psychometrics, psychoanalysis, and the neurophysiology of temperament comes directly from my experience as a graduate student (more than a few years ago) in the Department of Psychology at the University of Minnesota, particularly under the tutelage of Professors John Darley, Marvin

Dunnette, Auke Tellegen, Paul Meehl, David Lykken, and David Weiss. Under their influence I wound up, oddly enough, a psychometric researcher with an interest in the interaction of neurophysiology, psychoanalysis, and social psychology (Doyle, 1972). For their contribution to this inclination, I am truly grateful.

My emphasis on the *Quaternary* flows from an unlikely source for an academic psychologist: sales training. Restless after ten years as a psychometric researcher, I took a sabbatical leave in 1981-1982 to join a financial planning firm with which I had been familiar for quite a long time. My first shock came early, when management dispatched me to a sales-training seminar. I was mortified. After all, I had a Ph.D. in psychology and a therapist's license—what could some sales trainer teach me? What he could teach me, and did, was "social styles," in a quaternary form that reminded me of the patterns Professor Selvaggi had talked about. Even more important, he taught me to see how the quadrants work in relationships between husbands and wives, parents and children, and business associates, as well as between sales agents and prospects.

At the end of my sabbatical year I was simply too attracted by the complexity, earthy realism, and potential rewards of the financial world to give it up completely, yet too drawn to variety, intellectual stimulation, and financial security to leave the Academy, so I divided my professional life between the two. It was my friend and business associate Al Rashid who planted the seed for an integration of psychology and money. Patiently listening to yet another of my lamentations about the fragmentation in my life—finance in the morning, psychology in the afternoon—he said simply, "You could combine them." Many other good friends and colleagues at Strommen and Associates and Swenson Anderson Associates fertilized that seed, especially Bob Tufford, Dave Bosselmann, and David Williams.

My colleague, mentor, and "big sister," Beth Wales, led me to many clinical insights about money and family, and first called money a *talisman*. She, and Bill Wells, Irv Fang, Bill McKeachie, Tom Garman, Tom Crump, Matt Lamb, Paul Rosenblatt, Victoria Secunda, John Merrill, Phil Tichenor, Jin Wulun, Wang Shuren, Shota Gurchumelidze, and Don Gillmor, not only endured my chatter about this effort but read every page of one draft or another, goading me always to tighten my thinking, clarify my expression, and defend my assertions.

Thanks also to the people at Sage Publications who helped bring this project to light. First and foremost, to George McCune—*in pace requiescat*—and Sara Miller McCune, who first urged me to write this book; to Linda

Klein, who introduced me to the McCunes and provided lasting encouragement; to Harry Briggs and Peter Labella, who guided me along the way; to Diana Axelsen, who, as senior midwife in what we have come to call the "birthing process," dealt personably and effectively with the demands of this anxious father; and to Kate Peterson, copy editor *par exellence,* who kept my propensity for disarray under control without making me feel boxed in. But however much I might want to share with all these people the responsibility for my errors, and for my more controversial assertions, for all of those I have only myself to blame.

Speaking of controversy, I want to preview a few matters that will surely rub some people the wrong way. The first is my practice of emphasizing differences between groups, and downplaying differences within. The reason I do this is that I'm trying to stimulate research, which requires advancing hypotheses simple and sharp enough that people can test them rigorously. So I need to cut through some of the murkiness of real life, sacrifice some of the subtlety. The price of rigor is making life seem simpler than it really is.

The second potentially controversial matter is that I connect particular propensities with certain groups of people, for example, acquisitiveness with people of European descent. In doing so I not only concentrate on differences between groups, but I connect those patterns with some of today's most sensitive topics: gender, ethnicity, and race. This comes dangerously close to stereotyping, which some people say is serious sin. On the contrary, I contend that the evil in stereotyping is not the creation of the generalized or abstracted image, because that's our natural way of dealing with a complex world; rather, the evil lies in the malevolent use of that image. If I use a generalization (stereotype) to deprive particular kinds of people of jobs without getting to know them as individuals, it is my use of the image that is evil, not the image itself. For I can just as easily use that image to understand and even celebrate different people's identities—which is precisely what I am attempting to do in this book.

Similarly, my attention to European acquisitiveness does not mean that I don't see other propensities in people of European descent, expressiveness, for example, or orderliness or affiliativeness. Most individuals and groups are a dynamic mix of inclinations, though in every mix one or two generally stand out. Again for the sake of building theory, I need to concentrate on the predominant.

I also suspect that my emphasis on the biological basis of attitudes and values will excite some passions, for biology implies heritability, heritability implies determinism, and determinism suggests all manner of real and imagined mischief. My view is that, as everywhere else in the nature-nurture controversy, the extremes repel. Whether for motives good or motives ill, we cannot dismiss biology any longer, as so many of us did in the 1960s and 1970s and some are still trying to do in the 1990s. There is simply too much information now about the anatomical and chemical basis of personality. But neither are there grounds for becoming biologically fatalistic—identical twins reared apart do not think, feel, and behave in exactly the same way. The best estimate these days seems to be that slightly more than half of human variability is explained by biology (nature), slightly less by environment (nurture); so we still have plenty of room for choice. I understand the pain and fear and compassion that motivates some socially active students and colleagues to resist the introduction of biological phenomena into social science. With due respect, I suggest that a better use of time and energy would be to work with biological and evolutionary psychologists to spell out the interplay of genes and will, rather than fight the incoming tide of biopsychological data.

One of the most difficult things about writing a book like this is knowing when to stop. Nearly every paragraph could be doubled or tripled, nearly every idea expanded in many directions. Did I pay enough attention to the Jewish contribution? The Egyptian? The Arabic? What about other periods of history, for example, feudalism? And other disciplines, for example, linguistics and social geography? My best reply is that I think I have described enough ideas and experiences, I hope, that interested readers will be able to fill in where I have left gaps, to pick up where I leave off. Along with these errors of omission, there are surely errors of commission. I want to acknowledge the likelihood that, despite my best efforts to the contrary, this book contains at least its share of interpretative and even factual errors. Among the joys of multidisciplinary work is the enormous satisfaction that comes when disparate elements fall into place; among the sorrows is the certainty that through ignorance or accident, you will mislead your readers, and embarrass yourself. Finally, to everyone on whose work this book is built, on whose strong shoulders this work stands, my most sincere respect and gratitude.

June 19, 1998

This by his Name I swear, whose sacred Lore
First to Mankind explained the Mystick *four,*
Source of Eternal Nature and Almighty Pow'r.

—Pythagoras, Golden Verses

PART I

PROSPECTUS

In which I define my niche, spell out my intentions,
and offer a precis of what is to come.

Chapter 1

Exchange Versus Communication

W̶hat could be simpler? You have tomatoes and I have potatoes, and you
want what I have and I want what you have. If you're willing to give
up[1] some of your tomatoes and I'm willing to give up some of my potatoes,
we can simply exchange our produce[2] and go home happy.[3]

Down the ages and around the world, exchanges like this, barter[4] exchanges, have involved virtually anything buyers wanted and sellers were
willing to give up and upon the values of which people could agree—sheep,
for example, or silver, spices, slaves, spouses, and (of course) sex.

Suppose I were a shepherd and my wealth were in sheep. As life becomes
more sophisticated, barter grows progressively less satisfactory. First, it
proves inconvenient to take my keep of sheep to the theater, to the beach, or
on a business trip. Second, no matter where I hold my herd, it will be at risk
from predators and pestilence. Third, as the variety of available goods and
services broadens and my desires blossom accordingly, it becomes more and
more difficult to find someone who will accept my sheep in exchange for
what she or he purveys. Fourth, it becomes inefficient at best (and otherwise
unappealing) to carve out a portion of my wealth whenever what I want is
worth much less than one complete animal. Finally, it becomes clear quickly
that some sheep (to say nothing of some spices and some spouses) are more
desirable than others and should therefore figure differently in the exchange.

One solution might be tokens, like seashells, or pebbles, or clay or metal
disks. These would surely be more portable, durable, and divisible[5] than my
sheep, and probably more aesthetically appealing. But they might not be so
widely acceptable: A merchant in Madagascar, or even one in the next village
or just down the street, might value my tokens differently than I do, or might
not value them at all. Moreover, the supply of tokens might increase or
decrease, leaving me with a deflated or inflated store of wealth. Depending
on what token I happen to be using, I might even find that the village villain
is minting his own and diminishing the value of mine.

3

For better or worse, as my need for a dependable instrument of exchange increases, I am likely to find myself more and more under the sway of some commercial or political power that can standardize these tokens, control their supply, and protect their authenticity. This mogul or monarch might manufacture medallions that contain a specified measure of something we all value and upon the value of which we can agree, like copper or silver or gold. Or, if an abstract thinker with a cooperative constituency, she or he might mint medals that do not contain but merely represent specified amounts of those valued commodities. It is when these tokens become standardized that we begin to call them *money*. More precisely, they are coins, or specie. They are "full-bodied" if they contain their total value of the supporting commodity: for example, twenty dollars' worth of gold.

I should find these coins[6] quite suitable for everyday needs. But for extraordinary needs, for example, major purchases or commercial transactions, coins could quickly remind me of sheep—they would be inconvenient to cart around in large quantity. Paper money solves the convenience problem; the liquidity problem too, as long as you and I are both confident that the slips of paper we exchange are backed by copper, silver, gold, or some dependable promise thereof.

But I will quickly discover that paper money, like sheep, is vulnerable to the elements and villains. It can decompose or mysteriously disappear, and it can surely be stolen. What I need is some secure institution, call it a "bank," with which I can make a contract: You keep my money safe till I need it; in return, you can use it, while you have it, in that special way that profits you and creates new money[7] in the process.

This is a good and lasting system, though not without its faults. On the credit side, I get the benefit of safe and convenient money, and the bank gets the benefit of money with which it can manufacture more. On the debit side, the bank, as business grows, will eventually find its paper-processing (and people-pleasing) costs oppressive, and I will discover that the farther and wider I roam from home, the more difficult it will be to convince a storekeeper that my signature is as good as gold.

What would help would be a guarantee of my solvency and trustworthiness, perhaps in convenient, wallet-sized plastic card form.[8] Whether built on credit or debt, whether inert or "intelligent," these plastic cards could, at least in theory, create a nearly cashless society. If the entrepreneur is sufficiently inventive, these cards could interact in astonishing ways with computer terminals around the world. Only by eliminating the card itself in favor of exclusively electronic exchange (e.g., Internet banking) could money and wealth become more abstract (see Weatherford, 1997).

These intermediary devices—tokens, coins, paper money, plastic money, electronic money, and the like—facilitate *giving and taking* and *saving and spending,* the fundamental transactions through which we acquire, manage, and distribute things. Throughout this book, we shall talk about these devices—which economists call "money"—and about the things money can buy—which they call "property," or, more inclusively, "wealth." However, we shall talk about money and property (wealth) not as economic exchange but as social exchange, or communication (Babe, 1995; Bernard, 1996; Leiss, Kline, & Jhally, 1986).

BEYOND ECONOMICS

Most of us engage in economic exchange on a regular basis. We exchange work for compensation, taxes for services, dues for membership, board for bed. But we engage in social exchange even more frequently, and often with greater emotional involvement. Day in and day out, most of us use money and property *to send messages to one another.*

Some of this communication is simple and direct, like a greeting card to wish a happy birthday. Some is coded, or symbolic: a red rose for passion, a white one for condolence (Doyle, Hanchek, & McGrew, 1994). And some is shrouded, and very, very personal. It is the shrouded and personal meanings of money and property that are the principal subject of this book.

If I observe, for example, that my portfolio is bigger than yours, I may consciously or unconsciously interpret this as a sign that I am stronger than you, more attractive, or in some other fashion better. But the reason the size of my portfolio is important to me is not necessarily that I can do more with it for the benefit of my friends, family, and self, or for society in general; the reason may be that the larger it is, the less impotent I feel, the less frightened.

If I see that yours is bigger than mine, I may feel as though I am personally deficient in some important way. And if I see that you don't have a portfolio at all, I may feel that you are not a force with which I need to reckon. In all these cases, the fundamental motivation is fear.

On the other hand, you might find my concern with the size of my portfolio distasteful, even offensive. You might dislike it not because you think I will necessarily use the money and property to do evil; you may simply have come to believe that money is tawdry and to fear that the more I cleave to money, the more likely I am to abandon you. In your eyes, my interest in money may be a form of betrayal, or adultery.

If I argue that because my portfolio is bigger than most other people's, I deserve privileges of which less moneyed people aren't worthy, I may be saying that I need still more "badges of competence," perhaps an infinity of them, to keep my fear under control. If you, on the other hand, insist that the privileges should go rather to the truly poor, that the very presence of a portfolio makes me unworthy of social esteem or preference, you may be saying that my potency stirs up an equally profound fear in you. I may need all the gold of Croesus to shore up my fearful ego; you may need to strip yourself barer than bare to subjugate your own scary inclination toward oppression. We may send these messages to each other on a continual basis, and with enormous intensity. Yet neither of us may ever understand what the other is trying to say, nor understand ourselves.

In the chapters that follow, I will propose that the key to decoding the meanings of money and property is to identify the salient threat against which we use money and property as protection. First, especially for readers of technical bent, I will briefly review earlier thinking.

PRIOR CONCEPTIONS

Of the social scientists who became interested in the world of money and property, there were and are two opposing camps. The first is comprised mostly of economists (though not all of them), along with some sociologists and anthropologists who were especially interested in economic systems; the second is made up mostly of sociologists, anthropologists, and psychologists (not all) and the occasional maverick economist.

Briefly stated, the mainstream economists and economic sociologists and anthropologists paid homage to *Homo oeconomicus*, Economic man, John Stuart Mill's totally rational construct whose only goal is to acquire wealth in the most efficient way and whose only need is unbiased information about how to do so; they committed themselves to reducing income and consumption to tidy formulas, the simpler the better, and to shunning the emotional excursions of those less enlightened than themselves. The students of psychology and communication, on the other hand, preferred a juicier, more complete creature, far harder to tame, frothing with all the irrationality and emotionality of which the human species is capable.

The Economic Thrust

Though scholars in both camps were descendants of Jeremy Bentham, the English philosopher who had identified pleasure and pain as the two "masters of mankind," economists and psychologists grew to have little else in common. The economic group was and still is a formidable force, inspired by Mill and led by luminaries like Adam Smith, Stanley Jevons, John Maynard Keynes, Joseph Schumpeter, and Milton Friedman, all in economics; Georg Simmel and James Coleman in sociology; and Thomas Crump in anthropology. Their forte was and still is rigor, though (outsiders might say) at the cost of realism, and their centerpiece, "rational choice theory," a.k.a. utility theory: People make reasoned choices to maximize their overall well-being, or "utility." To this day, rational choice theory holds sway among economists and other students of Economic man (e.g., Coleman & Fararo, 1992).

Despite their commitment to rigor, most if not all of these scholars left the door open to occasional trysts[9] with members of the other group. If this dalliance did not lead to marriage, it at least begat a more vital focus for economic formulas than would otherwise have been the case.

For example, although his *Wealth of Nations* (1776/1953) would become the Bible for those who clung to the theology of Economic man, Adam Smith himself had mused in his earlier *Theory of Moral Sentiments* (1753/1976) about a distinctly psychological motive, the "drive for esteem":

> The rich man glories in his riches, because he feels that they naturally draw upon him the attention of the world. . . . At the thought of this, his heart seems to swell and dilate itself within him, and he is fonder of his wealth, upon this account, than for all the other advantages it procures him. (pp. 50-51)

He also believed that what keeps self-interest from becoming excessive and capitalism from becoming oppressive is a proper balance between Moral man's sympathy (in *Theory of Moral Sentiments*) and Economic man's competitiveness (in *Wealth of Nations*).

But Smith did not build these notions into his economic theories; rather, he left it to his disciples either to assume, by default, that this motivation was constant across individuals or to refine and extend his work to include this "irrational" drive. Most of his followers "simply presumed that people wanted the goods that the nation produced and that in their own self-interest they acted in ways to get them" (Finn, 1992, p. 660).

Stanley Jevons, more the utilitarian[10] than even Smith, shifted the goal of economics from the acquisition of narrowly defined *wealth* to the attainment of a more general *welfare*.[11] Jevons (1931) opened the door (just a crack) to the softer side of money when he introduced into his utility equation a degree of Epicurean (and Benthamian) subjectivity: "The object of Economy is to produce happiness by producing *pleasure,* as it were, at the lowest cost of *pain*" (p. 27; quoted in Finn, 1992, p. 661, emphasis added). By expanding wealth to include emotional satisfaction, he enabled subsequent theorists to include progressively more alien "moral calculations" in utility theory.

John Maynard Keynes, whose law of diminishing marginal utilities[12] helped establish economics as a modern social science, should be among the last to admit that any psychological "wanderings"—his word—might deserve a place in a theory of saving and spending. Yet halfway through his *General Theory of Employment, Interest and Money* (1936), Keynes described what psychologists Murray (1938) and McClelland (1961) would later call "need achievement":

> If human nature felt no temptation to take a chance, no satisfaction (profit apart) in constructing a factory, a railway, a mine or a farm, there might not be much investment merely as a result of cold calculation.
>
>   Most . . . of our decisions to do something positive . . . can only be taken as a result of . . . the spontaneous urge to action rather than inaction—and not as the outcome of a weighted average of quantitative benefits multiplied by quantitative probabilities. (Keynes, 1936, p. 161)

Joseph Schumpeter (1954/1994), economic historian *par excellence,* affirmed the importance of social and psychological considerations even though he insisted on their exercise outside the confines of the calisthenic logic of true economic science:

> Most of us would find it extremely difficult or at least highly inconvenient to avoid entirely all reference to motives, expectations, comparative estimates of present and future satisfactions, and the like, however fervently we might hope for an economic theory that would use nothing but statistically observable facts. (p. 1059)

In addition, Schumpeter's editor ascribes to Schumpeter the position that "so-called rational ends are not what motivate human behavior, but rather that the fundamental volition arises from impulses which appear from the economic (rational) viewpoint to be nonrational or irrational" (Sweezy's Introduction in Schumpeter, 1951, p. vii).

Milton Friedman, in his "theory of permanent income," stretched utility theory out of the present moment and into the more general recognition that rational consumers make decisions not just in terms of the immediate future but in the light of their whole life span. Friedman (1957) argued that emulation and the availability and usefulness of superior goods is what can lead to economic betterment among nations as well as among individuals (p. 232), that is, that people imitate what other people do, especially when they see the chance to improve their standard of living. Money thus means something to them more than subsistence, convenience, and comfort: it means social status, hence communication.

Georg Simmel (1900/1978) and James Coleman (1990), the most analytic of the sociologists interested in economic phenomena, are nevertheless both very much aware of individual psychology. Both devote considerable energy to description of individual psychological process—but both also demur on incorporating these individual processes into their theories. Simmel approaches money as an aesthetic phenomenon, like a piece of art. In his view, money, distinguished from property or even pre-money currencies like cattle, stands more and more separate from the individual, the further civilization advances:

> The more it stands before us in its own dignity, the more we attribute to it a significance that is not exhausted by haphazard subjective enjoyment, and the more the relationship of valuing the objects merely as means [utility] is replaced by a feeling of their independent value [beauty]. (p. 75)

Simmel keeps wealth objective and distant from the subject. Only on the rarest of occasions does he acknowledge any link at all, as between having and being. Even then he argues that the connection, however strong it may be with property, dissolves when it comes to money (Simmel, 1900/1978, p. 307; see also 1971).

Coleman (1990), too, makes it clear (p. 505) that individual irrationality and inconsistency will not be addressed in his analysis, but later (p. 932) he admits that treating people as "unanalyzed entities characterized by a utility function that each actor seeks to maximize" is not completely satisfactory, for it provides no insight into such "deviations from rationality" as interest psychologists.

Thomas Crump, tax lawyer turned economic anthropologist, begins to bridge the gap between the exchange theorists and the communication theorists. He proposes that money is a "deep ritual" that reflects the endless facets of the culture in which it occurs. He describes it further as anything that can complete the "ritual of payment" and lists among its functions the distribution of power within a community and the connection of the community to the outside world. He also notes the occasional connection of money with death and evil (Crump, 1992, pp. 671-673; see also Bloch & Parry, 1982).

> The ritual of money is always about something else. . . . What the actual ritual means must therefore be defined extrinsically, and the possibilities once again are endless. The anthropologist will note that the meaning, once chosen, tends to become a self-fulfilling prophecy, so that those who operate within a given monetary system develop a tunnel vision which makes them blind to the possible existence of alternative systems. (Crump, 1992, p. 674)

Elsewhere, Crump (1981, pp. 16-18) provides a brief history of money as a symbolic system and asserts that it lies within an individual culture's power to convert money to whatever "sacred symbol" it chooses. For a similar analysis, see Einzig (1949/1966).

Thus some of the most analytic minds in modern social science have at least acknowledged that money and property might mean something beyond rational economics and might even play a role in human motivation, if only the additional variables could be measured objectively and efficiently.[13]

The Parry

From the start, social scientists interested in money and property tried to identify their symbolic meaning. Early among those who saw money and property as much more than media of exchange was Karl Marx, who viewed wealth as a tool of oppression, the extension of the same bourgeois and proletarian personalities that Nietzsche would later call the personality of the "master" and the personality of the "slave" (MacIntyre, 1968, pp. 56, 167-168). Marx attacked Mill, Smith, and other classicists for the unrealistic quality of their formal theoretical assumptions. By suggesting that everyone was interested in maximizing wealth, and particularly that everyone was interested in it to the same degree, the economists, he insisted, were covering up the nefarious goal of the capitalist classes, namely, to secure their own financial advancement by stealing from the masses (Finn, 1992, p. 661). Whereas Smith's meanings for money and property were stacked vertically, in terms of progressive levels of achievement and efficiency, Marx's were arrayed horizontally, defining the solidarity that should make all individuals equivalent. Habermas (1989) and Giddens (1990), among others, have carried Marx's philosophy into the present. They view money as the source of corruption, and they argue—curiously—that money has the power to impose its corrupting qualities on other spheres of life but that the rest of life is incapable of affecting money.

Max Weber, too, complained that classical economic thinking stripped the human element out of money and resulted in life lived according to an artificial calculus, a "bean-counting" disposition to look at life like a utility function. In his often-quoted *The Protestant Ethic and the Spirit of Capitalism* (1934/1976), Weber sought meaning in the inclination to amass wealth that emanated from Protestantism in general, Calvinism in particular:

> We are interested in ascertaining those psychological *impulses* which originated in religious belief and the practice of religion, gave direction to the individual's everyday way of life and prompted him to adhere to it. (pp. 91-92)

The meaning he found was money-as-power, money particularly as a weapon in the price-system struggle of man against man (Weber, 1922/1978, p. 108; see also Baker, 1987, pp. 322-333).

Thorstein Veblen, like Weber before and Parsons after, connected money to competition and achievement. Early on, he observed "a direct propensity in human nature for one man to barter with another" (1896/1976, p. 244). Later, in his *Theory of the Leisure Class* (1899/1976), he described property as "the most easily recognised evidence of a reputable degree of success, . . . [the] 'badge of efficiency' [which is] itself intrinsically honourable and confers honour on its possessor" (p. 78). He pointed out that it is the unslakable thirst for honor that accounts for the fact that the desire for money and property is never satisfied:

> If . . . the incentive to accumulation were the want of subsistence or of physical comfort, then the aggregate economic wants of a community might conceivably be satisfied at some point in the advance of industrial efficiency; but since the struggle is substantially a race for reputability on the basis of an invidious comparison, no approach to a definitive attainment is possible. (p. 81)

Finally, Veblen connected achievement and failure with honor and dishonor and concluded that the main motive that drives people to accumulate wealth is imitation of the wealthy and honorable:

The propensity for achievement and the repugnance to futility remain the underlying economic motive. . . . Among the motives which lead men to accumulate wealth, the primacy, both in source and intensity, continues to belong to this motive of pecuniary emulation. (p. 82)

Sigmund Freud and other early psychoanalysts also repudiated Economic man, though from an entirely different angle. As we shall see in more detail later, they connected money to the "great underworld of vital, unseen forces which exercise an imperious control over the conscious thoughts and deeds of man" (Hall & Lindzey, 1957/1970, p. 30; see Freud, 1900/1965, and Borneman, 1976); that is, the analysts connected money to the "irrational" forces that were so troubling to the classical economists. In his characteristic effort to keep body and psyche close together, Freud shocked Viennese society in 1905 by postulating a biopsychological connection between hoarding and "anal eroticism," such that the adult's pleasure in holding onto money—"filthy lucre"—was equivalent to the child's in retaining feces (Freud, 1905/1976). Freud's protege, Sandor Ferenczi (1914/1976), said it even more forcefully:

Whatever form may be assumed by money, the enjoyment at possessing it has its deepest and amplest source in coprophilia [fascination with feces]. Every sociologist and national economist who examines the facts without prejudice has to reckon with this irrational element. Social problems can be solved only by discovering the real psychology of human beings; speculations about economic conditions alone will never reach the goal. (p. 86)

More recent social scientists concentrated on the role of money and property in the development of individual and social identity. George Herbert Mead (1934) proposed that people construct their personalities by interacting not only with other people but with material things; in short, that things as well as people contribute to the "generalized other," whose inferred attitudes toward him come to define his personality (pp. 154-155n). Money and property thus contribute to the development and identification of the self by bringing to light a broader range of goals and values.

James Duesenberry, whom Mary Douglas would later call one of the few major economists with "sophisticated views about the social nature of human needs" (Douglas & Isherwood, 1979, p. 44), explicitly expanded the economic focus from money per se to the things money can buy. He argued (1949) that it is culture that defines which consumer goods are appropriate for particular purposes, and how appropriate they are, and that the only freedom the individual actually enjoys in choosing goods is a choice within a relatively narrow range that culture specifies for each purpose. At the core of his formulation, like Veblen's, is the idea that consumers "emulate" each other in their choice and use of consumer goods. Citing psychoanalyst Horney (1937) and psychologist Festinger (1942), Duesenberry (1949) explains that the roots of emulation must be psychosocial:

> When the attainment of any end becomes a generally recognized social goal, the importance of attainment of this goal is instilled in every individual's mind by the socialization process. In psychoanalytic terms the goal is incorporated into the ego-ideal. (p. 28)

Mary Douglas (Douglas & Isherwood, 1979, pp. 58-59) argued for a complete redefinition of consumption, a change in emphasis from economic exchange to social communication. She maintained that consumption reflects the free choice of consumers to express themselves and that consumer decisions, in the final analysis, are "moral judgments about what a man is, what a woman is, how a man ought to treat his aged parents . . . , [the individual consumer's statements] about himself, his family, his locality, whether in town or country, on vacation or at home" (p. 68).

Mihalyi Csikszentmihalyi and Eugene Rochberg-Halton (1981) extended Meadean thinking into a conception of "personhood" characterized by the lifelong struggle between individuation and conformity. Despite being the most abstract of properties, money is also the "most social of all things" (p. 31), because it stands for the exchange of any property or activity. Like Simmel, they approach money (as well as property) through aesthetics, but they find a closer connection, in that, through a flow of psychic energy between subject and object, the object itself "imposes certain qualities on the viewer that create new insights" that lead to creative accomplishment (p. 45). Csikszentmihalyi (1990, 1996, 1997) extends this conception of subject-object connection into this theory of "flow" (see Buber, 1958/1966).

Adrian Furnham and Alan Lewis (1986) approach financial and economic topics through traditional social-psychological analysis. Through their examination of a host of studies on poverty, affluence, saving, spending, gambling, and the like, they lay a foundation for identifying the social meanings of money.

Viviana Zelizer (1989, 1994, p. 18) demonstrated that social factors are indeed capable of "investing [money] with meaning." Expanding Polanyi's (1957) notion of special-purpose money, she argued that "people earmark different currencies for many or perhaps all types of social interactions." She showed, for example, how a wife's "pin money" had different psychosocial value and a different range of potential use than her husband's salary. She described restrictions on money from the vantage both of the giver and the recipient (e.g., Do not give cash gifts to your boyfriend; do not accept cash gifts from your employees). Finally, she pointed out the strings we attach to welfare payments, how and why the old-fashioned dole metamorphosed into an entitlement, who constitutes a worthy recipient for unrestricted cash relief, and for what may welfare payments "properly" be used (groceries, yes; cigarettes or lottery tickets, no). In the same vein, Wayne Baker argued that "money, primitive or modern, can be understood only in its context," no more and no less dispassionate than the contexts in which it is experienced. That is, its meaning, like that of any other social institution, is subordinate to society itself (Baker & Jimerson, 1992, p. 679; see also Baker, 1987).

Occasional thinkers in the various disciplines called for a more cross-disciplinary approach to understanding the meanings of money and property. Talcott Parsons (e.g., Parsons & Smelser, 1956), among the most analytic of the sociologists and arguably the closest, spiritually, to modern economics, advocated the integration of psychology as well as economics into sociology (see, e.g., p. 232 on the consumption function, p. 236 on the investment function). In his view, sociology provides the general theory of social systems, of which economic theory is a special case, and psychology helps explain motivation and role expectations within systems (pp. 181, 232). In money he saw two components, the "wealth" aspect, which indicates the power to control decisions about exchanging goods, and the "prestige" aspect, which describes attitudes:

> If it cannot *command goods and services* money is not acceptable as wages; if it cannot *symbolize prestige* and mediate between detailed symbols and a broader symbolization it is not acceptable on other grounds. Only with this dual significance can money perform its social functions. (Parsons & Smelser, 1956, p. 71, emphasis added)

George Katona, the father of behavioral economics, tried to tear down the wall that separated economics and psychology. Psychology without economics, he insisted, fails to address important segments of human behavior;

economics without psychology fails to address those segments in a realistic fashion (1951, chap. 1, see also 1964, 1980). Katona's work focused on the differences among people that his colleagues routinely dismissed as random error, on those "wanderings" that Lord Keynes had so assiduously avoided. Katona opened the door particularly to differences that had to do with aspiration and motivation. He also provided empirical evidence that challenged the universality of Keynes's law of diminishing marginal utilities. Furnham and Lewis (1986, chap. 12; see also Lewis, Webley, & Furnham, 1995) advocate a similarly encompassing approach.

Tibor Scitovsky (1976, 1986) tried to build a bridge between economics and *physiological* psychology. Recalling Hawtrey's (1925, p. 191) well-known distinction, Scitovsky proposed that the "creative" satisfactions (pursuit of pleasure) and "defensive" satisfactions (avoidance of pain) are connected with the pleasure and pain centers in the brain (1976, p. 120). From that vantage he addressed many contemporary social issues that are usually beyond the reach of economic analysis. In urging more attention to the study of creative satisfactions, Scitovsky (1976) summarized the argument of the entire psychosocial camp:

> Economic quantification is attractive and useful, but we must not let it seduce us into attaching more significance to the measure of quantity and to what is quantified than they deserve. The national income is, at the very best, an index of economic welfare, and economic welfare is a very small part and often a very poor indicator of human welfare. (p. 145, see also 1986, p. 194)

Finally, a handful of psychologists challenged the centerpiece of traditional economic theory, rational choice theory, also known as utility theory. Daniel Kahneman (Kahneman, Knetch, & Thaler, 1986; Kahneman, Slovic, & Tversky, 1982; see also Zeckhauser, 1991) showed that rational choice theory could not handle some common psychological phenomena, and in doing so laid the groundwork for a great deal of research on the psychological aspects of decision making, which culminated in a possible alternative for rational choice theory, namely, Herrnstein's "matching law." Richard Herrnstein (e.g., 1990; see also Rachlin & Laibson, 1997) confronted the fact that people frequently behave in ways that do not seem to reflect "reasoned decisions to maximize well-being": they smoke, they eat and drink too much—and they use their money foolishly. Unwilling to dismiss such widespread misbehavior, Herrnstein and associates devised an alternative to rational choice theory: the matching law. The matching law proposes that rather than try always to maximize utility, people choose behaviors in direct proportion to the value they derive from each. Moreover, individuals change their behavior to reflect changing rates of reinforcement. So far, the matching law seems to do a better job than rational choice theory of explaining certain important kinds of choices—for example, to refrain from criminal activity, to do what's healthful, and to strengthen character (Prelec & Herrnstein, 1991; Williams, 1988; see also Rachlin & Laibson, 1997).

REFLECTION

The present book sits squarely in the psychological camp. Taking money's economic meaning only as its starting point, it quickly focuses itself on the more slippery study of symbolic communication. In the spirit of Marx, Weber, and Veblen, it will try to identify and systematize the meanings people communicate through money and property. In the spirit of Freud, it will try to dig below the surface to find the unconscious motives that influence those meanings. In the spirit of Mead, Duesenberry, Douglas, and Zelizer, it will concentrate on meanings that contribute to individual and social identity. And in the spirit of Parsons, Katona, and Scitovsky, it will try to take a step in the direction of a cross-disciplinary view of money and property.

This book strives to devise a conceptual framework that accounts for differences in the meanings various individuals, families, and cultures attach to money and property, and to propose a model that shows how they go about doing so. Coincidentally, it will also suggest a modification of the matching law to connect that theory with the "other" discipline of scientific psychology (Cronbach, 1957, 1975), namely, the individual differences tradition. The same framework that moderates our model can moderate the matching law, requiring both theories to account for the ways different people think, feel, and behave about money and property.

We are now ready to contemplate the origins of thought and attitude about money and property. In the next chapter, we shall examine the early history of our species, beginning in the African cradle thence separating into what we now call Europe, Asia, and the Americas. On the basis of differences in art, myth, and ritual, we shall begin to associate with Europe a particular interest in acquisition and accumulation; with Asia, a distinctive inclination toward order and frugality; with the Americas, the pre-Columbian Americas, a special emphasis on kinship and community; and, finally, with prepenetration Africa, a propensity toward expansiveness and social extravagance. Nowhere do I mean to suggest, of course, that *all* Europeans are acquisitive, *all* Africans flamboyant, and so forth, nor that any culture is exclusively of one propensity of another. Rather, I suggest that these four "archetypal" propensities are the basic dimensions of personality and culture that, in differing degrees, describe to this day the essential character of individuals, families, and cultures. While I know this wide-ranging "continental" approach will furrow some brows, I offer it in the spirit of Marvin Harris, distinguished Columbia University anthropologist, whose explorations in cultural materialism were painted with equally broad strokes. My intention, like his, is to ascend above the marshalling of facts to the creation of general and comparative theory[14]. To this end, I ask the reader's indulgence.

Now we shall begin to connect those ancient propensities to natural selection, on the one hand, and to the meanings of money and property, on the other. While doing so, I shall assert that *fear* is the root motive underlying how we think, feel, believe, and behave about money and property, and *protection* the root meaning.

Chapter 2

The Beginnings of Differentiation

W e were all born in Africa[1]—not in the north, along the Mediterranean seacoast that would become culturally more European than African, and not in the far northeast, along the Fertile Crescent that separated Africa from Eurasia. We were all born in the forests and savannas of east Africa, in what today we call Ethiopia, Kenya, and the Sudan. There, more than four million years ago, *Ardipithecus ramidus* and *Australopithecus afarensis,* perhaps contemporaneously, swung down from trees and first walked upright to carry their children to the better forage across the savanna. More than two million years ago, in nearby Tanzania, *Homo habilis*—Handy man, the first member of our genus—used stone tools to separate meat from scavenged carcasses. And more than one million years ago, *Homo erectus*—Upright man, Erect man, Straight man—tamed fire.

Fire gave *Homo erectus* many advantages that his ancestors had not enjoyed, not the least important of which was the ability to cook. In turn, the ability to cook led (I suppose) to the establishment of the community hearth and, with that, the benefits of the first social ritual, the common meal. As a result of that ritual, what started as simple functional banding probably began to incorporate increasing degrees of voluntary and involuntary structure, which quickly gave birth (I also suppose) to the experience of vertical (hierarchical) versus horizontal association. This, I suggest, is the first expression of capitalism versus socialism, the tension between which would, a million years later, become one of humankind's great preoccupations.

Life was hard for *Homo erectus.* It involved few satisfactions—food, water, sex; the touch of the sun's warmth or the refreshment of a cool breeze; companionship and the occasional brush of another being. But it entailed many threats. In thunder, lightning, rain, and floods; in sun, moon, stars, and comets; in disease, pestilence, pain, and death—in all these natural phenomena *Homo erectus* must have seen a world far larger than himself, and he must have feared that world (Garrison, 1929, chap. 1; James, 1902/1961, *passim*; Parrinder, 1983, pp. 32-34). Innocent of philosophy and psychology,

19

neither could he distinguish conscious from unconscious, dream from reality, subjective from objective (Lamb, 1992; Lonergan, 1988; Popper, 1972). Untutored in medicine and natural science, he lived at the beck and call of vague spiritual forces beyond his comprehension. In this shadowy existence, the center of his life was fear, and the pursuit of ways to quell that fear.

What role did money and property play in the life of *Homo erectus*? Clearly, money played no role at all, for the invention of coins and paper money still lay a thousand thousand years in the future. However, although the origins of wealth are conventionally associated with the surplus production of the (much later) first agricultural settlements, it is hard to imagine bands of hominids or proto-humans in which some notion of wealth did not emerge early, and it is difficult to conceive even that degree of wealth without some degree of envy and jealousy.[2]

What precipitated these first "deadly sins" we have no way of knowing. It could have been a larger or more choice morsel of food, or a more commodious accommodation, or a more cooperative consort; it could even have been greater skill at hunting or other valued occupation. My simple point is that at some time in paleohistory, someone had *more* or *better* than someone else, and that difference constituted the first discernible wealth. Because of the atmosphere of fear and brutal subsistence that surrounded *Homo erectus,* it seems likely that the response to difference was not altruism but narcissism— the fear that someone might have more than I do (envy) or the fear that someone might take my goods from me (jealousy). In short, these earthy emotions, envy and jealousy, probably existed in some form long before the first agricultural surplus.

SELECTIVE MIGRATION AND THE BEGINNINGS OF TEMPERAMENT

Another advantage of fire was that it enabled *Homo erectus* to tolerate the shocking cold of the Eurasian Ice Ages. As social groups became too large for the browse or too diverse to countenance, the more restless, the more put-upon, and perhaps the more cantankerous broke off from their communities and migrated north- and westward through the then-jungled Levant and into Eurasia, then to the world beyond, where some branches of the evolutionary bramble died out and others thrived. In due time,[3] that is, about 40,000 years ago, *Homo erectus* yielded to Peking man in Asia and Neanderthal man in Europe and Africa, *Homo sapiens pekinesis* and

Homo sapiens neanderthalensis, the first in the genus *Homo* and the species *sapiens.*

Peking man and European Neanderthal man encountered climatic hardships unknown to their African cousins. The bitter and barren plains and mountains of Siberian Asia and northern Europe caused new attitudes, values, and skills to emerge. These included greater competitiveness for the scarcer resources; more structured social organizations, to increase efficiency; more pronounced social hierarchies, to maintain order; fewer offspring,[4] with more attention to each of them; and greater attention to one's own needs and those of the immediate family: in short, to a general hardening and narrowing of vantage (after Rushton, 1995, p. 203; see also Jung, 1923, chap. 8). Those who followed the new competitive and structured ways survived; those who didn't, died out.

During this same period, although his precise origins are obscure, another creature in the species *sapiens* appeared on the scene and coexisted with Peking man and Neanderthal man for tens of thousands of years. *Homo sapiens sapiens*—Self-reflective man, our most direct ancestor— inaugurated a more refined society. He displayed a surprising degree of social sensitivity and capacity for symbolic communication, though he still lacked fully developed language and cognition. Although Neanderthal man and Peking man had sometimes buried their dead and occasionally even decorated the graves, it was *Homo sapiens sapiens* who first placed meat and tools on the graves, apparently to assist the deceased in a sacred voyage, and, later, laid the bodies on beds of boughs and branches, surrounding them with flowers. With these gestures and gifts, something like wealth began to play a part in human communication.

In these earliest material rituals, then, we find foreshadowing of the most basic social messages: affection, respect, mastery, and control. We shall watch these messages crystallize as our ancestors work their way around the archaic world. We shall see those messages also in the ancient legal principles, religious teachings, and philosophical tenets that became a part of the culture of every continent. Indeed, we shall see them in contemporary social science and medical science as we pursue a modest synthesis of these areas of knowledge and try to build upon that synthesis a theory of the meanings of money and property. In short, as a result of this survey, I shall suggest an "archetypal" value for each of the four principal cultures and argue that it is this value, founded in fear, that governs the principal meanings the majority of people in each culture attach to money and property. For an economic analysis of this period, see Finley (1973); for an ethical analysis, see Spengler (1980).

ARCHAIC EUROPE: ACQUISITIVENESS

As I have already suggested, the people who came to populate the different parts of Earth were in all likelihood not simple random samples from the original African population. Rather, they probably differed from the original population in many important ways: willingness to take on the risks of emigration; ingenuity and hardiness to survive the rigors of the trip; behavioral propensities that occasioned the need, desire, or drive to emigrate; and so forth. As a result of this natural selectivity, systematically different varieties of *Homo sapiens sapiens* evolved around the world: distinctive varieties or strains in Europe, Asia, Africa, and the Americas.

Ever since Descartes, conventional wisdom has been inclined to separate body and mind, and paleoanthropological conclusions have unfortunately emphasized the former to the exclusion of the latter (see Mithen, 1996, for a refreshing exception). Since body and mind travel with each other—in a sense, *are* each other—it seems reasonable to suggest that with each of these strains there evolved not just a distinctive physiognomy and physiology but a predominant temperament, along with distinguishable attitudes, values, and behavior patterns that help give meaning to the life experience. Part of the life experience, of course, is money and whatever money can buy.

As the Eurasian Stone Age was drawing to a close, nomadic kinship bands hunted vast territories, because the land could not yet support fixed habitation. Roughly 10,000 years ago, people in Africa and in the Americas discovered ways to improve the land's production of root crops, not yet true agriculture but "vegeculture." Not long thereafter, farmers in the Fertile Crescent, that strip of land arching west from the Levant to Anatolia and east to Iran, began to cultivate wheat and barley. Nearly simultaneously, people in eastern Asia began to cultivate millet, wild rice, and taro root. Both vegeculture and agriculture enabled the bands to limit their peregrination, with the result that by about 6000 B.C. the proto-Mesopotamians and proto-Chinese had begun to form settlements in which they grew crops and raised animals (Scarre, 1993, chap. 5, p. 76).

As with fire, the effects of agriculture on Western society were breathtaking. For the first time, man acquired stability, because agriculture not only permitted but required the establishment of settlements. He acquired social structure, because settlements demanded some degree of order; economy, because agricultural production was easier and more effective with division of labor; and wealth—not just the choicer morsel or mate but a true surplus production that could be spared for exchange[5] or stored for later use (Scarre, 1993, pp. 66-74).

Mesopotamia and Babylonia

Perhaps the first settlements on Earth, and surely the first in the West[6] appeared as early as 8500 B.C. in the form of scattered collections of huts in the Mesopotamian hills and in the vast marshlands left by the receding Persian Gulf (Kramer, 1963, p. 46; McNeill, 1979, p. 11). By the mid- to late fourth millennium, these communities had developed into high civilizations, complete with agriculture, religion, art, medicine,[7] and commerce (Hawkes, 1973).

The most important of these early city-states were Sumer and Babylon. Around 3000 B.C., the cross-fertilization of the barbaric Semitic nomads and the indigenous proto-Euphratean settlers produced Sumer, the first great city-state in the West. The industrious Sumerians built cities and decorated them in gold, silver, and lapis lazuli. They entertained themselves with games of chance[8] (Hiltebeitel, 1987). They established a trading network that spanned Anatolia (Turkey), Egypt, and Ethiopia (Kramer, 1963, chap. 3). They formalized their religion and gave it great power over the people and, as city dwellers seem always to do, divided themselves into social classes and labor specialties. They inaugurated a system of taxation that, not unlike our own, compelled the lower classes to work part of the year for the governors and the priests, to enable those elites to "memorialize" their achievements in temples and palaces (McNeill, 1979, p. 17).

The Sumerian economy before 2500 B.C. was a mixture of socialist and capitalist, state-controlled and free market. The Temple and the Palace owned much of the land, but large and small individual businessmen owned a substantial portion too, apparently the first capitalists on Earth. In their business transactions, the Sumerians employed both barter and "pre-coins," silver disks or rings[9] of known purity and weight (Kramer, 1963, pp. 74-75; Spengler, 1980, chap. 2). They exhibited the first instance of what became the classic financial sequence: labor specialization, barter, and money (Kramer, 1959).

At the same time this early capitalism was taking shape, the religion of the day was lamenting the oppression of the poor by the wealthy, foreshadowing a perpetual tension between money and religion. The opposition of God and Mammon is clear in Mesopotamian mythology. In the best-known Mesopotamian religious saga, Gilgamesh[10] has been oppressing his subjects, so they appeal to the gods for help. The gods create Enkidu, the archetypal noble savage, and send him to keep Gilgamesh in check. Enkidu has intercourse with a prostitute, who introduces him to civilization. From this exposure Enkidu loses his innocence, and he and Gilgamesh become friends, each eventually saving the life of the other (Heidel, 1946; Langdon, 1931; Shelmerdine, 1995; Willis, 1993, pp. 58-60).

From this and other Mesopotamian myths emerge two themes that will recur continually throughout history, particularly in the succession of European cultures: the enmity between the wealthy masters and the impoverished slaves (see Nietzsche), and the tension between the innocence and integrity of nature (noble poverty) and the corruption, artificiality, and fractiveness of moneyed urban life.

The Babylonians (2400 B.C.) were even more businesslike than the Sumerians. Except for pastureland held in common, they owned property individually, and, like the later Romans but unlike the Hebrews, they could buy, sell, lease, and bequeath it at will. They treated their slaves humanely, permitting them to own property and earn money and thus eventually to buy their freedom. They paid taxes on their property, and they exacted customs duties on imports (Driver & Miles, 1956). As a fundamentally agricultural society turning commercial-industrial, they still employed in-kind exchange, but they were coming to prefer copper, silver, and even gold as money.

Marriage in Babylon was entirely commercial. The groom paid a bride-price to the woman's father, and the bride brought to the marriage a substantial dowry. Divorce was simple in principle; it required only a public declaration. But the fact that the dowry had to be returned intact (unless the wife were a shrew or otherwise the certain fault) surely served to discourage dissolution (Goodspeed, 1921, pp. 79-80). Quiggin (1949, p. 321) argues that, nearly universally, the bride-price contained significant psychological elements: It paid for loss of affection, and it signified the groom's promise of present and future affiliation with and respect toward the bride's family, perhaps even affirmed his role as effective master of the new household.

This strong sense of justice the Babylonians turned into their greatest contribution to civilization, the first written laws in at least the Western world: the Code of Ur-Nammu, the Code of Bilalama, the Code of Lipit-Ishtar, and, best known of all, the Code of Hammurabi (see Chapter 4 in this volume). In these codes, the suggestions of capitalism that we first saw in Sumer become substantially more apparent.

Egypt

Egypt was a bridge between the East (India) and the West (Mesopotamia). The country was settled by Eastern peoples, probably ancestors of the same "Asiatics" of whom Hippocrates would speak 2,500 years later. But the society was modeled on—better, adapted from—the earlier Mesopotamian experience. With the help of Mesopotamian adventurers, the Egyptians were able to build in a few hundred years the kind of refined and economically prosperous society that Mesopotamia had required a thousand years of trial and error to develop (McNeill, 1979, pp. 28-29).

The first money used in Egypt (roughly 2800 B.C.) was the cowries[11] that accompanied trade with India and China. Soon the Egyptians began to use gold dust or flakes or nuggets from their Nubian mines. Later, they employed coin-shaped stones (nummulites), pieces of baked clay or porcelain (scarabaei), and gold wrist and ankle bracelets and finger rings, eventually the metal coins of the Lydians and Greeks (Del Mar, 1885/1968, pp. 146-148).

As elsewhere, Egypt's myths offer some insight into the character of the culture and its attitude toward wealth. In particular, the Osiris myth contains two pericopes that are especially pertinent to wealth and money. The first concerns a rich woman who closed her door against Isis and Horus, and the poor fisherman's wife who aided them. Isis' scorpions stung the rich woman's son with venom so powerful that it set the house afire. When Isis took pity on the anguished woman and cured her son, the woman regretted having closed the door and, out of remorse and gratitude, gave her wealth to Isis. In the other passage, Osiris, having condemned a rich man to eternal torment for his cruelty, gave the rich man's possessions to a poor but virtuous man, and made that poor man a blessed spirit (Willis, 1993, pp. 49, 55).

For at least 5,000 years, then, people have connected money and wealth with self-interest, oppression, and cruelty; viewed divestiture as a good deed; and believed (hoped?) that the evil rich would get their comeuppance. At the same time, however, they looked at wealth as a reward for virtuous behavior. This conflict between wealth as vice and wealth as a reward for virtue persists to the present day.

Continental Europe

Acquisitiveness has been the hallmark of the continental Europeans since earliest times. During the eighteenth and seventeenth centuries B.C., Phoenician adventurers bent on conquest and commerce measured the coastlines of the European continent and began to penetrate its virgin forests. Del Mar (1885/1968) is succinct in his description of these colonists:

> [They] were brave, reckless, adventurous, and cruel; they fought one another with ferocity; they imperiled their lives for the most trifling advantages; they pushed their way into the forests and explored the newly found continent from

the Mediterranean to the Alps; they forced the natives into their mines and slew them without remorse. (p. 158)

Not long thereafter, Europe was invaded from the north as well. As the southerners established mines and tried to obliterate the indigenous people, the northern invaders created agricultural settlements and tried to enslave them. The result, Del Mar tells us, was precisely the opposite of the intention: The attempt to destroy the natives in the south resulted in amalgamation, and the attempt to enslave them in the north resulted in their destruction. He attributes (pp. 159-160) the toughmindedness of the northern Europeans to the replacement of the aborigines by the conquering Phoenicians, and the tendermindedness of the southern Europeans to the intermixture with the native peoples.

The northern colonies, without native mines, came to rely on money of the clay and porcelain, and bell and ring, sorts that had originated in the China and India trades. The southerners made use of the same precious metals that had initially attracted the Phoenician explorers to European shores. Examples of northern coins were found in the Neuchâtel lake dwellings in Switzerland (Del Mar, 1885/1968, p. 160). These coins seems to have circulated throughout ancient Europe until they were replaced by the Lydian/Greek varieties in the sixth century B.C.

Europe's geography contributed to its inhabitants' propensity for acquisition and competition. Land on this smallest of the major continents was always in relatively short supply, and this paucity contributed to the nearly continuous warfare for which early Europe is well known. Around the beginning of the Bronze Age, that is, about 2200 B.C., European tribes began to build stockades and other fortifications. Not long afterward, they fenced the lands. Strikingly like their modern descendants, they lived on small parcels and defended those parcels fiercely (Scarre, 1993, pp. 112, 115).

Though the mythologies of most if not all cultures contain fearsome figures, northern and western European myths center in strong and threatening,[12] even bellicose, gods, like the Celtic Daghdha, the "Mighty One" who mates with the goddess of war to learn the martial arts, and the Germanic/Anglo-Saxon Donar and Wodin, gods of thunder and the underworld, respectively. They tell the story of strength and weakness, in which the gods create wealth and provide riches, perhaps the first mention of these as divine functions (Willis, 1993, pp. 178-179, 190-192). The Celtic and Germanic gods tended to have all the attributes of great leaders (Parrinder, 1983, p. 104), and the capitalist inclinations that germinated in Mesopotamia flourished under that leadership.

Greece

The ninth century B.C. saw the beginning of the Heroic period, in which Homer and Hesiod[13] sang songs that laid the foundation for all Greek civilization and (many say) for much of the civilization of the Western world. In their epic poems, the focus was on *virtue,* individual excellence in the pursuit of the duties required by one's role in society,[14] for example, courage, piety, fidelity, and even prosperity (MacIntyre, 1984, p. 121). In Homer's poems we see the first signs of a formal, more intellectual, Western moral philosophy, in which each virtue is paired in dialectic with a corresponding vice. Accordingly, prosperity is a virtue and as such deserves pursuit, but acquisitiveness and prodigality are vices to be avoided. Homer's gods punish men not only for pride and insubordination but for intemperance (Stumpf, 1971, p. 4).

Two of the most important of these dialectics are represented by Apollo/Dionysius[15] and Hermes/Hestia.[16] Apollo was the most Homeric of the gods,

who ever brought fair order and harmony out of confusion, who stood for moderation and sobriety, upon whose temple was graven the great Delphic saying, "Nothing in excess." (Hamilton, 1930/1983, p. 214)

In contrast, the post-Homeric Greeks invented Dionysius as an antidote to excessive Olympian rationality (Hamilton, 1930/1983, p. 213). Even the later, more temperate Dionysia were

full of primitive fertility magic: the sacrifice of a bull[17] or goat; the eating of his flesh for the purpose of receiving his mana or power; the phallus carried on a pole from door to door; the songs and mimetic dancing. (Friess & Schneider, 1932, p. 219)

The other principal dialectic pitted business and material abundance against the warmth and intimacy of home. Hermes was the god of trade, the god of wealth and abundance. A kindly fellow and popular with the Roman people, Hermes (Mercury) enjoyed attributes useful in the marketplace—he was cunning, diplomatic, and technologically expert. His name derives from the archaic *herms,* phallic towers spread around the countryside to help travelers find their way. Hermes himself was often portrayed as a sexually alluring athlete (Jost, 1996).

Hestia, closely associated with Vesta, was goddess of the hearth, the source of literal and figurative warmth. The "orbis umbilica," she swore to lifetime virginity and served as the guardian of innermost secrets (Mikalson, 1996; Walker, 1983).

We shall return to this subject repeatedly in what follows, because it represents the core of our framework for the meaning of money and property: liberation/constraint and acquisitiveness/affiliativeness.

Greece was a trading nation as well as a philosophical center. During the sixth century B.C., Greek mariners came across two practical problems and devised two solutions. The first problem was the more efficient exchange of ideas; the second, the more efficient exchange of goods. The first problem they solved by inventing a phonetic alphabet, far simpler (as we shall see) than the older Chinese calligraphic system.[18] The other problem—more efficient trade—they solved with the help of the inventive Lydians of Asia Minor: They used coins.

From the Sumerians and Babylonians to the continental explorers and island mariners, the peoples of the archaic West exhibit a distinctive aggressiveness and acquisitiveness. As a result of that spirit, each of these peoples built a lively economy based on trade with other nations. They laid the foundation for Western capitalism on which subsequent cultures would build. And they provided what I take as one of the fundamental meanings we attach to money and property: an instrument of competition, achievement, and acquisition.

ARCHAIC ASIA: CONCENTRATION

Just as in the West we could differentiate the Greeks and the Anglo-Saxons, in the East we can distinguish the inhabitants of China from those of India. Also as in the West, the "personality" of the Eastern cultures provides the basis for one of the foundational meanings of money and property (see Cattell, 1948, on "syntality").

China

About 4000 B.C., when the Mesopotamian villages were still young, Banpo villagers in what is now the city of Xi'an in central China arranged their mud-and-wattle dwellings in what were apparently kinship clusters, and they decorated their jars and pots with remarkably exact symmetrical patterns and stylized animal and plant designs, as well as kinship and lineage symbols. They surrounded their village with walls and a deep moat, and they used smaller walls and moats to demarcate areas within the village.

This inclination toward precision, hierarchy, and demarcation carried over into later settlement planning. Newer villages were even more orderly and symmetric than earlier ones, with designated areas for living, working, and burying. Even in the older villages, the wealthier residents had the largest houses in the most desirable locations. Similarly, in the burying areas, wealth and social status determined what was placed in the graves, and the buriers took pains to align the deceased according to the four cardinal directions (Fairbank, 1992, p. 32; Scarre, 1993, p. 85). Solid walls became the hallmark of the Chinese city, village, neighborhood, compound, and dwelling.

These tidy settlements would gradually evolve into dozens, then scores, then hundreds, of walled cities, each city housing a particular family, each collection of neighboring cities a particular clan. Marriage, migration, and military force led to a clear pattern of subordination and superordination among the cities and between the cities and the remaining towns and villages. Eventually, an overarching central government capped the social pyramid and produced generations of hereditary rule, the dynasties (Fairbank, 1992, p. 37).

The first archaeologically verified dynasty, the Shang (1750-1040 B.C.), was best known for its practice of foretelling the future through highly ritualized readings of the webworks of heat-induced crackings on their famous "oracle bones." The Shang also built a wide-ranging trade network based on cowrie shells (Fairbank, 1992, p. 35). These shells were apparently the oldest of the widely circulated pre-coins (or tokens) in China, as in so much else of the world, older, even, than the little clay cylinders that were popular in some locales. *Hae-fai,* or "fat of the sea," they were already being imported from India in 3000 B.C. and were first used in those provinces which abut the subcontinent. Del Mar (1885/1968, pp. 19-20) observes that metal coins came into use soon afterward. He cites DuHalde (1736, in Del Mar, 1885/1968, p. 16), who reports that coins were introduced by Emperor Hoang-ti in 2687 B.C. and that a prince in about 2119 B.C. had workers bury his coins for safekeeping, then killed them so they could not reveal the hiding place. And, as we shall see in a later chapter, as early as 2200 B.C. convicts could use metal coins to buy their freedom.

These earliest metal coins, Sung dynasty coins, were bell shaped and *tong king ho,* "good for gold," that is, based on a gold standard. A thousand years later appeared the well-known knife- and hoe-shaped coins, and, later still, the familiar disk-with-hole, or "cash." In short, coins (broadly defined) were widely used in China more than 4,500 years ago, even before Sumer, and long before Lydia. See Pan (1950) for enormous detail on ancient Chinese coins.

The Zhou dynasty (771-256 B.C.) was one of the most influential in all of Chinese history because Zhou views and ideals later exerted a major influence on Confucius, the most respected of all Chinese philosophers. The Zhou gentleman became the model for Confucius' moral philosophy: refined, dutiful, composed, respectful, attentive to ancestors, and aware of his place relative to other people as well as their places relative to him. At the same time, the Zhou king, as Heaven's representative, was responsible for keeping the world in order through rituals designed to ward off storms, crop failure, and infertility. The *Book of Songs,* an anthology of early poetry, archived those rituals and became the foundation for all Chinese poetry, dance, and mime.

The same Zhou tidiness is evident in the old Chinese use of language. Like the incisings on the Banpo earthenware, archaic Chinese calligraphy emphasized how individuals ranked in their families, how workers ranked in the workplace, and how families ranked with respect to one another, all the way up to the central government and its claim of direct access to Heaven and the heavenly spirits (Fairbank, 1992, p. 40). We see it also in the remarkable Chinese system of civil-service examinations, in which young people throughout the empire took tests in arts and letters to determine who was best qualified to hold government positions (DuBois, 1970).

In Chinese philosophy, cosmic order[19] turns on the harmony of two fundamental principles: Yin represents femininity, passivity, cold, wetness, and softness, and yang represents masculinity, activity, heat, dryness, and hardness. An extension of this principle is based on the ancient mystical significance of the number 5. Thus the Five Directions—two opposing pairs, plus center—correspond with the Five Seasons and the Five Elements (Willis, 1993, pp. 89-90, 264-277). The Heroic notion of temperance led to a stylistically similar system in classical Greek philosophy notably with Hippocrates and Galen.

Thus was Bronze Age China a land unto itself, pure (to the point of xenophobic) in culture, religion, and language, composed in attitude and behavior, serious and dutiful in internal relations, and surrounded by barbarians who could not appreciate or even comprehend Chinese quality. This attitude is reflected in the high masonry walls that still surround homes, villages, and cities and that once surrounded the entire nation. The walls do their job extraordinarily well: They not only keep alien fabrications at arms' length, but they keep Chinese thoughts and feelings under control (Holm, 1990, p. 55).

Early China was notable for its delineation and differentiation, for its controlled language and culture, and for its orderly connection to Heaven and the ancestral spirits. These qualities laid the foundation for the philosophies of Confucius, Mencius, and Lao-Tsu, all of which we shall examine more closely in a later chapter (see also Fairbank, 1992, p. 31).

India

In the middle of the second millennium B.C., heavily armed waves of Aryan charioteers began to sweep over the Indus Valley and level everything in sight. By 1200 B.C., virtually the only traces that remained of the indigenous Indus civilization were those maintained by simple rural folk (McNeill, 1979, pp. 35, 77).

India languished in its own Dark Ages until about 800 B.C., when centralized monarchies began to emerge, not in the Indus Valley but along the Ganges. One of the most important developments under these monarchies was the caste system, though apparently Aryan (Caucasian) in origin. Although formal Brahmanical teaching specified four castes (priests, warriors, workers, and the unclean), in practice there were hundreds if not thousands, organized on geographical, ideological, ethnic, and occupational distinctions (McNeill, 1979, pp. 78-81). Through its hierarchical arrangement and detailed enumeration, the caste system reveals a characteristically Eastern attitude and cognition, reminiscent of the Chinese family and clan hierarchies.

Vedic mythology, also like Chinese, focused on dialectic, the tension and complementarity between chaos and the world order. The Devas (gods) are opposed by the Asuras (antigods). Krishna's darkness and Radha's, his lover's, golden beauty complement one another. Shiva has both his ascetic and his erotic sides, as well as his shepherd and avenger roles. There is a flavor of abstract arithmetic and geometry in primitive Hindu religion and art, which will surface again in the Hindu propensity toward quantification— 8 of this, 4 of that, and 12 of the other—possibly even related to the contemporary Indian penchant for mathematics. As Willis (1993) observed, "In Indian thought the origin of the world was not an act of creation, but an act of arrangement" (p. 70).

Coinage in India is at least as ancient as that in China (Del Mar 1885/1968, p. 58). In the earliest times, India supplied cowries for China. As in China, the earliest Indian coins were of clay (p. 73). Possibly as early as 1700 B.C., the coins were fashioned of copper, silver, and gold, carefully weighed and related to one another (pp. 60-61). The Code of Manu specifies among its regulations the proper use of money. It and the older Vedic writings (see Chapter 5) provide additional insight into the Indian attitude about money and property.

China and India, the prototypic cultures of the East from which Japan, Korea, Thailand, and the other Asian nations derive much of their cultures, share a bent for demarcation and a special desire for order and harmony. In their art, their politics, and their religion, they count, they arrange, and they balance. There is a dispassion in these cultures that contrasts with the feisty aggressiveness we saw in the early Europeans, the reflectiveness we shall see in the ancient American Indians, and, even more, with the flamboyance we shall see among the archaic Africans. This dispassion provides the basis for the second archetypal meaning of money: an instrument of order and control.

THE ARCHAIC AMERICAS: AFFILIATIVENESS

The early indigenous Americans[20] established extensive trading networks[21] in both North and South America as far back as 7000 B.C. Although these networks eventually came to rival in extent those of the Europeans, there was a fundamental difference in purpose. The goal of the native enterprise was to support the community, not to generate individual wealth. Wealth, like individuality, was a concept foreign to most Indian people (Dye, 1984; Dye & Cox, 1990; Mason, 1957, pp. 30-32).

The guiding principle among many if not most early American Indians was their animistic spirituality. Because the Spirit pervaded all of creation, everything in creation deserved respect—animal, vegetable, and mineral. The ideal of universal respect led to the principle of inclusiveness. Thus the Indian community comprised, first, the traditional extended family; second, all members of the band or tribe, living and deceased; and, third, the whole of creation (Deloria, 1944).

American Indian people focused their energy inward. The sun dance, for instance, in which the people of nearly thirty North American tribes sought connection with the universe, consisted of slow and steady dancing[22] to the soulful beat of a hide drum (Gill, 1987; see also Metraux, 1946, and Steward, 1949), not the dramatic movements of the African dancers. Similarly, the South American Indians (e.g., the Tucano), in their important mourning liturgies, expressed themselves in melancholic "vocables," untranslatable syllables of the sort one still hears in native music (McAllester, 1980, 1987; see also Kirchoff, 1946). Even the "Dionysian" dancing that Benedict (1934, p. 72; see also Powers, 1987) ascribes to the vision-quest tribes is designed to encourage an interior experience. Her Apollonian Zuni (chap. IV) stand in even starker contrast to their African counterparts: the Zuni did not dance at all.

The ideal of respect was also the foundation for the emphasis on the communal economy that is evident in ancient Indian cultures throughout the Americas. Long before Marx, Indian mores provided that each member should receive what he needed, and each contribute what he could.[23] Except for those Indians who lived in the old cities[24] of Central and South America, this familial/communal culture persisted until the European penetration a mere 500 years ago.

The most important money- or property-related rituals among Indian peoples were just the reverse of those that were popular among Europeans. For example, the Lakota and Dakota Sioux, the Ojibwe, and other tribes in the interior of North America practiced (and still practice) the "give-away," or *otu'han,* a ritual in which the host gave gifts to the guests in honor of some important event, like a granddaughter's naming or a grandson's first hunting success. Families (then and now) might save for a year or more in preparation for a give-away. The Chinook, Kwaikutl, and other tribes of the American Northwest practiced *potlach,* a form of ritualistic combat in which the only armament is property and the only competition is giving. In potlach, one person gives a gift to another, usually a blanket, and the other is then obliged to reciprocate with a gift of twice the value, either at the moment or on promise of future payment. The giving cycles back and forth until one participant or the other acknowledges that he cannot proceed. The key to understanding the potlach is to view it not as competition for property but as entertainment, excitement, and the pursuit of respect (Boas, 1895/1970; Harris, 1974, pp. 111-132; Mead, 1937; Waldmar, 1994, pp. 86, 183; Whitling, 1967).

If early European culture was characterized by individuality, early American Indian culture was characterized by collectivity (Attneave, 1982). If the early Europeans were acquisitive and practical, the early Indians were communal and reflective, even melancholic. In many ways, these two cultures seem diametrically opposed[25] to one another, contrasting ends of the same continuum. From this opposition to acquisition comes the third archetypal meaning of wealth: an instrument of affiliation.

ARCHAIC AFRICA: EXPANSIVENESS

Much of sub-Saharan Africa's primordial cultural development remains unknown, even unknowable, because the forests have hidden or the climate has destroyed many traces of *Homo erectus'* descendants. The majority of the people of Black Africa, Bantu speakers, are agriculturists, but archaeologists believe that the nomadic Bushmen and Hottentots of southern Africa still live the life of their ancient forebears, employing archaic techniques in their pursuit of wild game and subsisting on a hunter's diet supplemented by reptiles, rodents, locusts, and termites (Scarre, 1993, pp. 78-79).

The ancient African agricultural settlements did not take on the formal characteristics of either the European or the Asian settlements, but they did provide companionship, defense, and some degree of economy. Particularly in the south, the African communities were less entrepreneurial than the European settlements, less ordered than the Asian, and more individualistic than the American Indian. Indeed, as the Bantu people from the north spread down the continent displacing the aboriginal people and establishing settlements, they introduced a social structure that was initially based on kinship groups. This structure quickly evolved into monarchies governed first by ancient leaders of fertility cults and other primitive associations and later by sacred rulers or kings. The kingdom, or chiefdom, with all wealth and power concentrated in the hands of one individual, is far more characteristic of Africa than either forest villages or hunter camps (Maquet, 1972, p. 93). The relations between today's war lords and the common folk seem a distant mirror of this ancient inclination.

Control of surplus production also enabled the chief to expand his sway to other villages, which produced additional workers for the fields and soldiers for the military, and to engage in trade,[26] primarily with nearby chiefs. Wealth consisted sometimes in cattle, sometimes in grain, sometimes even in slaves, and trade was generally pure barter. The most common form of money was beads and shells, along with salt, iron, and later, cloth. Beyond that, different localities at different times employed different moneys (Quiggin, 1949, chap. IX).

African art grew out of the ancient fertility cults. In both visual and aural forms, African creation was dynamic and stylish, marked by brilliant color, dramatic scale, and vital, often sexual, energy. The oldest pieces of African art concentrate on animal and human forms, and one famous old figurine shows the human genitalia in great detail. The early artists, like their successors, apparently tried less to represent reality and more "to express what the artist conceives intellectually and feels emotionally." Later versions emphasized color and flair as well. Even the African cave-wall figures were different from the European ones, more dynamic in expression and animal tension (Maquet, 1972, pp. 36, 71, and *passim*).

Not only art but myth was expressive, full of free-flowing sexuality,[27] humor, and optimism. Less metaphysical and cosmological than Asian myth in particular, African myth concentrates instead on the phenomena of every-day life, especially interpersonal phenomena, particularly sexuality and marital discord.

African and American Indian spirituality were similar in important respects, for example, connection with nature. But they were very different in style. African people directed their energy outward, in their music, their dance, their general demeanor. Biebuyck (1987) describes the dramatic religious practices of tribes and bands from all over Africa—Pygmies in the south and the Bobongo in the west, among others. American Indian people turned their energy inward. And, in a very general sense, African religions sought to control nature (Gehman, 1989, p. 67), whereas Indian religions sought to get along with nature, to become a part of it.

Wealth itself enters into tribal spirituality in limited ways. The Indians tried to enter into union *with* Nature; the Africans prayed and sacrificed *to* Nature. To the Africans, sacrifice was the most profound way of communicating with the invisible world. For that reason, the people sacrificed that which they especially valued: chickens, goats, and even cattle (Zahan, 1987).

African tribal religions do not involve the formal theologies or moral philosophies of the European or Asian religions. They are more akin to the naturalism, the animism, of American Indian spirituality, but directed outward. Also in contrast to European and Asian constructions, the Supreme Creator in African tribal religions is benevolent; he takes care of people because they need him, and he intervenes directly when asked. The fact that Africans created a benevolent[28] deity might reflect the relative ease of the African environment, or it might reveal a greater natural sanguinity.[29]

As American Indian culture contrasts with European American, so African contrasts with Asian. Asian cultures are characterized by precision, hierarchy,

TABLE 2.1 Summary of Early Cultural Propensities

Race	"Caucasoid"	"Mongoloid"	"Sub-Mongoloid"	"Negroid"
Locale	Europe	Asia	Americas	Africa
Values	Acquisitiveness	Concentration	Affiliativeness	Expansiveness
Art	Practical	Precise	Animistic	Expansive
Myth	Bellicose	Ordered	Familial	Sexual

ness is the basis for the fourth and final archetypal meaning of money and property: instruments of expressiveness.

REFLECTION

By roughly the beginning of the first millennium B.C., then, the four strains[30] of *Homo sapiens sapiens* had differentiated themselves into peoples distinct not only in geography and appearance but in values, attitudes, and general lifestyles (see Table 2.1). The push for urbanization and social stratification—along with what we generally view as the "civilized" uses of money—was more characteristic of the so-called Eastern and Western worlds, of China and India in the East, Mesopotamia and continental Europe in the West, than of either Africa or the Americas. The earliest residents of sub-Saharan Africa and the primordial Americas for the most part perpetuated the old nomadic ways, hunting and gathering, rather than subscribe to the aggressive economic values, disciplined styles, and authoritarian structures of the European and Asian cultures.

My notion is that this cultural differentiation was more biological than we generally think; not completely biological, by any means, but more so than conventional wisdom would have us believe (e.g., Rushton, p. 1995). Through selective migration and propagation, that is, through natural selection, each of the four prototypic peoples gradually evolved not only its own physiognomy but, more important, its own increasingly homogeneous neuroanatomy and neurochemistry. People of a given strain not only developed such facial and bodily structures that they came to look more like each other than like other people, but (I hypothesize) they were at the same time developing neurotransmitters, neuroreceptors, and neuronal codings more like one another's than like the other peoples'. As much as social and like one another's than like the other peoples'. As much as social and environmental factors, this biological differentiation[31] contributed to systematic differences among the strains.

Just as biology in the face of environment gradually produced the four types of people who populated Europe, Asia, Africa, and the Americas, so those same forces combined to produce subgroups within the continental groups, still smaller groups within the subgroups, and so on, perhaps down to the level of the individual. Thus, over thousands and thousands of years evolved the people we now call, for example, Italians and Swiss, Japanese and Thai, Yoruba and Ibo, and Iroquois and Shoshone—different temperaments within the archetypal cultures, but always fewer in number and influence than the archetypal people themselves.

How it happened that these four propensities—acquisitiveness, concentration, expansiveness, and affiliativeness—became the principal dimensions upon which individuals vary remains a mystery. For the sake of discussion, I hypothesize that each propensity is largely (not entirely) the result of heritable neurophysiological structures and processes, and that dominant and recessive forces within each of the four strains produce offspring in accordance with the laws of Mendelian genetics.

If biology exerts a substantial influence[32] not only on differences in appearance (to which we are excessively alert) but also on these far more important differences in social structure, attitudes, and customs, it is a small step to propose that biology also influences our perceptions and interpretations of the social and material worlds in which we live, including money and property. I do not mean to suggest that there is a gene for capitalism or coveting or liking-to-budget (see Lykken, McGue, Tellegen, & Bouchard, 1992, on "emergenesis"). I do propose that there are biological foundations for perceptual mechanisms and the attitudes and values that flow from those; that biology inclines some individuals to find satisfaction in expressing aggression and acquisitiveness, others in practicing demarcation and enumeration, others in experiencing affiliation and cooperation, and still others in enjoying flamboyance and extravagance; and that these propensities play themselves out in the financial domain as well as other domains of human life.[33]

In later chapters, we will pursue this line of thought by examining three of our ancestors' most important constructions: law, religion, and philosophy. We shall see, for example, that the laws our ancestors created were remarkable reflections of the propensities we have just noticed in ancient mythology, art, and economy: In Europe, the focus was property law, to support the ascendancy of the individual; in Asia, governmental regulation, to maintain political and psychic harmony by keeping the people under control; in Africa, not formal law but less structured customs for the protection of individual dignity; and in the Americas, customs for maintenance of family and community solidarity. We shall see that the values these laws and customs reveal are the values that determine how various types of people dealt with money and property: The Europeans amassed it, the Asians regulated it, the Africans displayed it, and the American Indians disregarded it. To the Europeans, wealth became a badge of success; to Asians, a symbol of security; to Africans, a means of self-expression; and to American Indians, an instrument of affiliation. Only later shall we look beneath these surface meanings, for money as talisman against particular fears.

Chapter 3

Overview

Having surveyed the evolution of thinking about money and property as media for social communication (Chapter 1) and having begun to see how the social meanings people attach to money and property reflect values, attitudes, and inclinations that are buried deep in personality and culture (Chapter 2), we can now speak to the intended benefit of this book and to its purpose, audience, and plan.

BENEFIT, PURPOSE, AND AUDIENCE

This is a book about the meanings of money and the things money can buy: houses, cars, clothes, jewelry, and all the other goods with which we occupy ourselves. In economists' terms, it is a book about the meanings of wealth.[1] It is not a book about how to make money, accumulate property, or amass wealth, though it should be of at least some value to people with those interests.

Briefly put, understanding more about the meanings of money and property can be useful in any arena in which individuals, families, and groups send social messages with, or take those messages from, money and property. It can be particularly useful in business, where advertisers, marketers, and salespeople often capitalize on social meanings to persuade people to buy their products; in mental health, where counselors and therapists frequently help patients understand themselves through powerful symbolic meanings hidden below the surface of even the most mundane possessions; and in social relations, where racial, ethnic, and political groups compete or cooperate over various forms of money and property. Learning more about the meanings of wealth can also be useful simply to help interpret the world around us.

My principal goal is to encourage empirical research and other disciplined inquiry into the meanings of money and property, a field of study that remains curiously untouched by researchers despite our culture's limitless interest in the subject. To this end I bring together a rather varied collection of material, ordered in a simple framework and a less simple model. It is important that much of this material be approached as a set of hypotheses in need of rigorous testing, not a body of documented results, because most of the work required to support the framework and model still remains to be done. In short, this book is a research agenda more than a research report.

It is probably clear by now that this book is not primarily for analytic economists and others mainly interested in expressing people's experience with money and property in efficient models and tidy mathematical formulas, though it will suggest some variables that might eventually be measured with sufficient objectivity that they might enter into and improve the validity of econometric efforts, along with the individual-differences framework. The book is rather for psychologists, sociologists, anthropologists, and other social scientists; legal scholars; scholars in literature and the humanities; and others who want to draw on a variety of disciplines to think about the social meanings we attribute to money and the things money can buy. It is also for the serious lay reader who is willing to endure the occasional dry and dusty academic moment in return for perhaps a different way of looking at the material world.

The view of early human history described in Chapter 2 not only sets the stage for later chapters, but it introduces enough terms and concepts to allow me to describe the basics of my proposal, and it unveils the principal values and attitudes that underlie this book. The purpose of the rest of this chapter is to preview the basic moderator and model, along with the values and principles that support them, to provide a roadmap for what is to come.

PLAN OF THE BOOK

Values and Principles

Biological Basis. It may come as something of a surprise that a book on the meanings of money and property should refer as much to biology, evolution, and natural selection as this one does; more precisely, to the evolution of neuroanatomical structures and neurochemical processes in human perception and valuation. The reason for this emphasis is simple: I propose that meaning rests on perception, which in turn rests on the temperament of the perceiver. That is to say, perception is governed by neurophysiological activity moderated by temperament, and temperament is the result of genetic and environmental influences accruing over long periods of history. This is far from a universal view, but I believe it does a good job of accounting for the available data (e.g., Bridges, 1978; Cloninger, 1991; Davidson & Sutton, 1995; LeDoux, 1995; Wilson, 1992).

Perhaps the most interesting of the biological assertions we will encounter is that our propensities for saving/spending, giving/taking, and so forth are rooted not in social experience, but rather in neurophysiological propensities operating in a social context. I propose that natural selection has led some people to develop perceptual mechanisms that favor one style; other people, others. I also suspect that these propensities evolve over the lifetime of the individual.

To be sure, this is not a book on neurophysiology. It merely tries to close the gap that has come to separate social science and psychological science from brain science, thus to offer a conceptualization that is more satisfying, more realistic, and more consistent with contemporary knowledge than a simpler, more purely social or psychological conceptualization.[2] The disadvantage of my approach is that it acknowledges serious limitations on our ability to remedy problems and improve experience—and in that acknowledgment can elicit adverse political reaction.

Fear and the Talisman. In my formulation, the central psychological purpose of money and property is to defend against threats to the ego; hence, the central motive is fear and the central meaning is protection. I settle on fear as the basic human motive not (I hope) out of any personal perversity or propensity toward pessimism, but because the fear mechanism is the most sensitive component of the brain, and the fear response the most swift, powerful, and durable. Moreover, clinical experience seems to confirm the powerful motivational properties of fear.

Fear in the domain of money and property centers in the anticipation that someone will take away what we already have (jealousy), or the perception that someone has or will have something we don't (envy). Besides explaining much individual, family, and large-group behavior, these two motives— jealousy and envy—illuminate the greatest philosophical dialectic of our day, capitalism versus socialism.[3] From the jealous urge to retain that which we possess, comes capitalism; from the envious need to strip property from others and even from ourselves, comes socialism. Moreover, from the discomfort we feel at clinging to our money and property especially when others have less, comes guilt; from the discomfort of having no wealth of our own and at the same time wanting to strip others of theirs, comes shame. Thus capitalism and socialism are not social or economic philosophies deduced through the cool processes of reason, but institutionalized responses to emotional experiences with money and property, emotional experiences that are as much governed by biological propensity as by social experience. It goes without saying that this is not the conventional interpretation of the roots of socialism and capitalism.

When people find themselves unable to neutralize a threat, they attempt to control it by creating talismans. A *talisman* is a charm or amulet that we imbue with the power to protect ourselves from that which we fear. There are many potential talismans, including religion, sex, food, education, and exercise, as well as money and property. If Wittgenstein (1953) is right, that the meaning of a thing resides in its function, then *to protect* is central to the meaning of money and property. In short, the intended economic function of money and property may be to facilitate trade, but the fundamental *psychosocial* function is to protect us from the threats that go against the very core of ego.

The relationship between individuals and their talismans can become so intimate that the talisman becomes, in effect, an extension of the self. I am not my house, but when my house is broken into, I feel violated. I am not my car, but when someone compliments it, I feel full, and when someone insults it, I shrivel. I am not my bank account, but when my bank account swells to a particular level, I feel strong or safe or important or lovable. Thus money and the things money can buy take on additional meanings as parts of the selves through which we operate on the world.

The Moderator Framework. The purpose of this framework is to moderate the model, that is, to make sure that the model recognizes that different kinds of people assign different meanings to money and property and go through different processes to do so. In my view, different types of people have their own characteristic fears against which they use money and property as protection. The most general types of people are represented as a quaternary, a fourfold arrangement built on the intersection of two independent dialectics. Authors from Horace to Hegel have considered the dialectic a dynamic and intuitively appealing expression of the human experience; authors from Pythagoras to Schopenhauer (1974) have considered the quaternary an even more profound depiction.

The particular quaternary I employ crosses acquisition/affiliation and convergence/divergence, reminiscent of the Hermes/Hestia and Apollo/Dionysius myths and consistent, as we shall see, with a great deal of the teaching in ancient law, religion, and philosophy and a great deal of research in contemporary neurophysiology, psychometrics, and psychoanalysis.

This quaternary is perhaps most interesting when it describes types of people. The Hermes/Hestia dialectic is defined at one end by high acquisitiveness, at the other by high affiliativeness. People in the Hermean segment of this continuum we shall call *Drivers*;[4] those in the Hestian segment, *Amiables*. But there is more to these types of people—these dimensions— than meets the eye. Acquisitive people (Drivers) do the things they do not only because they experience pleasure at competition and accomplishment, but even more because they experience the pleasure of feeling protected from threats against their fear of being found incompetent. Similarly, affiliative people (Amiables) behave as they do not only because they enjoy feeling nurtured and nurturing, but even more because they feel especially good when protected against their fear of abandonment. This perspective is similar to Freud's, exhibited in his definition of happiness as the fulfillment of a long-held wish. Thus acquisitive people, or Drivers, take money and property from others to convince themselves that they aren't so incompetent as they fear they are. In sufficient numbers, they create cultures that reflect the same fear, that is, capitalism and (in the extreme) imperialism. They are biologically and socially inclined toward differentiation, placing people into hierarchies of performance and ownership.

Affiliative people, or Amiables, avoid wealth because they fear it will cause those close to them to think they are tainted, hence to reject them. They create cultures that emphasize collectivity, socialism and (in the extreme) communism. They are disposed toward "equivalencing," or minimizing differences among people, so no one will feel "disaffiliated."

The Apollo/Dionysius dialectic is defined at one end by concentration people (*Analytics*), at the other by divergent people (*Expressives*). Concentration people behave as they do because they enjoy staying focused, but even more because they fear losing control. Divergent people engage in lively and spontaneous behavior because they enjoy such behaviors, even more because they feel threatened by anything that smacks of constraint.

Concentration people, or Analytics, guard their money and property because they are afraid it will slip from their grasp (control). Divergent people, or Expressives, spend their wealth in ways which attempt to prove that they are free spirits.

Figure 3.1 presents the individual version of the general-temperament quaternary,[5] along with Galen's temperaments, the characteristic fears, and, for illustration, some occupations that seem to attract people of the different types.[6] (For Galen's original discussion, see *On the Natural Faculties,* II, 8-9.)

II	I
Acquisitiveness/Driver	*Expansiveness/Expressive*
Galen's Choleric	Galen's Sanguine
Fear of incompetence	Fear of constraint
e.g., entrepreneurs, military officers	e.g., entertainers, sales representatives
III	IV
Concentration/Analytic	*Affiliativeness/Amiable*
Galen's Phlegmatic	Galen's Melancholic
Fear of disarray	Fear of abandonment
e.g., accountants, "hard" scientists	e.g., clergy, child care workers

Figure 3.1. The Basic Quaternary of Temperaments

In Chapter 9, I shall also present a group version that depicts small groups like families and larger groups like cultures.

Figure 3.2 presents the basic financial-temperament version of this quaternary, crossing giving/taking with saving/spending. Farther out from the temperate midpoint lie divesting/wresting and hoarding/dissipating, analogous activities but more intense. (The behavior gets increasingly intense as one moves outward from the center.) In addition, Figure 3.2 suggests that taking and spending are manifestations of jealousy and produce guilt, whereas giving (needing) and even saving are manifestations of envy and produce shame. We shall discuss these implications in more detail in Chapter 9.

(Jealousy, Guilt)	*(Jealousy, Guilt)*
Wresting	Dissipating
Taking	Spending
Saving	Giving
Hoarding	Divesting
(Envy, Shame)	*(Envy, Shame)*

Figure 3.2. The Financial Quaternary

Wresting/Imperialism	Dissipating/Imperialism
Taking/Capitalism	Spending/Capitalism
Saving/Socialism	Giving/Socialism
Hoarding/Communism	Divesting/Communism

Figure 3.3. The Social Relations Quaternary

Figure 3.3 extends the quaternary into political philosophy, or social relations. The most important parts of this version are the distinction between traditional capitalism/socialism and the more extreme imperialism/communism, the differentiation of two varieties of each of those, one "harder" than the other, and the predominant connection of each to one of the archetypal cultures discussed in Chapter 2. Because all these figures are analogous to one another, they may be superimposed to generate further interpretation.

One of the quaternary's most important uses is to describe individuals, families, and groups in terms of their position on the crossed acquisition/affiliation and concentration/divergence coordinates. Any individual, family, or group can be located in reference to those two dimensions. With suitable cut-off points, arbitrary or natural, the classification can also be categorical. In either case, the more "basic" these dimensions are, the more powerful the classification is. Thus Parts II and III of this book will concentrate on evidence that these dimensions are as close as we can presently come to basic dimensions of personality and culture.

The Model. Finally, the model describes the process through which we attribute talismanic meaning to money and property, moderated by the quaternary framework that specifies the various types of people for whose distinctive patterns of behavior the model must account and from whose distinctive fears the talisman must protect. This model rests on my own tentative extensions of Edelman's (1987) theory of neuronal group selection, Bruner's (1990) view of cognitive process, and Jung's (1923/1971) (as well as Galen's; see Siegel, 1968) theory of psychological types. The core of the model is that meaning results from the pairing of social experience with bodily sensation. The labels we attach to those pairings define what we mean by meaning.

In brief, I propose that natural selection creates, and cultural influences reinforce, particular neurophysiological structures and processes that lead various people to perceive different aspects of the world more clearly, as an artist sees color more vividly than a CPA but a CPA perceives order more clearly than a comedian. Through survival alarms encoded in our neurons, we are programmed to fear most intensely the loss of that which we see most clearly. Because of the intimate connections among parts of the human brain, that which threatens us in any significant way, that which triggers our survival values, results in experiences that we label anxiety or fear, the absence or removal of which we label pleasure or relief. Different survival values are what distinguish the quaternary of temperaments and cause different types of people to attribute different meanings to money and property. Therefore biology is the basis for the different meanings, and the operative mechanism is the fear reflex.

Arrangement of the Book

Because its objective is to identify the different meanings we associate with money and property, this book focuses on the quaternary framework from which (I propose) meanings are derived.

In Part I, after showing that the social meanings we attach to wealth lie buried deep in natural and cultural history, I present the basic versions of the framework, on which I will elaborate in later chapters.

In Part II, I look for naturally occurring patterns in the form and structure of ancient law, the great religions, and classical philosophy that reveal who our ancestors were, hence who we are, on the notion that a framework built on such patterns will be a more valid depiction than one built on some arbitrary psychometric or philosophical foundation. I emphasize historical data over contemporary, in the hope of identifying patterns of cross-cultural similarity and difference that took shape before communication and transportation began to attenuate our world. At the same time, I provide a compendium of legal, religious, and philosophical tenets, which should help us flesh out the meanings that different people have come to associate with money and property.

In Part III, I use the foregoing information to devise more elaborate versions of the quaternary framework, and I support those versions with evidence from my own synthesis of contemporary neurophysiology, psychometrics, and psychoanalysis. Along with these more elaborate frameworks, I present a model for the process through which the different kinds of people represented in the quaternary attach meanings to money and property. Thus the framework serves as a moderator for the model, requiring the model to show how it applies differently to the four temperaments.

Finally, in Part IV, I discuss implications and applications of this work and contemplate where we might go from here.

CAUTIONS

To avoid misunderstanding, it is important to emphasize that there is (of course) enormous variability beneath the simple quaternary schema. First, most individuals, families, and groups exhibit attitudes, values, and behaviors associated with more than one quadrant. As Jung and others have observed, real people are not textbook-pure types; they are characterized by primary and secondary inclinations, and, in Jung's view, even by unconscious opposing ones. Some of the variability within a quadrant may itself form a quaternary: Within the Driver quadrant, for example, some Drivers who are more Amiable than others, some more Expressive, and some more Analytic, all in addition to the relatively pure "Driver Driver." Thus we may think about quadrants within quadrants, and perhaps quadrants with those, all in addition to unique individual variability.

Second, an individual's position on the coordinates probably changes over time, in terms of life stage, education and learning, and even shifts in the relative contribution of heredity versus environment.

Finally, people's values and behaviors change in response to situational factors such as role, context, and relationship, and how free they feel "to be themselves."

In short, individual variability defines the richness of the human drama— but science requires patterns. Although I surely appreciate individuality and uniqueness, for present purposes I shall err more in the direction of generalization than specification.

PART II

LEGAL, RELIGIOUS, AND PHILOSOPHICAL ANTECEDENTS

In which we examine form and substance
in ancient law, the great religions, and
classical philosophy in search of natural patterns
of attitudes and values regarding money
and property to serve as evidence regarding
the validity of the proposed framework
and elaboration on the associated meanings.

Chapter 4

Patterns in Ancient Law

As the agricultural settlements in Mesopotamia and Asia expanded and
the bands of wanderers in Africa and the Americas enlarged, it became
clear that rules of conduct would be necessary to enable the communities to
live and function together and to interact with others. For with size came
diversity, and with diversity came more ways that people who lived and
worked together could offend one another (Hoebel, 1954, chap. 12).

As civilizations advanced,[1] the trend in authority was away from family
and toward government. As agriculture evolved from basket to hoe to plow,
the influence of the *paterpostestas,* the all-powerful head of the clan, diminished, yielding to some form of chief or king or council. Whether the root
was new relationships too distant for immediate and concrete redress of
grievances, new social classes too diverse for family control, or simply that
the kind of temperament that advances technology also suffers less gladly
those who see the world differently, the result was the same: a movement in
the direction of dispassionate and impersonal rules under the aegis of a
central, hierarchical authority (Hoebel, 1954, p. 321; Maine, 1931, p. 141;
Newman, 1983, chap. 5).

The earliest laws reflect what philosophers and theologians call natural
law,[2] the human inclination toward good and away from evil[3] that Nature
hath writ "not in books but in the hearts of man" (Ryan, 1965, p. 15). In some
cultures, these natural inclinations evolved into bodies of oral customary
law; in others, they evolved further, into codes of written formal law. By and
large, Europe and Asia favored written laws; Africa and the Americas, oral
laws.

While the majority of natural law proponents continue to debate the nature
versus nurture[4] origins of man's inclinations, the occasional maverick acknowledges the joint action of the two. Davitt (1968), for instance, tells us
that laws rise from customs, customs from values, and values from both
physiology and psychology. It is not a large step to suggest that *temperament*
has had considerably more to do with the evolution of law than we generally

assume. To say that natural law resides "in the hearts of man" may simply turn out to be another way of saying that natural law is the result of biopsychosocial propensity, that is, temperament.

From this foundation, the peoples of the Earth gradually developed their own characteristic bodies of custom, customary law, and formal law. If my thesis is correct, if law is indeed "the distilled essence of the civilization of a people" (Anderson, 1976), we should see in these different codes clear reflections of the quaternary framework proposed in the preceding chapter. More specifically, we should see among the acquisitive Europeans more laws that relate to property; among the convergent Asians, more that emphasize enumeration, arrangement, and protection; among the divergent Africans, more that protect free individual expression; and among the affiliative American Indians, more that relate to the establishment and maintenance of harmonious family relations. I argue that we find exactly this arrangement in both the form and the substance of ancient law.

EUROPEAN LAW

It will come as no surprise that, from the beginning, European law has been about individual money and property. The thrust of the Babylonian and Roman codes in particular was to protect the individual from those who would diminish his or her property rights, especially the government.

With the accumulation of wealth comes the temptation to take advantage of those of lesser means, and the history of European law is replete with efforts to protect the poor and powerless. Exploitation by rulers and governors of subjects and citizens has been a matter of record for thousands of years. For example, nearly 4,500 years ago the Mesopotamian people, as we have already indicated, enjoyed a civilized and prosperous life, though at considerable cost. To maintain their society, they constructed an effective trading economy built on a "highly developed system of business and family laws witnessed by hundreds of contracts and other legal documents" (Steele, 1948, p. 1).

In time, the government officials and bureaucrats whose work these documents supported began to take advantage of the people. The city of Lagash, near Sumer, was nearly paralyzed by a corrupt civil bureaucracy that, in response to the rulers' need to raise armies with which to expand their sway, taxed the citizens beyond the limit, continuing those taxes even after the military need passed and diverting much of the money into the bureaucrats' own pockets. Ultimately, the citizens of Lagash overthrew the rulers and installed the reformer-king Urukagina,[5] who canceled the taxes, fired the "parasitic" civil inspectors and "ubiquitous" tax collectors, and in general reaffirmed the social and economic power of the citizens (Kramer, 1956, chap. 6).

The Babylonian Codes

At about the same time, government in Babylon too had run amok. Civil inspectors often confiscated the property they inspected—animals, crops, edible oil—and bureaucrats applied a confiscatory system of taxes and tariffs. If a man divorced his wife, he paid a tax; if a perfumer made an oil preparation, he paid a tax; if a man died, he paid a tax—sometimes well over half his estate went to the palace, along with an array of "gifts" for the bureaucrats. By 2400 B.C., debtors and tax resistors languished in prisons beside common criminals (Kramer, 1963, pp. 77-81).

Into this morass came a series of rulers each more or less bent on protecting the poor[6] and the weak yet maintaining the primacy of property: the Babylonian lawgivers Ur-Nammu, Bilalama, Lipit-Ishtar, and, most famous of all, Hammurabi.

Code of Ur-Nammu (ca. 2050 B.C.). To present knowledge, the earliest written legal code[7] is not that of Hammurabi but of Ur-Nammu, more than three hundred years earlier (Kramer, 1956, pp. 48-51). The Ur-Nammu Code, although it exists only in the most fragmentary form, tells a great deal about the culture of the time, hence about the backdrop against which law and meaning developed.

Recalling that meaning resides in function, it is striking that the first functions ascribed to money in a legal code were to oppress the poor and thus, presumably, to magnify the wealthy. The preamble of the Ur-Nammu Code recounts some of the oppressive "functions" for the prevention of which Ur-Nammu demanded praise:

> The orphan did not fall a prey to the wealthy man.
> The widow did not fall a prey to the mighty man.
> The man of one shekel did not fall a prey to the man of one mina.

The Ur-Nammu Code also specified the first known schedule of money damages for personal injury:

> If a man, in the course of a scuffle, smash the limb of another man with a club, he shall pay one mina of silver.

Thus money was not only something people coveted, it was something that could be severed, as an arm or leg might have been severed in another place or another age. More than 4,000 years ago, then, money and property had already come to mean oppression of the poor and the weak, magnification of the rich and the powerful, and compensation for victims of some kinds of crime. Because paying compensation could substitute for amputation of a limb, separations both, the people of Babylonia apparently saw money as some kind of extension of themselves.

Code of Bilalama (ca. 1920 B.C.). A hundred and thirty years after Ur-Nammu, King Bilalama of Eshnunna compiled a code of laws that focused on life in an agricultural economy, with perhaps even greater emphasis than Ur-Nammu's on the business side of life, specifically rent, payments, and interest. More important for our purposes, the Code of Bilalama also showed how the early Mesopotamians used money and property to express social values, particularly with regard to the importance of the family (Bilalama, 1969, p. 162; see also Yaron, 1969):

Bilalama Law 26: If a man gives bride-money for a[nother] man's daughter, but another man seizes her forcibly without asking the permission of her father and her mother, and deprives her of her virginity, it is a capital offence and he shall die.

Bilalama Law 59: If a man divorces his wife after having made her bear children and takes [another] wife, he shall be driven from his house and from whatever he owns and may go after [the woman] whom he loves.

It is clear in these laws that the husband is still the seat of power in the home, though not with the unlimited authority of the paterpotestas. But it is equally clear that the community will hold him responsible for his wife's well-being. He may divorce her, but the cost of pursuing his new love will be substantial. Even in the face of love and lust, then, money means not only ownership but responsibility, supported by some potential for redress on the part of the community for violations of community standards, especially along sexual lines. Four thousand years ago, then, jurisprudence began to notice the tension not only between individual and community but also between money and love, and between money and religion. If money is opposed to love and religion, money must be evil.

Code of Lipit-Ishtar (1860 B.C.). About sixty years after Bilalama, Anu, the "father of the gods," and Enlil, the "lord who determines destinies," are said to have given a collection of laws to Lipit-Ishtar "to establish justice in the land" and "bring well-being to the Sumerians and Akkadians." Though only 200 years more recent than the Code of Ur-Nammu, the Code of Lipit-Ishtar contains a much wider range of laws, the bulk of which deal with business and commerce, plus a few that concentrate on family responsibility.

For example, on business and commerce (quoted in Steele, 1948):

> Lipit-Ishtar Laws 34 and 35: If a man rented an ox and injured the flesh at the nose ring, he shall pay one-third of its price. . . . [If he] damaged its eye, he shall pay one-half its price.

> Lipit-Ishtar Law 12: A man who is caught in [someone else's crop-field] during the daytime shall pay ten shekels of silver. He who is caught in the [crop-field] at night shall die, he shall not get away alive.

On family relations:

> Lipit-Ishtar Law 142: If [the divorced wife] have been a careful mistress and be without reproach and her husband have been going about and greatly belittling her, the woman has no blame. She shall receive her dowry and shall go to her father's house.

> Lipit-Ishtar Law 24: If the second wife whom he had married bore him children, the dowry which she brought from her father's house belongs to her children, but the children of his first wife and the children of his second wife shall divide equally the property of their father.

Through gradations of severity of damages and recognition of competing rights, the Lipit-Ishtar Code attempts to formulate a more refined sense of justice[8] than its predecessors. Lipit-Ishtar's laws begin to control the flow of money and property from member to member on the basis not just of power but of equity.

Code of Hammurabi (1690 B.C.). Just as the gods gave the laws to Lipit-Ishtar and would give them to Moses, so they also gave a code to Hammurabi. The overall goals of Hammurabi's Code were "to cause justice to prevail in the land, to destroy the wicked and the evil, to prevent the strong from oppressing the weak . . . , to enlighten the land, and to further the welfare of the people" (Prologue in Hammurabi, 1904).

Like Ur-Nammu and the other lawgivers, Hammurabi provided, in his Prologue, a self-description that gives further insight into Babylonian temperament, at least the temperament of the leaders:

> The elect shepherd of Bel am I, dispensing riches and abundance . . . the hero king . . . the avenging warrior . . . the protector of the land . . . the grave of the foe . . . possessor of sceptre and crown . . . the far-seeing one . . . the royal ruler of the city who has subjugated the districts . . . the renowned potentate . . . the promulgator of justice . . . the crusher of enemies . . . the exalted one, who humbles himself before the great gods. (quoted in Edwards, 1934, pp. 13-16)

A collection of 282 laws inscribed on stone monuments, the Code of Hammurabi promulgates a still more refined conception of social justice (Hammurabi, 1904):

> Hammurabi Law 198: If one destroy the eye of a [working-class] freeman . . . , he shall pay one mina[9] of silver.

> Hammurabi Law 199: If one destroy the eye of a man's slave . . . , he shall pay one-half his price.

Hammurabi is even more strict than Lipit-Ishtar about punishment for failures of responsibility:

> Hammurabi Law 218: If a physician operate on a man . . . and cause the man's death . . . , they shall cut off his fingers.

> Hammurabi Law 229: If . . . the house which [a builder] has built collapse and cause the death of the owner . . . , that builder shall be put to death.

> Hammurabi Law 233: [If] . . . a wall fall in, that builder shall strengthen that wall at his own [expense].

Mesopotamian law is natural law in that it reflects the propensities of the influential members of the community. On the one hand, it supports the capitalistic values on which the Mesopotamian society depended; on the other, it tries to hold in check the inclination of the wealthy and powerful to oppress the poor and impotent. These messages are embedded not in some vague and unreliable impressions but in a well-defined conception[10] of social justice (Schmidt, 1987, chap. 3).

The Mosaic Code

Moses flourished about 1250 B.C., nearer in time to Homer than to Hammurabi. The Mosaic Code was similar to the Babylonian codes in some respects, very different in many others. The Torah, the first five books of the Old Testament (particularly Exodus and Deuteronomy), is the law of a theocratic people, highly influenced by religious ethics.[11] It is, in addition, a response to an achieving people's occasional propensity to go too far.

But the Torah is also an invitation to positive behavior. The thrust of the Torah is prescription about how people should relate to one another and to God (Parrinder, 1983, p. 401). Hillel's (1918) summary of the Torah (ca .100 A.D.) is consistent with the Christian and Confucian Golden Rules:

> What is hateful to yourself do not do to your fellow-man. That is the whole Torah. All the rest is commentary. Now go and study. (Babylonian Talmud tractate Shabbat, p. 31a; quoted in Neusner, 1988, p. 23)

The social idealism learned during the Exile and Return permeates laws regarding the treatment of land and the treatment of the poor.

The emotional significance the Hebrews attached to the land in which their ancestors were buried defined the Hebraic approach to land law, which bridged the evolution from Mesopotamian (largely) communal ownership to Roman (largely) individual ownership (Genesis 47:29). The hallmark of later Roman land law would be the owner's absolute right to use, to alienate, even to abuse his property. The Hebrews, in contrast, were forbidden to abuse land, not only because it is where the ancestors are buried but, even more important, because it belonged to God. In fact, they must let the land lie fallow every seventh year (Exodus 23:10-11; Leviticus 25:2-4) and return the title to God every fiftieth, during the Jubilee. And they must never sell rural land in perpetuity. The calculation of land values took account of these limitations (Gonzalez, 1990, p. 20).

The Mosaic Code also prohibited usury,[12] regardless of the rate of interest, and in doing so set an example that Christians would follow until the Enlightenment, Muslims to the present day. To this prohibition it added a call for compassion toward those who have to borrow:

> If ever you take your neighbor's garment in pledge, you shall restore it to him before the sun goes down; for that is his only covering, it is the mantle for his body; in what else shall he sleep? (Exodus 22:26-27 [all biblical quotes are from the New English Bible, 1970])

The code also prohibited obviously dishonest practices like falsifying weights and measures (Deuteronomy 25:13).

The social idealism of the Hebrews is even more evident in the Mosaic Code's prescriptions for dealing with the poor. They let the poor gather gleanings from any untended land (and left what the poor didn't take for hungry wild animals), and they followed detailed guidelines[13] about how much to leave behind during harvesting, never less than one-sixth of the total crop (Pe'ah 5-6, in Gonzalez, 1990, p. 21). Every third and sixth year of the seven-year cycle, the Hebrews paid special land tithes. During Jubilee years, they freed slaves and forgave debts, or at least they viewed these as ideal Jubilee practices (Gonzalez, 1990, pp. 21-22). *Tsedaqah,* almsgiving, and *gemilut hasadim,* or philanthropy, are still pillars of Jewish observance.

This degree of sensitivity to the Hebrew poor, more than any other feature, distinguished the Mosaic Code[14] from its Mesopotamian predecessors and helped make it the basis for later Christian and Muslim law.

If the Mosaic Code was a reply to early capitalism, the Essenian code was a revolution. The Essenes stripped themselves of private property and lived the truly communal life. Philo explains:

> First of all then, one's house is not his own in the sense that it is shared by all, for besides the fact that they dwell together in communities, the door is open to visitors from elsewhere who share their convictions. Again they all have a single treasury and common disbursements; their clothes are held in common and also their food through their institution of public meals. In no other community can we find the institution of sharing roof, life and board more firmly established in actual practice. And that is no more than one would expect. For all the wages which they earn in the day's work they do not keep as their private property, but throw them into the common stock and allow the benefit thus accruing to be shared by those who wish to use it. (*Quod Omnis Probus,* 85-87; quoted in Gonzalez, 1990, p. 23)

More clearly than its predecessors,[15] the Mosaic Code teaches us that there is a moral dimension to money and property. In it we see the beginnings of a long tradition of disdain for money and property, what Schmidt (1987) describes as the Judeo-Christian "hostility to wealth." From a broader vantage, we can see a relativity in the morality of wealth: To affiliative types, of whom the Essenes would be an extreme example, the presence of wealth is evil, the absence good, but to acquisitive types, like the Mesopotamians (and Romans and Germanic Europeans and European Americans), the absence of wealth is evil, its presence good. This dialectic sets the basis for the much of the conflict and turmoil that seem so often to accompany money and property.

Greek Custom and Early Law

The values that Homer and Hesiod attributed to their Heroes evolved into customs, customary laws,[16] and eventually, the written laws of the of the fledgling democracy. The Greek poets (and occasional rulers), like the Mesopotamian rulers (and occasional poets), railed against the rich and the mighty for oppressing the poor and the weak. Of poor and weak in preclassical Greece there were many, for Greek agriculture had cycled into depression, largely because the small farms on rocky soil could not compete with cheaper produce from abroad. By the seventh century B.C., the customs and customary laws were reminiscent of the Mesopotamian codes in that they favored capitalistic enterprise. The eupatrids, hereditary aristocrats, controlled the state, and they operated it to their advantage and at the expense of the small farmers. The farmers could, and did, mortgage their ancestral lands; in addition, they could, and did, mortgage their wives, their children, and themselves. Wealthy investors took advantage of this opportunity and bought up the mortgaged lands. Eviction, starvation, and debt-slavery became the order of the day (Groseclose, 1934, p. 14; Thorlief, 1960).

As in Lagash, acquisitive excess provoked a series of reactions. In this instance,[17] the first reaction was that of Draco (621 B.C.), who attempted to break the eupatrid power monopoly by formalizing what had previously been custom and customary law. Among the better-known of his measures was doing away with hereditary power in favor of power as a function of productivity (measured as wealth). Eventually, however, the old approach regained its force, Draco's reforms lost public support, and the depression returned.

In 607 B.C., the power of government passed to Solon, a salubrious combination of masterful leader, masterly orator, and idealistic poet. As soon as he became archon in 594 B.C., he decreed his *seisachtheia*—shaking off the burdens. He invalidated all loans, real as well as personal; he forbade pledging oneself or one's family as collateral for a mortgage, freed debtors from prison, even brought back those who had been enslaved abroad. Finally, he devalued the currency to reduce the cost of living—and drove many businessmen and landlords into bankruptcy (Groseclose, 1934, pp. 15-26; Harrison, 1971).

Roman Law

Roman law is the perfection of the property law that began with the Mesopotamians.[18] Starting with the Council of Ten, the Decemviri, and culminating with the Emperor Justinian, Roman law became the foundation on which most later Western law would be constructed, including the laws of Germany, Holland, Great Britain, and, eventually, the United States (Sohm, 1907, esp. p. 48).

The Twelve Tables (450 B.C.*).* Like the Greeks two centuries before, the Romans wanted laws fixed in writing so magistrates could not alter them to the disadvantage of the people. According to legend, a delegation of legal scholars went to Greece to study the possibility of adopting Draco's laws. More likely, the Council of Ten memorialized Roman customs and customary laws, with some Greek influence. Although the tables (tablets) themselves were lost when the barbarians sacked the city, we know from secondary sources that the collection promulgated a range of laws[19] covering realty and personality.

Grueber (1886, pp. 186-187; see also Colquhoun, 1851) notes that the Twelve Tables used the human body as metaphor for property, distinguishing damage to an extremity (*membrum rumpere,* or "break an extremity") from the more serious damage to head or torso (*os frangere,* or "break a bone in head or trunk"). In either event, though the amounts differ, payment of money and property constitutes absolution:

Table VII 14: If someone "break an extremity" of another and not make peace, it is *talio* (and a mediator shall decide money damages, the payment of which absolves the defendant).

Table VII 15: If someone "break a bone in head or trunk" of a freeman, he shall pay the victim 300 ewes, if of a slave, 150.

Property transactions formed the centerpiece of the Twelve Tables. Every valid transaction involved either the *mancipatio* or the *nexum.*[20] Mancipatio, literally, taking-in-hand, was a solemn buy/sell ritual in which the buyer, in the presence of five witnesses, grasped the item to be purchased in his hand and simultaneously poured a certain amount of copper flake into the hand of the seller, all the while reciting a formal incantation. As time went by, the mancipatio was used only for purchases important enough to require the binding force of the formal liturgy, much as real estate transactions today are valid only if they are in writing and follow the prescribed verbal formulas.

Nexum, a net, or—by extension—a binding, was an equally solemn liturgy for making a loan. Again in the presence of witnesses, the lender poured the proper amount of metal flake into the hand of the borrower and received in return a solemn promise that the loan would be repaid. The nexum was a particularly oppressive contract. If the borrower should default, the lender could have him sold into slavery, or even killed—presumably discouraging further default. If he should default against several lenders, they could literally cut him into proportionate pieces.

The tenor of both these transactions was that property rights and title should be protected at all costs. The mancipatio and nexum liturgies were very complex as well as concrete, and any violation of the formula could invalidate the transaction. Thus the Romans were even more serious about property than the Mesopotamians had been, and from the very beginning they dedicated their talent for jurisprudence to the service of property rights. The contrast between the Roman and Hebrew attitudes toward loan repayment could not be more stark.

Code of Justinian (534). In the nearly 1,000 years[21] between the Twelve Tables and Justinian's time, the body of law on which the Roman state stood grew so large and complex, so hard to access, so internally inconsistent and even contradictory that few legal scholars, and fewer practicing lawyers, could master it. Thus one of Justinian's principal motives grew from his lawyerly mind, to codify the body of Roman law. A second motive reflected his conversion to Christianity: his Code was to create a new world order that would be the perfect union of the Roman and Christian traditions (Ure, 1951, pp. 140, 167).

Justinian's Prooemium is remarkably similar to the Prologues of the Mesopotamian codes, recounting victories and promoting the ruler's finely honed sense of justice—and of self:

> In the name of Our Lord Jesus Christ. The Emperor Caesar Flavius Justinian, conqueror of the Alamanni, Goths, Franks, Germans, Antes, Alani, Vandals, Africans. Devout, fortunate, renowned. Victorious and Triumphant. Forever Augustus. To Young Enthusiasts for Law: Imperial Majesty should not only be graced with arms but also armed with laws, so that good government may prevail in time of war and peace alike. The head of the Roman state can then stand victorious not only over our enemies in war but also over troublemakers,

driving out their wickedness through the paths of the law, and can triumph as much for his devotion to the law as for his conquests in battle. (Justinian, 1987, p. 33)

In essence a grand elaboration of the Twelve Tables, the bulk of the Code of Justinian concerns the safeguarding, preservation, and transmission of private property. Ure (1951) attributes this emphasis not to "the selfish interests of a moneyed clique but [to] the long unbroken tradition" of the Roman legal profession "exercising its ingenuity in perfecting one particular system" (p. 142).

But Justinian's conception of social justice is more encompassing than that of his predecessors. Justinian's goal of merging Roman law with Christian values is clearly evident in his attempts to maintain the sanctity of the sacrament of matrimony. Like the Mesopotamians, Justinian used threats to property (Hermes) to promote the integrity of the family (Hestia):

> When the crime of adultery has been established, We order the penalties prescribed by Constantine, of Divine memory, shall be inflicted upon those who are guilty; . . . so far as the property of the adulterer is concerned, if he has a wife, We order that the dowry and ante-nuptial donation shall be given to her. . . . The adulteress shall suffer corporeal punishment, and shall be confined in a monastery. (Justinian, 1973)

to protect womanhood:

> We do not permit a woman to be placed in prison, or guarded by men, on account of a fiscal obligation . . . lest her chastity may suffer violation. (Justinian, 1932, Collection 9, Title XVII, p. 143)

to discipline priests:

> We do not permit a deacon . . . or any other member of the clergy . . . to be appointed a receiver or collector of taxes, a recorder of public or private property . . . or an attorney to conduct legislation. . . . When [they] do this, a fine . . . shall be collected. (Justinian, 1932, Collection 9, Title VI, pp. 85-86)

and to protect and augment church property:

> We forbid lands belonging to holy churches . . . to be subjected to . . . extraordinary [taxes and tributes]. (Justinian, 1932, Collection 9, Title XIV, p. 126)

Finally, one of the most important contributions, indeed one of the hallmarks, of Roman jurisprudence was the introduction of the concept of individual rights:

> Justice is an answering and perpetual determination to acknowledge all men's rights. (Justinian, 1987, Book I, Title 1:1, p. 37)

Justinian's absolute property rights and greatly expanded individual rights were not only central to Roman law but established the foundation for virtually all subsequent Western law.

Just as the Mosaic Code was more abstract than the Mesopotamian codes, more apodictic, so the Roman laws were more abstract than their predecessors'. Indeed, Justinian's work was the first true *code* of laws, as distinguished from a simple collection. In both intent and accomplishment the first true *jurisprudence,* or "science of the just and the unjust" (Justinian, 1987, Book I, Title 1:1), it could not stand in starker contrast to Chinese (Asian) law, to which we now turn.

CHINESE LAW

Legal systems reflect, and then affect, the temperament of their cultures. If Western law was about property, Eastern law was about order. If Western law was about individuality, Eastern was about community. If Western law was about rights, Eastern was about "wrongs." If Western law protected the person from the state, Eastern law protected the state from the person (see Chen, 1973, pp. 9-10; see also Spengler, 1980, chap. 4, and Cohen & Cohen, 1980).

With law as with everything else in earliest China, it is difficult to distinguish between myth and history. According to myth-history, the Emperor Huang Ti—the same Huang Ti who apparently minted the first coins—issued the first regulations concerning human conduct in 2697 B.C. (on today's Western calendar), and the Emperor Yao instituted the "five corporal punishments" in about 2300 B.C. If these claims and dates enjoy any validity, the earliest Chinese laws were promulgated substantially earlier than the earliest known Mesopotamian laws, for Ur-Nammu's Code dates only to 2050 B.C. So far, however, there is no physical evidence to support this tradition.

Chinese law, like law throughout the world, surely began as etiquette intended to maintain comfortable functioning at home, at work, and in the public eye, then developed into the clan rules and the guild laws—customary law—and finally evolved into the dynastic codes, upon the earliest of which we shall focus here.

The Q'in Code

The first known written Chinese legal code[22] was that of the Q'in dynasty (221-206 B.C.; pronounced *chin,* whence China), of which only fragments remain.

The Q'in Code, like all subsequent Chinese law, was deeply influenced by the tension between Confucianism and legalism. Confucius (551-479 B.C.) had preached a fundamentally aristocratic etiquette of respect that emphasized tidy hierarchical differentiation as part of the traditional order of the universe. As a result of this structure, the privileges that accrued to the nobility did not apply to the common folk, and the punishments that applied to the common folk did not accrue to the nobility.

The legalists believed in rewarding good behavior and punishing bad without regard to personal station. They taught that laws should apply equally to prince and pauper, that neither should escape punishment or be deprived of rewards by virtue of his rank, and that both should be absolutely subject to the authority of the state (Chen, 1973, pp. 7, 27-28). Through the "unification of punishments," Kung-sun Yan, founder of the legalist school, proposed a system in which the law was applied equitably, dispassionately—and ruthlessly.

When Q'in Emperor Tsin united the empire in the third century B.C., he adopted the uniform and impartial philosophy of the legalists and laid the foundation of Chinese law for centuries to come. Written on bamboo strips because the invention of paper was still several centuries in the offing, the Q'in Code detailed a wide-ranging system that was essentially penal in nature[23] but that nevertheless covered not only what Westerners would call criminal law but much of civil and regulatory law as well. Punishment is the single most evident characteristic of this code and of Chinese law in general. Indeed, one of the old Chinese words for punishment is the same as one of the old words for law.[24]

The system of punishments was carefully thought out and articulated, and (of course) it was centrally controlled. For criminal infractions, or for failures to meet civil and regulatory procedural requirements, convicts could expect severe punishment: the death penalty (usually beheading; for more serious crimes, a slower death by slashing); hard labor (for men, building the famous Chinese walls and fortifications; for women, making bricks from rice); and also banishment, castration, and other mutilations (Hulsewe, 1985, p. 14).

In addition, the Q'in established an illuminating system of fines that deserves special attention. "Fine" was a much more inclusive concept in China than in the West. Its usual meaning, as in Babylonia, was simply a monetary punishment. But in its second meaning a fine was quantified as *time,* not money; for example, one could be "fined" two years' service building city walls. Finally, a fine was a fee paid as "redemption" against the traditional punishments. Indeed, convicts were often condemned to pay redemption against whatever physical punishment the court had ordered. If they could not pay the redemption on the spot, they could work it off, shoulder to shoulder with the hard-labor convicts; otherwise, they simply had to endure it. Presumably the richer and more able-bodied fared better; professors and others of low station and limited practical ability, worse: In 93 B.C., the historian Su-ma Ch'ien lamented, understandably enough, his inability to pay the redemption fee against his own castration (Hulsewe, 1985, p. 18).

Fines were paid not in cash but in suits of armor[25]—the entire suit, or just the shield, or perhaps just the laces that tied the whole suit together. Although this practice seems curious at first, it is consistent with the ancient Chinese practice of using tools, or miniaturized tools, as specie. No information exists as to the cash value of this armor (Hulsewe, 1985, p. 18).

The Q'in statutes penetrated even more deeply than the Mosaic Code into daily life. In addition, they involved not only the perpetrator but his or her superiors and associates. For example:

Q'in Statute C11: When the quality of manufactured objects upon inspection is poor, the Master of the Artisans is fined one suit of armor, the Assistant as well as the Head of the work-squad are fined one shield, and the men are fined twenty sets of laces.

After punishment, the most striking feature of the Q'in Code is the degree of central control it specifies for the administration of the country. For example:

Q'in Statute A1: Whenever the rain is beneficial and affects the grain in ear, a report in writing is to be made concerning the favored crop and the grain in ear, as well as the number of [acres] of cultivated fields and areas without crops.

Whenever it rains when the crop is already fully grown, also the quantity of rain and the number of [acres] which were affected are to be reported in writing. Likewise, in cases of drought and violent wind or rain, floods, hordes of grasshoppers or other creatures which damage the crops, the number of [acres] concerned is always to be reported in writing.

Q'in Statute A76: For one lubrication when repairing one cart, use one ounce of glue and two ounces of grease. When repairing pieces which have fallen apart, the glue is divided according to their number.

In addition, the Q'in Code contains a question-and-answer section intended to instruct civil servants in the use of the code and to standardize the application of the code throughout the country. For example:

Q'in Statute D150: If a wife has committed a crime for which she is arrested, are the slaves, clothes and vessels of her dowry warranted to be confiscated or are these returned to her husband? To be returned to her husband.

The infamous "checking" statutes governed the mandatory practice of informing on people who made mistakes or committed crimes. The purpose of checking was to maintain work quality and preserve government property. Workers were assigned to squads, and families were assigned to cells, not so much for companionship or teamwork as to make people responsible for overseeing, checking, and possibly denouncing each other. If one family violated a law, all families in the cell would be punished (Hulsewe, 1955, p. 273).

The Han Code

History becomes more reliable with the Han dynasty (206 B.C.–220 A.D.). The Han Code, consisting of some twenty principal statutes and many lesser regulations, is also preserved in fragmentary form. Beginning with the relatively simple "Statutes in Nine Sections," the Han Code[26] grew into 26,000 articles and, like the Torah, a commentary many times the length of the code itself.

Like the Q'in Statutes, the Han Code concentrates on punishment, from multiples of 100 strokes of the bamboo bastinado[27] on the bare buttocks to torture followed by "extermination of the clan" (Hulsewe, 1955, pp. 102-135). Although the Han punishments were for the most part corporal, they were occasionally monetary. At least one scholar believes that every ordinance included a provision for fines, but there are no texts to support that belief (Shen, in Hulsewe, 1955, p. 134). Occasionally, as in Q'in times, the convict could apparently purchase redemption from the corporal punishment.

In keeping with the legalist philosophy, there are very few signs of compassion in the Han Code. One ordinance provides that a hard-labor sentence for women can be commuted after six months if a fine is paid, another that foodstuffs are to be distributed to young mothers and to people eighty years of age and older (Hulsewe, 1955, pp. 45-46).

The form and content of the Q'in and Han codes foreshadowed those of all subsequent dynastic codes as well: the Code of the Sui (589-618 A.D.), the Code of the T'ang (the oldest code to have survived intact; 618-907 A.D.), the Code of the Ming (1368-1662 A.D.), and the Code of the Q'ing (1644-1911 A.D.); indeed, also the laws of Japan, Korea, and Vietnam. As time passed, the punishments became somewhat less ferocious, and the systems were organized into a tidy crimes-by-punishments matrix that enabled even uneducated magistrates in the farthest reaches of the country to apply the law with legalist precision and dispassion, and always under central control (Jones, 1994, pp. 12-13).

With all their enumeration, quantification, and dispassion, these measures must have produced a fearful and suspicious population in which prudent individuals would be reluctant to share their thoughts and feelings with friends and neighbors, perhaps even with family. As a result, the Chinese psyche became as impenetrable to outsiders as the Great Wall. Although it can be argued that Confucian philosophy exerted telling pressure on the development of Chinese society, the system of laws has been a reminder of central authority until this very day.

AFRICAN CUSTOMARY LAW

For better or worse, neither sub-Saharan African law[28] nor indigenous North and South American Indian law evolved in the same directions or at the same pace as did European or Asian law.

European and Asian law evolved relatively quickly into formal written compendiums, the former comprising precepts for protecting property, the latter rules for regulating wrongs. With regard to money, the Europeans were concerned with its commercial use, the Asians with its compensatory potential.

In contrast, African and American Indian law remained, and in many ways still remain, in the prejurisprudence, or customary law, stage (Palmer, 1970, p. 32). Customary law is more personal than geographical; it travels with the tribe no matter where the tribe may travel (Allott, 1960, p. 155). In the more remote parts of South and Central America and on some of the more traditional reservations and reserves in North America, daily life is still governed by customary law. Though American Indian customary law was by and large even less formal than its African counterpart, both the African and Indian versions paid more attention to family than to property and to tort law than to penal law. African and Indian law focused on the family as both the victim of wrong-doing and the agent for redress.

There is relatively little in the earliest African customary laws about property rights, because individual ownership[29] was an alien notion, and the clan's very survival, to say nothing of its wealth, depended on the people's access to cattle and land. As in other parts of the world, the patriarch, the paterfamilias, owned the clan's property, and all acquisitions throughout the family were on his behalf. He had absolute control over movable ancestral property, limited control over immovable ancestral property (could only alienate with elders' consent), and no control over "family" or "private" property (Palmer, 1970, p. 60). Later, after the Bantu occupation, the individual monarchs owned the land.

By way of contrast, much of African customary law focuses on family growth and harmony. Family growth is achieved through marriage and protected by laws against homicide and assault, also by laws against theft of those material things that support survival. Marriage, in turn, is advanced by laws that formalize the matrimonial contract[30] and discourage dissolution.

Marriage involved a series of property rituals from initial proposal through the nuptial ceremony itself. To initiate a proposal, an East African Kamba suitor, for example, should send two goats to the girl's family, and the boy's father should send two calabashes of beer. The acceptance of these offerings signifies consent to the engagement (Penwill, 1951, pp. 2-3). Kamba customary law spells out all the details of the marriage arrangement, right down to redress if one of the bride-price animals is barren. Similarly among the Fanti and Ashanti of West Africa's Gold Coast, acceptance of the suitor's initial request *and the gift* constitute acceptance of the marriage proposal. This process, *consawment*, is called "the price of the head" (Sarbah, 1904, p. 47; see also Rattray, 1929), though, as with the gift exchange, the transaction is more social than economic. The Kamba bride-price always includes one bull, two cows, and some number of goats (Penwill, 1951, pp. 2-3).

In addition to the consawment and bride-price, the bride's family could request a dowry. As the purpose of the consawment was to establish the marriage contract, and the purpose of the bride-price was to assure exclusive sexual rights for the husband, the purpose of the dowry was to protect the bride, her children, and even her family in the event of divorce or the husband's death. Accordingly, African customary law (like natural law) classifies adultery as a form of theft. The penalty for adultery is a fine paid by the interloper to the husband's family, in some tribes to the husband. The Fanti set the price of this fine equal to the consawment plus all marriage expenses (Rattray, 1929, p. 317; Sarbah, 1904, pp. 48, 73). For a thorough examination of bridewealth and dowry, see Goody & Tambiah, 1973).

Because the integrity of the family is compromised by homicide, adultery,[31] assault, or theft against any member, some kind of restitution to the offended family is necessary if clan strife is to be avoided. The value of the property used for compensation reflected the severity of the crime. For homicide and assault, payment of the "blood-price" would sometimes suffice, though some tribes accepted only talion payment, blood for blood— "If you spill blood, blood alone can right it," runs an Ashanti maxim. For murdering a man, a typical blood-price was eleven cows, one bull, and one goat; for murdering a woman, four cows, a bull, and a goat. If the homicide were accidental, there was still a monetary penalty: one pound in gold dust, the market value of a male slave. The blood-price for assault depended on the damage the victim suffered, though it was often more symbolic than economic. For example, compensation for loss of one finger was generally a cow, a bull, and a goat, but the loss of one hand was worth five cows, and a bull and a goat. Sometimes the damages were paid to the House Master (paterfamilias), clan leader, or tribal elders on behalf of the family or community (Palmer, 1970, pp. 24, 101; Sarbah, 1904, pp. 85). Some tribes permitted people to purchase redemption against assigned punishments.

Because theft was not only an offense against the family but a genuine threat to survival among a subsistence people, it resulted in severe penalties. For habitual theft, even of small items, the community would burn down the perpetrator's house with all his possessions inside. For serious theft, the penalty was death. However, if the father of the thief was determined to redeem his son, he could pay restitution to the victims—after which payment all the rest of *his* cattle would be slaughtered and *his* house burned down (Sarbah, 1904, pp. 88, 110).

Like most legal systems rooted in truly ancient times, African customary law permits usury. Any man can make a money debt, and the creditor can charge interest on the loan. Money interest is charged against money debts, but otherwise the produce of the borrowed property constitutes the interest (more like a limited partnership; see Islamic "interest-free banking," p. 85). In lieu of monetary discharge, the debtor can pawn some property or person to work off the debt. If the pawn is a person and runs away, interest is calculated until she or he returns; otherwise, the labor of the pawn is equivalent to interest. In pawning land, the mortgagee could ask for interest in the form of gold dust, because he may not live long enough to share the produce of the land (Palmer, 1970, pp. 50, 84-85; Rattray, 1929, p. 367).

Tort law in old Africa frequently includes a notion of responsibility. For example, if a man's cattle got out of their pen during the night and damaged someone else's property, the owner of the cattle incurred no penalty, but if the cattle escaped during the day, or if the fence was missing, inadequate, or damaged, he had to pay compensation. There is no fault at night because much that happens under cover of darkness is beyond a person's control (Palmer, 1970, p. 103). The Babylonians, Hebrews, and Romans, as we have seen, had made the same distinction but arrived at very different interpretations.

African customary law places its greatest emphasis on preserving the dignity of every member of the community, especially the elders. If an Ashanti man called his mother-in-law by too familiar a name, he had to pay a fine (one goat). If he inadvertently sat in her special place near the hearth, he had to pay a larger fine. If a woman called her mother-in-law by too familiar a name, she too had to pay a goat—and she would also be beaten by her husband. Outside the immediate family, an elder could protest to a tribunal that a young man had disrespected him, and the boy would be properly reprimanded or punished. Sarbah (1904) notes that in the old days, the elder would protest directly to the boy's father, but even by the turn of the last century paternal authority in tribal Africa had diminished beneath that point (pp. 110-111).

To the more ingenious Africans, however, the sanctions for disrespect could be turned into occasions for the enhancement of personal prestige. For instance, because it was considered particularly impressive to recline on the very bed where one's wife was born, occasionally during a beer party an Ashanti might enter his mother-in-law's bedroom and stretch out on her bed, his willingness and ability to pay the substantial fine a public demonstration of his wealth and courage (Sarbah, 1904, p. 112).

The great majority of quarrels and lawsuits in neighboring Shanti culture had to do with actual or perceived violations of personal dignity, including the dignity of parents and other ancestors. The greatest insults were special utterances: "Your mother!" "Your father!" "Your mother's genitals!" "Your father's genitals!" and the less colorful "Child of a fool!" (Rattray, 1929, p. 309).

Apparently in the spirit of the law of the talion, the punishment for violating another's dignity was humiliation. The offender might have to walk around the village carrying a live chicken in his mouth, preceded by a drummer or gong player calling the people to attention. Periodically, the drummer would stop, and the offender would have to recant his insult. In some areas, the offender carried a large rock in his arms, rather than a chicken (Rattray, 1929, pp. 372, 376; Sarbah, 1904, p. 114).

Indeed, "name" was as important to Africans as "face" was to Asians. A bad name in old African society was often more than a person could bear. It rendered life in the community intolerable, and it could result in suicide. An Ashanti proverb declares: "If it be a choice between disgrace and death, then death is preferable" (Rattray, 1929, p. 373).

For our growing thesaurus on the meanings of money, then, African customary law confirms some of the meanings we have seen elsewhere—theft of personal property is like assault or murder in that it represents an intrusion into self, or a taking away of self; money is sufficient restitution even for murder, even though the size of the fine indicates that it is more symbolic than economic; it is a measure of a man's mastery over his wife and respect for her parents; and it is powerful enough to seal an important deal, like uniting two families through marriage. African customary law's distinctive contribution is that money and property can be used to establish, maintain, and revitalize individual dignity.

AMERICAN INDIAN CUSTOMARY LAW

The indigenous Americans, North and South, are by and large the most communal of the cultures discussed here. In diametric opposition to the European case, the idea of private ownership is almost entirely absent from most traditional American Indian customary law. Indeed, Indian customary law generally assumes that community members in need will take what's necessary without embarrassment or obligation and that those who have more, even if what they have is less than they themselves need, will give without limit and without reluctance to those who have less.

Because land in the old Americas was something to be used and not something to be owned, there was no provision for purchase or sale. With regard to what we would call tangible personal property, individuals had principally the right of possession, although they could keep items they produced with their own hands unless the item was produced for a particular person. Thus a woman owned the clothes she made, unless she had made them specifically for her husband, children, or some other particular individual (Lowie, 1949a, p. 357). With regard to intangible personal property, some individuals did enjoy a kind of ownership or proprietorship: the right to sing a particular song, wear a particular garment, or use a particular magical formula sometimes accrued to individuals, usually on the basis of some heroic act.

There was similarly little need for any law of inheritance, because the whole community owned almost everything in common. Instead, the survivors viewed the decedent's possessions as a personal extension of himself. Accordingly, some people sent his personal items with him, to assist in the long journey; others hid the items, to do away with the painful memories; still others sought out the items, to keep as a reminder of the deceased himself (Lowie, 1949a, p. 363).

Like African law, American Indian law concentrated on preservation of the family. Given the less formal character of Indian society, wealth and property did not play quite so intimate or structured a role in betrothal in Indian society as they did in Africa, although there are similarities. During courtship, the woman might present the man with food or a pair of moccasins; if he accepted the offer, the couple were engaged. Despite this informality, bride-price was common. Suitors in some tribes paid a monetary bride-price; in others, they worked off the price in personal service to the bride's parents. The bride-price was often very high, but just as often it was offset by a similarly large dowry or trousseau (Lowie, 1949b, p. 316). The standard bride-price on the North American Plains was six buffalo hides or their equivalent (more, if the woman were considered especially industrious or hospitable). For the marriage ritual, the groom and his family, and the bride and her family, would all provide food for a feast. The dowry would often consist of a tipi, a pair of shoes, and various tools. The bride might also bring a trousseau, perhaps including a special dress of tanned deerskin decorated with porcupine quills and feathers (Walker, 1982, p. 51).

The most common punishment for adultery on the part of the woman was cutting off one braid of her hair, a punishment more severe to American Indians (as to Chinese) than is apparent to Europeans and those of European descent. If she repeated her offense, her husband might cut off her ear or her nose, as a permanent badge of her lack of character. He might also give her to someone else, or "throw her away," in which case he gave up all rights and privileges in her regard. If the adultery was the husband's, the wife could leave him and go live with her friends. If the friends felt her departure were just and proper, she could remain with them and keep all of her personal property, including the tipi, for she had fashioned the skins of which it was made. If the friends felt her departure unjust, she would have to return to her husband (Walker, 1982).

The thrust of the law was to maintain harmony in the face of whatever trials and tribulations might beset the community. Even laws about real and personal property, and inheritance, were really laws designed to maintain community affiliation. As a body of law almost totally disinterested in property and individual rights, American Indian law is the antithesis of European law, especially Roman law.

REFLECTION

In both form and substance, the bodies of custom and law down the ages and around the world surely do seem to reflect our quaternary framework. I suggest, as I did above, that the reason for this differentiation is more complex than usually assumed, that it is the result of biological and social forces working together on the individual and group levels. Specifically, I propose that natural selection has produced differences in neuroanatomical structures and neurochemical processes that cause some people to see some aspects of the world more vividly, others others. Carl Jung, in his *Psychological Types* (1923, 1923/1971), elaborates on this perceptual differentiation. He asserts that there are four types of people, distinguished on the basis of their particularly refined perceptual operations:[32]

"Sensing" people, who perceive empirical reality most fully, as an army general might see the deployment of his troops;

"Thinking" people, who perceive the world unemotionally and in detail, as a scientist might see the components of matter;

"Intuiting" people, who perceive the breadth and depth of possibility most easily, as an architect might envision possibilities for a skyscraper; and

"Feeling" people, who perceive the emotional features of situations most readily, as a therapist might observe the changing feelings of her clients.

TABLE 4.1 Connections Between the Prototypic Cultures and Their Laws

	Geographical Concentration			
	Europe	*Asia*	*Americas*	*Africa*
Operation	Sensing	Thinking	Feeling	Intuiting
Perceptual skill	Empirical Reality	Detail	Emotion	Possibility
Emphasis	Rights	Wrongs	Relationships	Freedom
Goal	Preserve property	Preserve harmony	Preserve community	Preserve dignity
Worst crimes	Taking life or property	Upsetting social order	Diminishing the community	Disrespecting the individual
Distinctive punishments	Confiscation	Shaming	Excommunication	Humiliation
Talisman against	Fear of incompetence	Fear of disarray	Fear of isolation	Fear of constraint

These skills seem to correspond with the distinguishing features of the four prototypic cultures (Table 4.1). Indeed, they may be able to provide some insight into the general direction of cultural development (Chapter 2) as well as the form and content of legal systems. For example, a people especially skilled at perceiving empirical reality might be expected to design a culture that centers in competition for property—empirical reality *par excellence*—and devise a system of law that protects property rights, whereas a people particularly able to see the world in detail and unemotionally could be expected to construct a tidy, hierarchical, even totalitarian culture and produce an especially ordered, dispassionate, and controlling legal code. Similarly, a people specially skilled at free-ranging, intuitive perception seem most likely to create an unfettered culture and establish a body of law that protects individuality and free expression, and a people distinctively skilled at emotional evaluation should be expected to build a culture centered in family ties and devise a body of law focused on the support of such affiliation. At the same time, living in such cultures should reinforce and refine those perceptual skills, at least for people of the majority temperament.

From a more clinical vantage, people fear most the loss of what they value most, that is, that which they see most vividly. It follows that

- The real foundation for acquisitive European law may be the fear of losing competence, against which accumulating property is a talisman;
- The real foundation for structured Asian law may be the fear of disarray, against which an ordered life is a talisman;
- The real foundation for affiliative American Indian law may be the fear of isolation, against which a tightly knit community is a talisman; and
- The real foundation for divergent African law may be the fear of constraint, against which free, even extravagant, personal expression is a talisman.

In a later chapter, we shall see that there are also neurophysiological explanations for these same propensities.

In our search to validate and elaborate on the moderator framework, we are now ready to turn our attention to the great religions of the world. We shall see in the structure of these religions the same signs of the quaternary that we found in secular law, and, in their content, parallel patterns of moral principle. But we shall also discover *within* each of the religions major tensions that represent the acquisition/affiliation dialectic.

Chapter 5

Patterns in the Great Religions

Down the ages and around the world, humankind has used religion "to coerce the spiritual powers [and] get them on our side" (James, 1902/ 1961). The religions we have devised, like the laws, reflect our temperaments in both structure and substance. They underscore differences between East and West, between city and countryside, and—most vividly—between the inclination to acquire and the inclination to affiliate. Perhaps because religion is closer to the hearts and souls of the people than is law, and hence a more intimate reflection, the history of religion exposes a deeper level of dialectical tension. Central to this tension is the quaternary, which, I propose, describes the basic "patterns of culture" (cf. Benedict, 1934; Weber, 1964) and "dimensions of personality" (cf. Halverson, Kohnstamm, & Martin, 1994), the pursuit of which has occupied the attention of social scientists for a long time. In this chapter, we shall make the transition from personality and cultural differences between groups to those within groups. At the same time, we shall see how the different religions' values, attitudes, and teachings about money and property clash with one another.

Before we begin to explore the religious antecedents of the quaternary structure, I should reiterate that in none of this do I mean to call all Europeans acquisitive, all Asians convergent, all Africans expansive, or all American Indians affiliative. Within-group variation is evident all around us: subcultures of each propensity in every one of the four archetypal cultures (e.g., German and Italian Europeans); subgroups within each of those groups (e.g., northern and southern Germans); and subgroups on down the line through societies, clans, families, couples, and individuals, along with all manner of unpredictable individual variability. Indeed, most individuals manifest different attitudes and behaviors at various times and under sundry circumstances.

In individuals and in groups, however, there is generally enough consistency of attitude and behavior that we can recognize people and predict, albeit roughly, what they will do in the future—enough that we can notice when they are "not like themselves." My intention is to write at a level of abstraction at which there is sufficient consistency for building theory, but without losing sight of the richness of individual differences. Nevertheless, because my purpose is to identify patterns from which to build that theory, I expect to err in the direction of too much generalization. At the same time, I want to stress that although I may talk of types, there are few if any pure types in this world: Virtually all individuals and groups can (and should) be described in terms of "scores" on the four attributes; better, on the two pairs of opposing attributes. When I speak of "types," I use the term for convenience, recognizing each comprises different hues, saturations, and intensities.

EARLY ANIMISTIC SPIRITUALITY

As law began in an essential unity of form, so did religion, with magical rites[1] centering in the elements of nature (Allott, 1960; Garrison, 1929, chap. 1). In Europe, Asia, Africa, and the Americas, the earliest liturgies concentrated on earth, air, fire, and water. Every quivering leaf, comforting breeze, glimmering star, and roiling cataract was a manifestation of The Power. As the peoples of Earth grew progressively more unlike one another, their religions came to reflect their varied attitudes and values, indeed, their natural propensities. European and Asian people, the people of the written word, created formal religions just as they had devised formal laws; African and American Indian people continued their more informal oral traditions, no less full than the expressions of their European and Asian counterparts, indeed perhaps more full, but generally absent the structured liturgies.

As we saw in Chapter 2, the earliest peoples attributed to their deities the qualities they most respected. The Europeans created gods who were leaders— fierce, imposing, and clever. The Asians created gods who were arrangers, who made the universe a harmony. The Africans created benefactors, and the American Indians created relatives. For reasons of space, and because the religions of Europe and Asia have had more influence on the maintenance of values and attitudes that contribute to the meanings of money in the industrialized world, we shall (regretfully) limit the rest of our discussion to these more formal religions. Because Confucianism and Taoism were more philosophies than religions, we will examine them in Chapter 6.

Most prominent among the religions of Europe and Asia were Hinduism, Judaism, Buddhism, Islam, and Christianity. We shall defer the discussion of Christianity until a later chapter.

Hinduism and Judaism

Hinduism and Judaism, the oldest of the surviving formal religions, are in some ways similar to one another, in other ways quite the opposite. They are similar, for example, in their employment of lengthy and complex rituals and their establishment of a priestly class (Heesterman, 1987, 1993). They are different in that Hinduism was born in military conquest; Judaism, in "exile and return." At least partly for those reasons, Hinduism began with an admiration of wealth, which evolved into suspiciousness and then into detachment, whereas Judaism started with a dislike that turned into a disdain and thence into outright hostility.

The Aryan warriors[2] who flooded into India's Indus Valley during the three centuries preceding 1200 B.C. brought not only their chariots but their priests. As the invaders settled in, the priests composed the hymns of the Rig-Veda, the oldest piece of religious literature in the world (Reinach, 1930, pp. 48-49). The Rig-Veda, the Later Hymns, the Upanishads, and the Bhagavad Gita contain passages that describe the four-stage evolution of Hindu thinking with regard to wealth.

Stage 1: Rig-Veda—The Acquisitive Stage. The Rig-Veda (ca. 2000 B.C.) comprises a thousand hymns to the Vedic deities. These hymns suggests a people who value strength in their gods and wealth in themselves, that is, the songs of a hungry and fearful people turning to external powers for satisfaction and protection. For example:

To Usas, Goddess of Dawn

Bring us to wealth abundant, sent in every shape,
to plentiful refreshing food,
To all subduing splendour, Usas, mighty one,
to strength, thou rich in spoil and wealth
—To Usas I.48.16, quoted in Griffith (1920-1926)

Stage 2: The Later Hymns—Genesis of Gentler Values. Later songs sound a softer, more tender tone. They promote generosity over acquisitiveness, and acceptance over effectance:

To Dana [Charity]

The wealthier man should give unto the needy,
Considering the course of life hereafter;
For riches are like chariot wheels revolving:
Now to one man they come, now to another.

—*To Dana X.117.5, quoted in Macdonnel (1922)*

Stage 3: The Upanishads—Wisdom Over Wealth. By the time of the Upanishads,[3] the eighth and seventh centuries B.C., the Hindu hymns had become not only antiacquisitive but very introspective, less focused on life's practicalities and more on the internal religious experience. Indeed, the Upanishads are viewed as a reaction against Brahmin sacerdotalism (Dandekar, 1987). In the *Katha Upanishad,* Yama, the leader of the departed spirits, tempts Naciketas with wealth and long life, but Naciketas resists worldly allurement in favor of knowledge. No longer are wealth and strength acclaimed; the new hero, Naciketas, is the one who disdains wealth:

Yama: Choose centenarian sons and grandsons,
Many cattle, elephants, gold, and horses.
Choose a great abode of earth.
And thyself live as many autumns as thou desirest.

Naciketas: Not with wealth is a man to be satisfied.
Shall we take wealth, if we have seen thee?
Shall we live so long as thou shalt rule?
—This, in truth, is the boon to be chosen by me.

—*Katha Upanishad, 23 and 27, quoted in Hume (1931)*

At this stage, Hinduism takes on the same hostility toward wealth that we will see in the majority of other great religions, particularly ancient Judaism and early Christianity. The Christian Bible's Temptation on the Mount will send the same message nearly 800 years later.

Stage 4: Bhagavad Gita—Complete Detachment. The Bhagavad Gita (Radhakrishnan, 1948/1957; see also Buhler, 1886) goes still further. It promotes the abandonment of desire[4] for the sake of equilibrium, stability, or interior peace:

He whose mind is untroubled in the midst of sorrows
and is free from eager desire amid pleasures,
he from whom passion, fear, and rage have passed away—
he is called a sage of settled intelligence.

. . .

He who abandons all desires and acts free from longing,
without any sense of mineness or egotism—
he attains to peace.

>   —*The Bhagavad Gita, 56 and 71, quoted in*
>   *Radhakrishnan (1948/1957, pp. 111-112)*

Like all the great religions, Hinduism struggles with internal conflict about money as good versus money as evil. The Code of Manu,[5] a collection of religious exhortations that occupies a place in Hindu tradition roughly similar to that of the Decalogue in the Christian tradition, is conflicted about wealth. In one place, Manu defines it as a reward for virtue:

> Through virtuous conduct he obtains long life, through virtuous conduct desirable offspring, *through virtuous conduct [he obtains] imperishable wealth;* virtuous conduct destroys the effects of inauspicious marks. (*Laws* IV:156, quoted in Radhakrishnan & Moore, 1957, p. 174, emphasis added)

But elsewhere he urges the Brahmin to avoid attachment to pleasure and wealth, for these are impediments to the pursuit of knowledge.[6] Indeed, he now applies the word *worthless:*

> Let him not, out of desire for enjoyments, attach himself to any sensual pleasures, and let him carefully obviate an excessive attachment to them, by reflecting on their worthlessness in his heart. (*Laws* IV:16, quoted in Radhakrishnan & Moore, 1957, p. 181)

In addition, while mainstream Hinduism at least tries to portray wealth as morally neutral,[7] two well known sects make it an explicit evil. The Vaishnavas, like the Essenes, the Chinese Taoists, and many of the American Indians, created a poetic and devotional religion that was the emotional antithesis of the intellectual Upanishadic tradition (Parrinder, 1983, p. 225). To the Vaishnavas, wealth would be an affront to God, a sign of distrust. The Jains, too, emphasized avoidance of wealth, also to the extreme—they had no money, no property, and no homes. Indeed, some of them had no clothes, partly to forsake the world and partly to assure that no small vermin could be crushed within the folds of any fabric (Parrinder, 1983, p. 249).

Thus did Hindu teaching do a complete turnaround: What had been good in the beginning became evil, and what had been evil became good. Money and property, initially the goal, metamorphosed into the impediment. Artha, wealth and power, initially the predominant emphasis, gave way to dharma, devotion to duty (Davis, 1987). Usury, initially not only tolerated but approved, came to be prohibited, except for religious purposes.

In his compelling essay on wealth in the Judeo-Christian tradition, Schmidt (1987) traces an increasing hostility toward wealth from the first indications in ancient Near East fragments, into the Jewish canonical and noncanonical literatures, and thence into the synoptic Gospels of the Christian era. He describes three evolutionary stages in the ancient view of wealth: First, he proposes a natural law principle that he calls the "justice imperative." Next, he identifies a series of progressively more encompassing definitions of injustice: initially, that *injustice equals greed,* later, that the mere *possession of wealth equals injustice,* and still later, that the very *existence of wealth equals injustice.* Last of all, he cites the "mandate to disdain wealth."[8]

In support for the first stage, that injustice equals greed, Schmidt (1987, pp. 44, 57) offers statements of which these are representative:

Hearts are rapacious, and everyone takes his neighbor's goods. (From *The Man Who Was Tired of Life,* line 105; see also Simpson, 1972)

For the wicked [man] boasts of the desires of his heart, and the man greedy for gain curses and renounces the Lord. (Psalms 10.3)

In support of his next stages—possession of wealth equals injustice and existence of wealth equals injustice—Schmidt (pp. 45, 57) provides a collection of fragments like these:

[The] rich [man] who heaps up goods [should be] burnt at the stake. (From *The Babylonian Theodicy,* lines 63-64; see also Lambert, 1960)

Behold, these are the wicked; always at ease, they increase in riches. (Psalms 73:12)

Finally, in support of his last stage, disdain wealth, Schmidt offers examples of this sort:

> Better, then, is poverty in the hand of God / than riches in the storehouse. Better is bread when the mind is at ease / than riches with anxiety. (From *Instruction to Amenemope,* 9.5-9; see also Simpson, 1972)

> Be not afraid when one becomes rich, when the glory of his house increases. For when he dies he will carry nothing away; his glory will not go down with him. (Psalms 49.16-17)

Buddhism and Islam

Buddhism and Islam are polar opposites (see Morris, 1942), the former teaching detachment from the things of this world, the latter urging involvement, especially commercial involvement. More even than Hinduism and Judaism, Buddhism and Islam seem to fit the natural inclinations of the cultures in which they predominate.[9] Strange bedfellows, they both seem to find wealth and morality perfectly compatible, though for very different reasons.

Buddhism teaches that the most morally pure action is also the most profitable action and that wealth signifies virtue, poverty vice. Islam teaches that wealth is a gift from God and that enjoying it is good, provided it always remains secondary to respect for Allah. But Buddhism advocates detachment and philanthropy as the means to prevent envy and jealousy from interfering with the pursuit of enlightenment, whereas Islam promotes active commercial activity and involvement. If one looks closely, however, one can find in both Buddhism and Islam the same kinds of conflicts about money and property and the same disdain for wealth, though to different degrees, that we saw in later Hinduism and Judaism, and will see in early Christianity.

The Buddha taught that too little money might stimulate craving (envy), but too much might promote attachment (jealousy). Accordingly, people who seek enlightenment need to detach themselves from money and property. Given such detachment, not only is wealth—even great wealth—compatible with the pursuit of enlightenment, but it is a positive sign of virtue, the reward for pious living.

The source for this idea is karma, the principle of retribution (deeds): Whatever is, is deserved. To use the famous example, a man lying robbed and beaten in a ditch has suffered that fate because he deserves it on account of some act earlier in his life or perhaps in a prior life. If a benefactor should rescue him, that, too, is because he deserves it (Sizemore & Swearer, 1990). By extension, if someone is languishing in poverty, it is because he deserves it on account of his impiety; if someone is luxuriating in wealth, it is because he deserves it by reason of his virtue. Hence, as in Hinduism, wealth in Buddhism is both an impediment to and a visible sign of a virtuous life.

To reach the goal-state of nirvana, the absence of worldly desire *(dukkha)*, pious Buddhist laypeople refrain from five categories of allurement: causing injury to living things, taking that which is not given (stealing), sexual immorality, falsehood, and using alcohol and drugs. Those who choose a stricter discipline also avoid taking food or drink after midday; dancing, singing, and amusements; and using garlands, cosmetics, and personal adornments. Finally, the monks themselves also aver accepting gold or silver and using a luxurious bed (Parrinder, 1971, p. 272). The higher the level of holiness one pursues, the more important it becomes to separate oneself from worldly possessions. Despite the principle of detachment, there seems to be in Buddhism a fundamental disdain for money and property.

Both Buddhism and Islam promote almsgiving. Much of Buddhism's ethical philosophy focuses on philanthropy, because giving is seen as the best measure of detachment. As we also saw in Judaism, there is in Buddhism a clear and distinct hierarchy of giving, not according to recipients' needs but according to their merit or virtue. The most salutary gifts are those given to most estimable recipients and with the most meritorious attitude. The best recipients are surely the Buddha and the holiest of the monks; after that come one's family and society at large. True nonattached giving is most virtuous; any accompanying vanity, reluctance, or ulterior motive tarnishes the gift, or even destroys it.

This emphasis on philanthropy led Max Weber to articulate his well-known paradox: The more detached the Buddhist laity become through giving, the more attached the monks are likely to become through receiving. The Buddhist theologian's reply to Weber is that, because wealth is the natural result of the virtuous life, it is proper that the monasteries should become wealthy and further that the monks more than anyone else should be able to receive philanthropy without attachment. Nevertheless, monastic wealth, like monastic power, has provoked criticism from the outside and discussion within.

In Islam, to give is good; to give out of the public eye is better.

Whatever alms you give *shall rebound to your own advantage,* provided that you give them for the love of God. (Koran 2:271-272, emphasis added. All Koran citations are from the Koran, 1993)

To be charitable in public is good, but to give alms to the poor in private is better and will atone for some of your sins. (Koran 2:271)

Islam pays more attention to practical financial matters than Buddhism does. Mohammed taught that wealth begins with labor and that business transactions are clearly a form of labor and therefore holy (Koran 4:28). From this conception flows a proscription against unearned income, and from that prohibition flow regulations against gambling, begging, renting out land, and most of all, charging interest, for "God has laid His curse on usury" (Koran 2:276). In addition, usury is just the opposite of almsgiving. It keeps one party always at a disadvantage and provides for debt that increases continually (Khan, 1989, p. 294).

In lieu of usury, Islam proposes *mudarabah,* interest-free banking (Khan, 1989, pp. 294-300). Under mudarabah, the banker contributes the capital and the borrower contributes the work. They agree beforehand on a percentage share of profits, so the debt does not compound. They further agree that if the enterprise should fail, the banker will lose his capital just as the borrower will lose his labor. In short, they form a partnership or joint venture in which both principals stand to profit, and both are at risk.

In the pursuit of earned income, the Koran commands social equity and honesty:

Do not devour one another's property by unjust means, nor bribe with it the judges in order that you may wrongfully and knowingly usurp the possessions of other men. (Koran 2:188)

Give full measure when you measure, and weigh with even scales. That is fair, and better in the end. (Koran 17:35)

Reminiscent of the Babylonian Codes, it speaks also to family justice:

You shall bequeath your widows a year's maintenance without causing them to leave their homes. . . . Reasonable provision shall also be made for divorced women. That is incumbent on righteous men. (Koran 2:240-241)

> Give orphans the property which belongs to them. Do not . . . cheat them of their possessions; for this would surely be a great sin. . . . Give women their dowry as a free gift. (Koran 4:3-4)

> If you wish to replace your wife with another, do not take from her the dowry you have given her even if it be a talent of gold. (Koran 4:20)

On the subject of communal versus individual ownership, Muslim thought is divided. Those scholars who advocate communal ownership argue that all land ultimately belongs to Allah and that man holds land only in trust from Him and on behalf of the community. Those who approve of individual ownership argue that different degrees of wealth reflect Allah's goodness in rewarding man's differential labor and that to redistribute property would be a challenge to God's goodness, as well as economically and socially disruptive to the community (Khan, 1989, pp. 152, 172-173, 184ff.). In Chapter 6 we shall trace more closely the conflicting philosophies of property ownership.

Even in Islam, disdain for wealth occasionally appears. For example, in *Zakat,* involuntary almsgiving through a progressive property tax, and in the Parable of the Rich Man and the Poor Man, Islam's underlying disdain for the riches it promotes comes to the surface:

> Riches breed stinginess, selfishness, mutual loathing and aversion and even moral degeneration. The best remedy against these evils is charitable disposal of one's money. (Khan, 1989, p. 240)

Rather than the wholly positive sign of Allah's bounty and a tool that should be enjoyed, albeit in moderation, money suddenly becomes corrupt,[10] the wellspring of "mutual loathing and aversion and even moral degeneration." So, even in entrepreneurial Islam there is the notion that wealth requires propitiation, a hint of unconscious guilt at the enjoyment, pursuit, or even possession of money and property.

REFLECTION

With regard to the quaternary framework, it seems clear that the religions of the West—Islam, for example, and old Hinduism—were "active," in contrast to the "contemplative" religions of the East, for example, Buddhism. It also seems clear that the religions of the cities were not only more active but more formal, more ritualized, and more cerebral than those of the countryside.[11]

But the most striking discovery here is within-group variation. The great religions of Europe and Asia seem generally arrayed along the diagonal acquisition/affiliation continuum, not surprisingly more at the affiliation end, perhaps as an antidote to political and economic oppression. The most ancient religions appear to have developed variants to accommodate the acquisition and the affiliation cultures. Judaism, for example, not only subsumed both the Pharisees and the Essenes, but it also provided the foundation for both Islam and Christianity. Hinduism evolved from the old observance to the new. Indeed, in both city and countryside, religion (and the culture that supports it) has undergone such "dialectical" evolution that the old is barely recognizable in the new. We shall see considerably more of this within-group acquisition/affiliation in the history of Eastern and Western philosophy, to which we now turn.

Chapter 6

Patterns in Classical Philosophy

In the history of philosophy, the fifth and fourth centuries B.C. were remarkable for the parallel births of the three greatest names of the Eastern (Chinese) literati school of philosophy and the three greatest names of the Western (Greek) classical school: Confucius and Socrates, Mencius and Plato, and Hsun Tsu and Aristotle. From their work grew bodies of moral philosophy, or ethics, that confirm the between-group and within-group tensions that pervade religion. Indeed, to paraphrase James, between religion and philosophy the line is often difficult to draw.

CHINESE ETHICAL PHILOSOPHY

In ancient days as now, Asia put more emphasis than Europe on social and intellectual hierarchy, order, and segmentation, on what Freud, in another context, referred to as tidy, stubborn, and parsimonious.

Confucius and Mencius

The foundation of Confucius' philosophy (551-479 B.C.) was the Chinese gentleman, that Zhou dynasty construct who personified courtesy, deference, loyalty, moral courage, and filial piety, and to whom "reasoned virtue" led to a life lived always in proper, orderly relationship with other people, especially family, especially elders. Confucius promulgated an Asian version of the Golden Rule:

> Tzu-kung asked, "Is there a single word which can be a guide to conduct throughout one's life?" The Master said, "It is perhaps the word *shu* [reciprocity]. Do not impose on others what you yourself do not desire." (Confucius, 1979, p. 135, *Analects* XV, xxiv)

But he also revealed a hint of parsimony:

> If there are many producers and few consumers, and if people who produce
> wealth do so quickly and those who spend it do so slowly, then wealth will
> always be sufficient. (Confucius, 1963, p. 94, *The Great Learning,* chap. 10)

Even though Confucius taught during a period of economic boom in China, when mercantilism was taking root, merchants were enjoying at least a temporary measure of respectability, and the various city-states were busily minting their own coins for domestic and foreign use, his writings do not offer a great deal of guidance about issues of wealth. However, occasional passages in *The Great Learning* and the *Analects* make a sharp distinction between wealth and virtue and suggest that the two exist in opposition:

> Duke Ching of Ch'i had a thousand teams of four horses each, but on his death
> the common people were unable to find anything to praise him for, whereas
> P'ih-e and Shuh-ts'e starved under Mount Shou Yang and yet to this day the
> common people still sing their praises. (Confucius, 1979, p. 141, *Analects* XVI,
> xii)

The central Confucian values are equilibrium and harmony, though the meanings of these terms are rather particular. Equilibrium exists in the absence of emotion, harmony in its temperate presence. Money is one of the stimuli that can upset equilibrium and defeat harmony. Consequently, money is at once a danger and, because it can occasion the practice of virtue, an opportunity. Thus Confucius takes a characteristically temperate position on money, very much like that of his Greek counterparts.

But, as we shall see so often, Confucius ultimately declares a disdain for money and property, for he associates wealth with "unrighteousness" and "shame." Unrighteousness he connects with the vast accumulation of wealth by evil rulers; shame, with any accumulation over and above mere sufficiency.

Mencius (ca. 371–ca. 289 B.C.) reiterated Confucius' concern that wealth would lead to disharmony and shame:

> Mencius replied [to King Hui at Liang], "Why must you use the term *profit*?
> What I have to offer are nothing but humanity and righteousness. (Mencius,
> 1963, *Book of Mencius* I.A.1)

Thus Confucius and Mencius drew together family, respect, and order, the most important inclinations that already existed in the culture, formalized and codified them, and turned them into a way of life. Money played a part in the way of life, not only for one's own subsistence but also for the care of one's parents and elderly people in general. Beyond that, however, money takes on connotations of shamefulness and unrighteousness, a commodity with the potential to distract from equilibrium, harmony, and the virtuous life.

Mohism and Taoism

The views of Confucius and Mencius attracted challenges from both the left and the right. From the left, both the Mohists and the Taoists attacked Confucian social segmentation, because they saw in it an insufferable snobbery, an affront to human equality. From the right, the legalists also attacked segmentation, though less for its snobbery than for the lesser privileges and greater punishments it loaded on the shoulders of some citizens, and the greater privileges and lesser punishments it accorded others.

The Mohists, after Mo Tzu (470-391 B.C.), despised Confucius' followers as self-important aristocrats out of touch with the common people. Instead, Mo Tzu preached a politics of universal love and communal responsibility. He advocated an almost monastic asceticism and condemned ritual, music, extravagance, nepotism, and most of all, oppression.

> Now at the present time, what brings the greatest harm to the world? Great states attacking small ones, great families overthrowing small ones, the strong oppressing the weak, the many harrying the few, the cunning deceiving the stupid, the eminent lording it over the humble—these are harmful to the world. (Mo Tzu, 1963, p. 39, III.16)

Taoists, too, sought equilibrium,[1] but they sought it through primitivism (Lao Tzu, n.d., perhaps legendary). In other words, do away with things that enlarge the self and you will do away with temptation; do away with temptation and you will reach equilibrium. Money, of course, and the things money can buy, are among the things that enlarge the self.

> Do not honor the worthy,
> So that the people will not contend with one another.
> Do not value hard-to-get goods,

So that the people will not turn robbers.
Do not show objects of desire,
So that the people's minds are not disturbed.

—(Lao Tzu, 1989, Tao Te Ching 3)

Legalism

Antithetical to Mohism and Taoism, legalism was a pragmatic, even anti-intellectual, reaction to what its adherents considered the softness of the alternative philosophies. Han Fei Tzu (d. 233 B.C.), the principal eponym for the legalist school, not only advocated severe and consistent punishment to restrain evil but also generous rewards to encourage whatever contributed to the well-being of the state. It is noteworthy that he found it important to augment economic rewards and punishments with honor and disgrace (Han Fei Tzu, 1959, 49). Legalism was a law-and-order philosophy designed to prevent disorder in the state. When he describes the disorderly state, Han Fei Tzu reveals his disdain for the essential self-interest of wealth:

> If forged money and faked articles can circulate in the marketplace, trades will no longer fall short of demands and supplies. If the profits they make thereby are twice as much as by farming and the honors they get thereby surpass those of tillers and warriors, men of firm integrity and strong character will become few while merchants and tradesmen will increase in number. (Han Fei Tzu, 1959, XIX.19)

Confucianism and legalism competed for a while for the favor of the emperor; neither Mohism nor Taoism was ever a practical contender. Legalism won, not surprisingly, because it offered more support for a strong sovereign; it has characterized Chinese politics since that time. Confucianism, ultimately proclaimed the "official" philosophy of the country, provided a better fit with the popular temperament. In short, since these early days, legalism has governed the Chinese people, but Confucianism has shaped—and reflected—their character.

The qualities of Chinese temperament that we see most closely associated with money are virtue and harmony, to which the craving for money is a threat; shame, of which the intemperate desire for wealth is an important source; and parsimony, which is defined (by implication) as the prudent management of just enough wealth—a sufficiency, not a superfluity. In all of these, money is at best an impediment. With regard to money and social segmentation, China seems deeply conflicted. On the one hand, Confucian values support temperate accumulation and the respect that derives from success; on the other, the legalist history (and more recent Marxist history) requires a privilege-free society: "The nail that stands out gets pounded down."

GREEK ETHICAL PHILOSOPHY

As Eastern philosophy emphasized the social cohesion of the community, Western philosophy emphasized the wealth of the individual. As in Asia, ancient European philosophy struggled with a tension between the tough and the tender. It found the hard side in the materialism of the Ionics (Hippocrates and Aristophanes), and later, the Romans, and the soft side in the Tao-like mysticism of the Italics (like Pythagoras and Phaleas) and Plato, eventually Augustine. From time to time, a middle position appeared, a synthesis: the best known of these have been Aristotle, much later Aquinas, later still and most recently, MacIntyre. Like Chinese philosophy, Greek philosophy consisted of thesis, antithesis, and synthesis.

The Beginning: Ionics Versus Italics

Western philosophy began with the study of the empirical world. There the Ionian philosophers sought to identify the fundamental matter of the universe. For the Ionians, the material world, the world of the senses, explained everything that needed explaining. Moist and dry, hot and cold— these qualities were the foundation of matter. Hence the universe was composed of four elements: fire, earth, air, and water. Later thinkers built on this quaternary. Hippocrates proposed that behavior was determined by the four humors: blood, black bile, phlegm, and yellow bile. Galen added psychological meaning: the sanguine (optimistic), choleric (irritable), phlegmatic (composed), and melancholic (pensive) temperaments. We shall make much use of this work later.

The spiritual world was as meaningful for the Italics as the material world was for the Ionics. For the former, soul surpassed body; indeed, the body constrained and tainted the soul. For the latter, soul was secondary.

Classical Greek views of wealth and property, like classical Chinese views, reflected this Ionic-Italic tension. In no matter was the tension more clear than in the question of property ownership, in which from these

beginnings the perpetual conflict between communal and individual ownership was sharp. Gonzalez (1990, p. 3) tells us that Phaleas of Chalcedon, a
follower of the great Italic numerologist Pythagoras, proposed an early plan
for the redistribution of private property, "for equity's sake." In Aristophanes' satirical *Ecclesiazusae* (The Company of Women), Proxagora, the
leader of the company, echoes Phaleas' principle:

> I [Proxagora] want all to have a share in everything and all property to be in
> common; there will no longer be either rich or poor; . . . I intend that there shall
> only be one and the same condition for all. . . . I shall begin by making land,
> money, everything that is private property, common to all. (Aristophanes, 1938,
> lines 589-598)

Through Aristophanes' pen, however, she goes on to destroy her credibility
in the eyes of the Ionic audience, by taking an intolerably extreme position:

> The poor will no longer be obliged to work; each will have all that he needs,
> bread, salt fish, cakes, tunics, wine, chaplets, and chick-pease. (Aristophanes,
> 1938, lines 604-609)

The stage was thus set for an individualist/collectivist dialectic that would
endure until the present day.

The Rise: Socrates and Plato Versus Protagoras and the Sophists

In Socrates' view, money distracts from the practice of virtue.[2] In *Apology,*
he laments:

> You, my friend—a citizen of the great and mighty and wise state of Athens—are
> you not ashamed of heaping up the greatest amount of money and honor and
> reputation, and caring so little about wisdom and truth and the greatest improve-
> ment of the soul, which you never regard or heed at all? (Plato, 1942)

To Socrates, doing away with the concerns that rise from property ownership[3] is essential to happiness (Plato, 1941, *Republic* V 464).

Plato was to Socrates as Mencius to Confucius: spokesman, chronicler,
systematizer. In his utopian *Republic,* Plato outlined a state in which reason
was king and where temperance, restraint, courage, wisdom, and justice
governed daily life. *The Republic* portrays an ideal state founded on "a

cosmic order *[dike]* which dictates the place of each virtue in a total harmonious scheme of human life" (MacIntyre, 1984, p. 142). This view reappears in Aristotle, still again, perhaps more faintly, in Aquinas and the medieval Scholastics.

This ideal state Plato saw threatened by "that insatiable craving":[4]

> In finding new ways of spending their money, men begin by stretching the law for that purpose, until they and their wives obey it no longer. . . . The more they value money . . . the less they care for virtue. (Plato, 1941, *Republic* VIII 550)

Luxury, because it is inherently intemperate, is a special threat:

> Is it not also disgraceful to need doctoring, not merely for a wound or an attack of some seasonal disorder, but because, through living in idleness and luxury, our bodies are infested with winds and humours, like marsh gas in a stagnant pool, so that the sons of Asclepius [patron of physicians] are put to inventing for diseases such ingenious names as flatulence and catarrh? (Plato, 1941, *Republic* III 405)

The solution, then, is temperance, although Plato's idea of temperance, like Socrates', is to possess little more than bare necessity. Indeed, he proposes that the rulers and guardians, that is, the upper classes, should hold the most important property in common: real estate, food, clothing—and spouses (Plato, 1941, *Republic* IV 417, 420).

As to money itself, Schumpeter (1954/1994, p. 56) credits Plato with being among the first to teach that money, a medium of exchange (*symbolon,* or "symbol-token," see *Politeia* II, 371), is independent of the material of which it is made. Beyond that—and his loathing for gold and silver—Plato had little to say about the nature of money.

As opposite as can be to Socrates and Plato were Protagoras and his Sophists. Socrates and Plato believed in moral absolutes; Protagoras (ca. 490-421 B.C.) considered all things relative, moral decisions included. Socrates and Plato were ascetics; Protagoras enjoyed the good life. Socrates and Plato disdained money and the things money could buy; Protagoras charged substantial fees[5] for his instruction—indeed, he seemed to seek out the rich and powerful to become his students. In philosophy, in values, and in practice, Protagoras the Sophist was antithesis to Plato and Socrates.

The Sophists were pragmatists. They arrived in an Athens in which power had recently passed from the aristocracy to the freemen, and the freemen were eager to learn the sophisticated political oratory the Sophists taught so well. They did not burden their students with the epistemology and metaphysics that Socrates and Plato valued. They taught skills that students could apply immediately.

With regard to money and property, the Sophists never tried to derive general principles, and certainly not a "natural law." One set of laws was no better than another, they taught; an argument could be made to support or refute any law or principle. The practical, *expedient* approach was to follow the laws and customs of one's forebears, not because those are necessarily better than anyone else's but simply to maintain a stable society (Stumpf, 1971, pp. 32-35).

The Synthesis: Aristotle

Aristotle argued that the proper goal of human life is happiness—more than happiness, *eudaimonia,* the state of happiness, fullness, prosperity. Now, prosperity does not require a great deal of money or property, just enough so one is burdened neither by want nor by luxury. The idea, of course, is temperance—neither the asceticism of Socrates nor the extravagance of Protagoras.

Like the Buddha, Aristotle worried about the effects of poverty as well as the effects of luxury:

> Those who have too much of the goods of fortune, strength, wealth, friends, and the like, are neither willing nor able to submit to authority. The evil begins at home, for when they are boys, by reason of the luxury in which they are brought up, they never learn, even at school, the habit of obedience.
>
> On the other hand, the very poor, who are in the opposite extreme, are too degraded. So that the one class cannot obey, and can only rule despotically; the other knows not how to command and must be ruled like slaves. Thus arises a city, not of freemen, but of masters and slaves, the one despising, the other envying; and nothing can be more fatal to friendship and good fellowship. (Aristotle, 1921, *Politica* 1295).

Aristotle disagrees with Plato on the subject of common versus individual property. "Aristotle has little respect either for the communism of the *Republic* or the oligarchy of the *Laws,* for both are impracticable in details and if practiced would lead to ruinous dissension" (Baker, 1947, p. 66). He settles on private ownership with some public usage (see also Gonzalez, 1990, pp. 4-10):

> While property up to a point should be held in common, the general principle should be that of private ownership. . . . Briefly it would work thus: each man has his own possessions; part of these he makes available for his own immediate circle, part he uses in common with others. For example, in Sparta they use each others' slaves practically as if they were their own, and horses and dogs too; and if they need food on a journey, they get it in the country as they go. Clearly then it is better for property to remain in private hands, but we should make the right to use it communal. (*Politica* VII, 11, quoted in Thompson, 1955)

With regard to private ownership, Aristotle argues against pure equality. He prefers "proportional distribution according to merit." Anything else is unjust, either more than the individual deserves, or less (Gonzalez, 1990, p. 10).

Nevertheless, he criticizes all business activity beyond that required to run one's own household. He distinguishes managing one's household ("economics") from trying to make money for its own sake ("chrematistics"):

> The former is necessary and honourable, while that which consists in exchange is justly censured; for it is unnatural, and a mode by which men gain from one another. (Aristotle, 1921, *Politica* 1258, quoted in Gonzales, 1990, p. 10)

Thus a shoemaker can barter his labor to a carpenter to have a house built, or can even take money[6] for his labor and exchange that money for the house. But he cannot go into the business of taking mortgages and charging interest,[7] even to help another build a house. Those who do so enter into that "most hated sort" of business, namely,

> usury, which makes a gain out of money itself, and not from the natural object of it. For money was intended to be used in exchange, but not to increase at interest. And this term *interest,* which means the birth of money from money, is applied to the breeding of money because the offspring resembles the parent. Wherefore of all modes of getting wealth this is the most unnatural. (Aristotle, 1941, 1258, quoted in Gonzales, 1990, p. 10)

But most of all, Aristotle advocates the cultivation of morality. Though moderation is the path to the virtuous life, the pursuit of virtue does not imply the battle against one's natural inclinations that the Christian philosophers will advocate (MacIntyre, 1984, p. 149). Rather, part of one's responsibility as a citizen is to live in such a way that one's natural inclination becomes the inclination to live virtuously, "for when we have decided as a result of deliberation, we desire in accordance with our deliberation" (Aristotle, 1985, *Nicomachean Ethics* 359; see also Festinger, 1942). This attention to the virtuous life held sway until Enlightenment thinkers two thousand years later decided that the pursuit of happiness is better guided by law than by ethics (MacIntrye, 1984, p. 157).

The Denouement: Epicurus Versus Zeno and the Stoics

After the Peloponnesian War, Greek civilization entered into decline, and Greek philosophy lost its metaphysical edge and began a gradual metamorphosis into religion, an evolution that would be perfected in the Middle Ages and endure until the Enlightenment.

The last two schools of Greek philosophy were the Epicureans and the Stoics, the eponyms for which were Epicurus and Zeno, respectively. Epicurus identified three kinds of desires: natural and necessary, like food; natural and unnecessary, like sex; and unnatural and unnecessary, like fame, popularity— and wealth. We should continually satisfy the first; we should sometimes satisfy the second; we should avoid the third (Gonzalez, 1990, p. 11).

Despite the indulgence that his name now suggests, his was a philosophy centered in classical Greek temperance and rationality. Pleasure is the absence of bodily pain and the presence of emotional repose. To minimize pain and maximize repose, one needs to subject experience to rational control. The goal is the highest *net* pleasure—pleasure that lasts; pleasure that, unlike overindulgence, does not result in pain; pleasure that does not produce desire, for desire destroys the joy in what one has.

We should avoid the desires for fame, popularity, and wealth not only because these are unnatural and unnecessary but also because they cannot be satisfied, because they lead ultimately to frustration, disappointment, and preoccupation. The very pleasure of controlling desire through reason is in itself more pleasurable than the satisfaction of the particular craving (Schmidt, 1987, p. 120).

Epicurus favored individual ownership over communal, but for a new and interesting reason: Communal ownership implies mistrust among people, and trust is fundamental to the harmonious state (Gonzalez, 1990, p. 11). He also recommended detachment from poor people, because with poverty and the poor come many problems that disturb emotional repose (Schmidt, 1987, p. 11). Finally, he discouraged both chrematistics and usury, for each of these can entangle the mind and rob the soul of repose.

Zeno, fundamentally a Platonist, maintained that wisdom comprises both reason and fate and that it is our responsibility not only to accept—"stoically"—whatever role fate gives us but to play that role as well as it can be played (Greek excellence).

Zeno favored communal ownership in a rather extreme form: In Zeno's *Republic,* which shared not only its name but many of its values with Plato's more famous work, "people would share common clothes, a common table, and a common marriage." Furthermore, there would be no need for money, because with common property there is no need for trade and the vehicles of trade (Gonzalez, 1990, p. 11).

The tension between tough and tender thinking is as clear in Greece as it was in China. The Chinese concentrated on social organization, with the toughminded legalists advocating a dispassionate social segmentation, the tenderminded Mohists and Taoists a passionate and inclusive universal love. The Greeks emphasized property issues, the toughminded Ionics preferring private ownership; the tenderminded Italics, communal ownership. The philosophers as a rule leaned toward communal ownership, but the philosophers (like the preachers) did not necessarily represent the inclinations of the people.

In both China and Greece, profit is virtually always evil, usury even more so. Behind the metaphysical reasons advanced against profit and interest—that these are artificial enterprises; that they involve money "birthing" money—always seems to lurk a fear that money will be a tool of oppression, either a tool through which the wealthy and strong will, as in Mesopotamia, oppress the poor and the weak or a tool that itself will oppress those who seek or possess it. In the tenderminded, there seems also to be a reluctance or inability to differentiate, to make distinctions, a fear of discrimination, of admitting differences among people, perhaps because acknowledging differences will necessarily pave the way to oppression. In the toughminded, there seems to be a corresponding fear of the indiscriminate masses, perhaps because they can be expected to smother one's individuality and interfere with one's success.

The difference between Greek and Chinese philosophy lies in their effects. As we have already noted, the Confucian system fit the Chinese temperament exceedingly well: orderly, firm, and frugal. The Chinese people took it up, and held it close. Greek philosophy, although it appealed to the academic mind, did not fit the European temperament so well. Whereas Greek thinking has had an enormous effect on the Western intelligentsia, it was the aggressive and acquisitive Roman lawyers who really personified the culture.

Chapter 7

The Judeo-Christian Foundation

To understand the Christian extension of Judaism requires at least a brief look at its antithesis, Imperial Rome. The foundation of ancient Rome was its economy, and the foundation of the early Roman economy was the small farm (Gonzalez, 1990, p. 29ff.). Many of these farms were owned by the Roman legionnaires, who left the lands untended during military campaigns. The returning soldiers found their lands so overgrown that many sold them at fire-sale prices, or even abandoned them, and moved to the cities. In addition, the armies brought back many slaves, whom the large landowners could buy to work those lands. Cheap land and cheaper labor thus contributed to the growth of the massive estates, or *latifundia,* the concentration of money and property into the hands of a few fabulously wealthy people, and the dramatic class differentiation that seems necessarily to accompany the development of cities.

ROMAN INDIVIDUALISM

Then as now, some of the wealthiest landowners were social philosophers, and many of the influential citizens were lawyers. Then as now, the tough-minded members of these professions spoke in favor of entrepreneurial values and individual property rights, while the tenderminded advocated redistribution of land and heavy taxes against the rich. Representative of the competing philosophies, that is, socialism and capitalism, were Catalina and Cicero.

Catalina (fl. 68 B.C.) was one of the first prominent Romans to propose land redistribution and a property tax. Dissolute scion of a patrician family that had sunk into poverty, he led a rebellion of slaves, bankrupt veterans, and others who had been driven from their lands, with the intent of destroying the latifundia and returning the land to the people (Ramsay, 1967). To attract followers, he promised to "destroy creditors' books" and to "banish the rich"

(Sallust, *Bellum Catalinae,* 17, 20, quoted in Wilkins, 1961; see also Badian, 1996).

Cicero (106-43 B.C.), famed orator and Catalina's mortal foe, vigorously opposed any suggestion of the sort, because these proposals violated the traditional Roman conception of individual freedom. He was an articulate, even virulent, opponent of land reform:

> But they who pose as friends of the people, and who . . . either attempt to have agrarian laws passed, in order that the occupants may be driven out of their homes, or propose that money loaned should be remitted to the borrowers, are undermining the foundations of the commonwealth; first of all, they are destroying harmony, which cannot exist when money is taken away from one party and bestowed upon another; and second, they do away with equity, which is utterly subverted if property rights are not respected.
>
> For . . . it is the peculiar function of the state and the city to guarantee to every man the free and undisturbed control of his own particular property. (Cicero, *De Officiis,* 2:21-22, quoted in Loeb Classical Library [LCL], 1912-)

In the waning centuries of the Republic, philosophers continued to struggle against legislators, but their abstract protests were lost against the practical needs of the state. Pliny's assertion that "the first crime was committed by the person who wore the first ring" (quoted in Gonzalez, 1990, p. 18) evaporated against the pressing needs of the crumbling empire. Under increasing pressure from the gentry, the Roman legislators made sure the laws supported each and every landowner's absolute right to use, to enjoy, and even to abuse his land, and to pass it on to his heirs without government interference. The Romans also resisted property tax, because they viewed it as a sign of weakness—only conquered peoples paid taxes. A Roman's home was his castle long before an Englishman's—his home along with his money and the rest of his property were the badges of his accomplishment, the measure of not only his economic but also personal worth.

THE EARLY CHRISTIANS

Partly in reaction to Roman individualism, a small but persistent sect of religious zealots formed in Jerusalem and spread north and west around the Mediterranean, to Rome and to Constantinople, bringing with them collectivist ideals[1] every bit as strong as the Essenes'. With those ideals came an amplification of the hostility toward money and property that Schmidt

(1987) had identified in ancient Judaism. As evidence for the final stage in his theory of the development of the Judeo-Christian disdain for wealth, Schmidt pointed to the New Testament parable of the Rich Young Man, a passage that also turned out to be the focus of a great deal of anxious debate during the formative years of the Christian religion:

> "Good Master, what must I do to win eternal life?"
> "One thing you lack: go, sell everything you have, and give to the poor, and you will have riches in heaven; and come, follow me."
> At these words, his face fell and he went away with a heavy heart; for he was a man of great wealth.
> Jesus looked round at his disciples and said to them, "How hard it will be for the wealthy to enter the kingdom of God!" . . . "It is easier for a camel to pass through the eye of a needle than for a rich man to enter the kingdom of God." (Mark 10:17-26; see also Matthew 19:16-24, 24-27; Luke 1:52, 9:23-26, 12:27-31, 18:18-30)

During the 2,000 years of its existence, Christianity's attitude toward money and property has evolved from the (nearly) single-minded disdain that originated in the Jewish tradition into a dialectical tension that continues to intensify even in the present day. As Schmidt identified four stages in the evolution of the Judeo-Christian disdain for wealth, I suggest three stages in the ebb and flow of attitudes toward wealth in the early Christian era.

Stage 1: Disdain Without Accommodation

The early Church taught that the last would be first, that the Church's wretchedly impoverished members would become the Elect, that the wealthy and powerful Roman military leaders and aristocrats would be hungry and despised, and (curiously) that the Elect would rejoice in the poverty and impotence of the fallen aristocracy.

Just as the Decalogue—The Ten Commandments—sums up the Old Testament, the Sermon on the Mount encapsulates the New. Of the different versions of the Sermon, the Mattean is the more frequently quoted, but the Lukan is the more powerful:

> Blessed are you poor, for yours is the kingdom of God.
> Blessed are you that hunger now, for you shall be satisfied.
> Blessed are you that weep now, for you shall laugh.

But woe to you that are rich, for you have received your consolation.
Woe to you that are full now, for you shall hunger. (Luke 6:20-21, 24-26)

Gonzalez tell us (1990, p. 94) that the communism of the early Church[2] was consistent with (though not necessarily a result of) the disdain for money:

There was not a needy person among them, for as many as were possessors of lands or houses sold them, and brought the proceeds of what was sold and laid it at the apostles' feet; and the distribution was made to each as any had need. (Acts 34:34-35)

The communal life style, the fear of the Romans, and the message of the Sermon on the Mount acted together to confirm the fundamental wickedness of money, more pronounced in Christianity than in any other religion:

But those who desire to be rich fall into temptation, into a snare, into many senseless and hurtful desires that plunge men into ruin and destruction. For the love of money is the root of all evils; it is through this craving that some have wandered away from the faith and pierced their hearts with many pangs. (I Timothy 6:7-10)

Gonzalez (1990, pp. 96-98) describes wealth and money as impediments to salvation, because interest in business distracts from attention to the faith and puts one in the company of people whose interests are mercenary.

Stage 2: Accommodation and Conflict— St. Irenaeus Versus St. Clement

By the late second and early third centuries, the Church had begun to attract small but increasing numbers of members from the upper classes. Some early theologians used the presence of these wealthy converts as an opportunity to preach an even more intense hostility toward wealth. Others preferred to be more accommodating.

Irenaeus of Lyons (d. ca. 200 A.D.) held firmly to the view that wealth is inherently unrighteous:

For in some cases there follows us . . . property which we have acquired from the mammon of unrighteousness. For from what source do we derive the houses in which we dwell, the garments in which we are clothed, the vessels which we use, and everything else ministering to our everyday life, unless it be from those things which, when we were Gentiles, we acquired by avarice, or received them from our heathen parents, relations or friends who unrighteously obtained them? (Adversus Haereticos 4.30.1, quoted in Gonzalez, 1990, p. 110, and in *Ante-Nicean Fathers* [*ANF*], 1908-1911)

But Clement of Alexandria (d. ca. 215 A.D.) took a gentler approach. Clement's position was that we should neither fawn over the rich nor condemn them, but show them the road to salvation, rugged and steep though it may be. He interprets the parable of the Rich Young Man more metaphorically than do other Fathers of the Church:

[Jesus] does not . . . bid him throw away the substance he possessed, and abandon his property; but he bids him banish from his soul his notions about wealth, his excitement and morbid feeling about it, the anxieties, which are the thorns of existence, which choke the seed of life. (*Quis Dives Salvetur?* 11, quoted in Gonzalez, 1990, pp. 112-113 [Who Is the Rich Man That May Be Saved?] and in *ANF*, 1908-1911)

Wealth is neither evil in itself nor good, Clement taught; what matters is our attitude toward it. We can give away all our possessions and then thirst after them, or we can keep them and learn to stay unattached. The poor can be as covetous as the rich, the rich as virtuous as the poor. To achieve virtue, the rich should not only give to those in need but should engage a wise and firm spiritual adviser to help them deal properly with their wealth. Wealth is like a "poisonous snake" that unless we know just how to control it, can come around and bite us. Despite this powerful imagery, Clement was accused of being "soft on wealth," another indication of the depth of hostility toward money and property in the early Church.

Of the remaining early Fathers whose teachings on the subject have survived, Cyprian (d. 258) and Ambrose (d. 397) reflect Irenaeus' view, while Lactantius and Jerome reflect Clement's. Cyprian, in *de Opere et Eleemosyns,* argues that the rich man should strip himself of his treasure on earth to lay up treasure in heaven. Lactantius, in *Divinae Institutiones,* proposes that wealth gives one the opportunity to practice virtue, which requires stripping away not just wealth but whatever it is that makes us feel superior to others. Lactantius also defends private property. People will not take care of communal property, he asserts (as Aristotle did and Thomas would), and they will lose all sense of frugality (*Divinae Institutiones* 3.22, recounted in Gonzalez, 1990, p. 137).

After Constantine's dramatic conversion to Christianity, the Church grew markedly more prosperous. Ambrose's rebuke to the wealthier members of the community evidenced the continuing hostility toward wealth:

> A harsh judgment awaits you, O rich! The people are hungry and you close your granaries. The people cry and you show your jewels. Woe to one who can save so many lives from death, and does not! (*De Nabuthe Jez,* 56, quoted in Gonzalez, 1990, p. 190; *Patrologiae Cursus Completus,* 1844).

The exegete Jerome (d. 420) distinguished between the commandments and the "counsels to perfection," between the obligations of monks and the less demanding obligations of the laity. In Jerome's view, the parable of the Rich Young Man is not a requirement of all Christians but an "invitation to a higher perfection":

> Do you wish to be perfect and be at the highest summit of virtue? Do as the apostles, sell all you have, give it to the poor and follow the Savior. . . . Do you wish not to be perfect, but to reach the second level of virtue? Divest yourself of all you have, give it to your children and to your relatives. No one will despise you if you choose the lower level, as long as you acknowledge that the first course is the most perfect. (Ep. 120.1, quoted in Gonzalez, 1990, p. 195; *Biblioteca de Autores Cristianos,* 1944-)

Stage 3: Synthesis—St. John Chrysostom

As shepherd to a flock that comprised both the fabulously wealthy and the wretchedly poor, John Chrysostom, Bishop of Constantinople (d. 407), preached a synthesis between the two prevailing sets of values. He chided the poor as well as the rich, "for they too rob those that are poorer than themselves" (*Homily in I Thessalonians 10,* quoted in Gonzalez, 1990, p. 208). And he lamented that fact that we seem to want to use property to fragment the community:

> But when one attempts to possess himself of anything, to make it his own, then contention is introduced, *as if . . . we are eager to separate ourselves by appropriating things,* and by using those cold words "mine and thine." (Homily in I Timothy, quoted in Gonzalez, 1990, p. 204, emphasis added; *Nicene and Post-Nicene Fathers,* 1886-1901)

The solution to this contention and fragmentation, Chrysostom taught, is *solidarity,* a concept that has remained central to Christianity (and socialism) to the present day.

MATURE CHRISTIANITY

After Chrysostom's synthesis, the old pattern emerged again: Roman individualism and its European descendants as thesis, but now with Augustinian collectivism the antithesis and Thomistic temperance the synthesis. We have already discussed Roman individualism, so we shall turn now to St. Augustine.

St. Augustine Versus St. Thomas Aquinas

Augustine's (d. 430) philosophy centers in ordered versus disordered love. In his view, people need to love, because to love is to go beyond one's own incompleteness. We may love (1) material objects, such as food, drink, or money; (2) other people; (3) self; and (4) God. But each love object can give satisfaction only in proportion to its rightful place in the overall order of the universe. Loving things leads to less satisfaction than loving people; loving people offers less satisfaction than loving self; loving self provides less satisfaction than loving God. Only loving God results in complete satisfaction.

"Disordered love" comes from trying to get more satisfaction from a love object than it is capable of providing. Disordered love results in an overall restlessness and desperate efforts to find satisfaction. It leads to disordered individuals, which in turn lead to disordered communities (Schmidt, 1987, pp. 153-156). The most expeditious way to produce disorder in individuals and communities is by expecting that material things will satisfy our longings (Gonzalez, 1990, p. 215).

On the practical level, Augustine condemns lending money at interest, as he condemns putting pressure on those who owe you money. Instead, he counsels generosity, both tithing and almsgiving. He teaches that

> God, the giver of all, requires back a tenth part from us; that He requires Tithes of whatever is our livelihood; and that they are due as a debt; and that whosoever would procure of God either pardon or reward, must pay for them, and *out of*

the nine parts remaining endeavor to give alms. (Fuller, 1890, p. 39, quoted in
Powell, 1962, p. 28, emphasis added)

He insists that we give away whatever we do not actually need, for "not to
give to the needy what is superfluous [to us] is akin to fraud" (Sermons 206.2,
quoted in Gonzalez, 1990, p. 216). If we cannot afford to give, we should at
least lend (but not at interest). But Augustine does not recommend complete
divestiture for all his flock, nor does he urge upon all of us the monastic life.
Like Jerome, he describes both those practices as an ideal, a reminder of
what true Christianity is like. Savvy sinner that he had been in his youth, he
also warns us not to view his counsel as permission to commit sins for which
almsgiving could then atone!

Augustine's philosophy is antithetical to the ancient Roman conception of
property—the right to use, the right to enjoy, and the right to abuse. In
Augustine's view, to abuse property is to violate the law of nature. To enjoy
property is to violate the basic principle that whatever can be owned can only
be used as a means toward true enjoyment. And the right to use can only
mean to use in pursuit of the proper end, enjoyment of God (Gonzalez, 1990,
p. 216). European Christianity remained essentially Augustinian, neo-
Platonic, until the thirteenth century, when Thomas Aquinas would supply
his Christianized version of Aristotle.

Thomas Aquinas (1225-1274) Christianized Aristotle[3] the same way
Augustine Christianized Plato. In Aquinas, philosophy finds its middle
course between communal Christian Platonism (Augustine) and pagan Roman individualism. In Aquinas' view, our moral experience turns on the
tension between the "concupiscent appetite," through which we perceive
sensations as pleasurable, and the "irascible appetite," through which we
experience sensations as painful. This tension, governed by reason, is the
basis for our experiences of love and hate, and good and evil (Baumgarth &
Regan, 1988; Bradley, 1997).

Aquinas taught that whatever is, is good, because it emanates from God.
Thus wealth, sexual pleasure, and power are all proper focuses of human
appetite. But money, sex, and power cannot result in complete happiness;
they are not capable of satisfying our deepest longings, for such things do
not "possess the character of the universal good that man's soul seeks"
(quoted in Schmidt, 1987, p. 200; see also Lamb, 1992).

Aquinas was adamant that to charge interest is sinful:[4]

To the Seventh Commandment, which prohibits theft, is added the precept forbidding the taking of interest, according to Dt. 23:19: "You shall not lend to your brother money at interest," and the prohibition against fraud, according to Dt. 25:13: "You shall not have diverse weights in your bag," and universally all prohibitions relating to peculations and larceny. (*Summa Theologica [ST]*, 1964, I-II Q 100, A 11)

Charging interest for money lent is unjust in itself, because this is to sell what does not exist, and this evidently leads to inequality, which is contrary to justice. (*ST*, 1964, II-II Q 78, A 1)

He would not even accept Islamic interest-free banking, because, he insisted,

just as it is a sin against justice to take money in return for lending money or anything else that is consumed by being used, so also it is a like sin . . . to receive anything whose price can be measured by money. (*ST*, 1964, II-II Q 78, A 2)

Aquinas agrees with Aristotle that it is natural and lawful to possess external things (*ST*, 1964, II-II Q 66, AA 1, 2); that robbery and theft are sinful; but that robbery, because of its violent component, is the more sinful (AA 4, 5, 6, 9). He allows that theft *(furtus)* is not sinful "through stress of need" (AA 7, 8).

Aquinas poses a challenge to parts of the modern business world by declaring that it is both unjust and against natural law to sell a thing for more than it is worth, because selling something for more than its worth is the very definition of inequity. However, if the object sold represents a great emotional loss to the seller, the seller may be justified in accepting a higher price, because the object's worth to the seller is greater that its inherent worth, or if the object represents a great benefit to the buyer, the seller may be justified in voluntarily paying a premium, again because the personal worth exceeds the inherent worth (*ST*, 1964, II-II Q77, A 1). To pay such a premium is a matter of the buyer's virtue.

Aquinas adds that it is sometimes laudable to sell something for more than one paid for it, and sometimes blameworthy. For example, if the purpose of an exchange is to provide necessities for one's family or community, the act is not trade per se, not chrematistics, but maintenance. If the purpose is to trade for profit, there can be no virtuous end, and the act must only be intended to satisfy the greed for gain "which knows no limit and tends to infinity" (*ST*, 1964, II-II Q77, A 4).

Like Aristotle, Aquinas believed that property should be owned individually but available for common use. The responsibility to manage, administer, and use (*potestas procurandi et dispensandi*; *ST,* 1964, II-II, 66, 2) is more likely to be met under individual ownership than communal. Thus the principle of individual ownership flows from "the natural course of things," that is, from natural law.

Neither law nor custom may contravene individual ownership, except that the authorities may intervene, first, to make sure that property activities are consistent with local custom, and second, in extreme cases, when individuals are failing in their responsibilities, for example, failing to use or develop the property (Evans & Ward, 1933/1976, pp. 47, 52). The laws and customs should emphasize the three things that constitute good work in a community: proper care in the administration of its goods, absence of confusion in work, and maintenance of the public peace (p. 58). Thus the Thomistic view of ownership occupies a middle, synthetic ground between the communal ownership of Plato and Augustine and the absolute individual ownership of the Romans and their successors.

Thomas' synthesis held sway until a series of social revolutions began to reshape the Western world: the Renaissance, the Reformation, and the Enlightenment.

The Renaissance: Erasmus Versus Machiavelli

Thomas' immediate descendants, the Scholastics, taught an economic philosophy more to the political right than their master's. They believed that politics should follow not just Revelation but the Public Good, that business profit was licit if it came from risk, even that charging interest was legitimate, provided only that the rate was not excessive.

Erasmus (1466-1536) challenged the Scholastics from the left, his contemporary, Machiavelli (1469-1527), from the right. Erasmus' goal was to return to the simplicity of original Christianity, without what he viewed as the excessive rationalism of the Scholastics. As Augustine before him, Erasmus saw considerable similarity between Plato's teachings and Christ's, and he sought to return the Church to her kinder, gentler roots.

With regard to money and wealth, Erasmus is best known for *Praise of Folly* (1941), his attack on the phariseeism of the clergy:

[A friar] will boast that for sixty years he never touched money, except when his fingers were protected by two pairs of gloves. . . . But Christ will say: "I

recognize one commandment which is truly mine, and of that I hear nothing.
. . . I promised the inheritance of my father . . . to works of charity." (pp. 87-88)

To Erasmus, disdain for money was no substitute for love of neighbor.
Machiavelli attacked Scholasticism from the opposite angle. More political pragmatist than philosopher, he decried the naiveté of trying to govern a
state according to Thomistic ethical principles. Like Marx, he considered
religion an opiate for the people. But governors cannot be constrained by
such fantasies; they must refine their skills in the art of deception, or they
will fall prey to the evil men who govern nations. Above all, they must stamp
out any inclination they might have toward generosity, for that trait necessarily leads to a severe weakening of princely power (Machiavelli, 1952,
p. 96).

The Reformation: Luther Versus Calvin

The needs of the Church and the wants of the churchmen required an
improvement in ecclesiastical cash flow, preferably with a proper doctrinal
foundation. The first solution was the doctrine of penance, which specified
suitable monetary satisfaction for each entry in a catalog of sins. The second
was the doctrine of indulgences,[5] which encouraged sinners to remit their
guilt by participating in the Crusades, making pilgrimages to Rome, or best
of all, contributing money to the Church. Indeed, St. Peter's Basilica was
financed largely through the sale of indulgences. The third and final solution
was the sale of relics[6] and related clerical services, including transaction
fees, guaranty fees, and pious offerings from the faithful (Collinson, 1990,
p. 241; Powell, 1962, pp. 58-61).

The chief critic of this commercialization of religion was Martin Luther
(1483-1546), monk, preacher, and Platonic idealist. With special vigor,
Luther attacked simony, that "wanton preaching of pardons," and of course,
usury (Collinson, 1990, p. 245; Marty, 1971).

Unwilling to offend either prelate or merchant, the mainstream philosophers and theologians of the day equivocated about the ethics of usury:

From city after city municipal authorities, terrified by popular demands for the
repression of the extortioner, consulted universities and divines as to the
legitimacy of interest, and universities and divines gave, as is their wont, a loud,
but confused, response. (Tawney, 1926, p. 81)

Luther, however, did not equivocate:

> The devil invented [interest], and the Pope, by giving his sanction to it, has done untold evil throughout the world. (quoted in Tawney, 1926, p. 95).

He would refuse usurers the sacraments, absolution, and Christian burial. See his Long Sermon on Usury (1519-1520/1931) and Sermon on Trade and Usury (1524/1931).

Luther's intent, like Erasmus', was to revitalize dogma and practice according to values "derived from the forgotten purity of primitive Christianity." Luther preferred the simplicity of the countryside to the sophistication of the city, for the peasant life was "least touched by the corroding spirit of commercial calculation." Thus Luther's Reformation was not only an attack on moral laxity and financial exigency but a frontal assault on the capitalism of the time. Sloth and envy are the two unforgivable sins, "the sins of the vagrants, the monks, and the capitalists!" (Tawney, 1926, pp. 85-92).

It would be difficult to find a cleric more different from Luther than John Calvin (1509-1564). Calvin's goal, like Luther's, was to return religion to its pristine beauty, before the taint of Scholasticism and Popism. But his theology, set against the already disciplined backdrop of Swiss society and abetted by the antiseptic likes of John Knox, radiated a colder, more legalistic, and more capitalistic aura than did Luther's (Calvin, 1936; Choisy, 1902; Dowey, 1971, p. 673; Rupp, 1971).

By today's standards, Calvin's notion of capitalism was restrained, but by sixteenth-century standards, it was radical departure. For example, with regard to the ever-sensitive subject of interest, he taught

> that interest is lawful, provided it does not exceed an official maximum; that, even when a maximum is fixed, loans must be made gratis to the poor; that the borrower must reap as much advantage as the lender; that excessive security must not be exacted; that what is venial as an occasional expedient is reprehensible when carried on as a regular occupation; that no man may snatch economic gain for himself to the injury of his neighbor. (quoted in Tawney, 1926, p. 106)

Thus his rule was a dramatic departure from status quo, but hardly permissive enough to warm Shylock's heart, or Adam Smith's.

Calvin also repressed mendicancy and indiscriminate almsgiving, encouraged industry and thrift, and turned business into almost a religious ritual. He required that authorities visit families who receive alms to make sure that no one was idle, or drunk, or dressed in luxurious clothes, or wearing ornaments, or playing cards (Calvin, 1989).

With Knox, Calvin also spelled out the canon for the English Puritans, who would soon ride the *Mayflower* to the New World and carry with them the Reformed values[7] of industry, responsibility, risk-taking, frugality—those values that produce economic success and that at long last had religious sanction.

Calvin's genius, the key to his longevity, was that he bridged the chasm between the world of economic achievement and the world of the spirit not by eschewing achievement but by dedicating it "to the greater glory of God" (Tawney, 1926, p. 110). Money for Calvin and his American Puritans was no longer evil: it was good, and its accumulation was a kind of prayer.

The Enlightenment: Capitalism Versus Socialism

With the dawn of the Enlightenment, our survey of the legal, religious, and philosophical foundations for the meanings of money and property begins to draw to a close, for we have come full circle back to the dialectic between John Locke, John Stuart Mill, and Adam Smith, on the one hand, and Ludwig Fuerbach, David Ricardo, and Karl Marx, on the other: Economic man versus Soulful man.

Since the Enlightenment, knowing self, not God, was the end, and reason, not revelation, was the means. The Enlightenment made man "the measure of all things." A man owned his own labor, labor justified private ownership, ownership led to social differentiation, and differentiation paired with ownership made money the index of individual and group worth (MacPherson, 1962, p. 243, cited in Lamb, 1992, p. 744).

Locke knew that without some intervening ethic, this focus on money and property would naturally lead to oppression (jealousy), on the one hand, and victimization (envy), on the other (Schmidt, 1987, pp. 287-288). The ethic that the Enlightenment thinkers chose to follow in their perfection of human potential was not the Homeric tradition of virtue but the new European disposition[8] toward civil, criminal, and regulatory law, a paradigm shift (Kuhn, 1962) in which the question is no longer "What are my responsibilities as a good citizen?" but "How far can I go and still stay within the law?" Under such an ethic, the focus is avoidance of the negative rather than pursuit of the positive; as a result, time obscures the original intent, and each successive generation discovers new gambits to test the limits. Under such an ethic, both the vertical differentiation that characterizes capitalism and the horizontal homogenization that represents socialism will intensify until, ultimately, society must split apart.

Syntheses: Nietzsche, and Thomism Revisited

Friedrich Nietzsche (1844-1900) noted how society protects itself from this disintegration by naturally putting a limit on excessive attitudes and behavior (Nietzsche, 1886/1989, 1887/1974). As the pendulum swings toward the extreme right, people gradually redefine as evil that which the masters see as good, and as good that which the masters see as evil. Thus assertiveness, independence, determination, and the like, which contributed to the power of the masters and the growth of the capitalistic economy, society comes to see as evil; and sympathy, patience, gentleness, and the like, which the slaves admire but the masters disdain, people come to see as good. Later, when the softer values become excessive, society will reverse that evaluation and shift the power structure in the other direction. It is not a difficult step to find jealousy and envy at work in this process.

Rather than a Nietzschean ebb and flow, the modern theologians of the Catholic Church have tried to maintain a Thomistic middle ground. The most recent manifestation of that position is the 1994 revision of the *Catechism of the Catholic Church (CCC)*. While this document certainly does not purport to speak for all Christendom, it does present a well-reasoned ethic of wealth that all Catholics are supposed to follow and that many other people try to follow. According to that catechism, Christians are not only supposed to obey the Ten Commandments and the Precepts of Jesus, they are supposed to pursue a life of "divine charity" and "human solidarity." Walzer's (1983, esp. chaps. 1 and 4) theory of pluralism and equality and Wuthnow's (1994) examination of the tensions between materialism and religion are contemporary interpretations of these ancient principles, beyond the boundaries of the Catholic Church.

Charity is "the theological virtue by which we love God above all things for his own sake, and our neighbor as ourselves for the love of God" *(CCC,* paragraph 1822). Charity informs and animates the moral virtues and "binds everything together in perfect harmony" (Col. 3:14). *Solidarity—* "friendship," in the classical Greek sense—is a respectful and loving fraternity among all members of the human race.

It is at the junction of divine charity and human solidarity that modern Christianity begins to focus on money and wealth. Christianity, like most religions essentially socialistic, advocates the sharing of material goods in proportion to need and in consideration of ability. It envisions the solution of social problems by cooperation among the poor themselves, between the rich and the poor, between the employer and the worker, and among peoples and nations of the world *(CCC,* 1940-1941).

In its precepts concerning money and wealth, Christianity focuses on the Seventh and Tenth Commandments (Exodus 20:15, 17; Deuteronomy 5:19, 21; Matthew 19:18):

Seventh: Neither shall you steal.

Tenth: You shall not desire . . . anything that is your neighbor's.

In its negative interpretation, the Seventh Commandment "forbids unjustly taking or keeping the goods of one's neighbor and wronging him in any way with respect to his goods" (*CCC,* 2401). Included among the prohibited practices are fraud, bribery, forgery, tax evasion, vandalism, waste, and work poorly done (*CCC,* 2409). The Seventh Commandment also prohibits gambling when the result interferes with the ability to provide for themselves or others for whom they are responsible (*CCC,* 2413). Finally, it forbids any form of slavery, for enslavement denies the dignity of the human being (*CCC,* 2414).

Positively, the Seventh Commandment mandates "justice and charity in the care of earthly goods and the fruits of men's labor" (*CCC,* 2401). It allows private ownership but mandates that owners share the benefits, starting with their families (*CCC,* 2403-2404) and that they "use them with moderation, reserving the better part for guests, for the sick and the poor" (*CCC,* 2405, 2407). It allows profit, but commands that business owners consider social good above financial benefit (*CCC,* 2432). It mandates that "everyone should make legitimate use of his talents to contribute to the abundance that will benefit all" (*CCC,* 2429). And it reminds richer peoples and nations that they have a responsibility "in charity and solidarity" toward those who are unable to provide for their own development, especially peasants.

Finally, the Seventh Commandment urges special love for the poor through the "corporal works of mercy"—feeding the hungry, sheltering the homeless, clothing the naked, and, especially, giving alms to the poor.

The Tenth Commandment prohibits coveting someone else's property, because coveting can lead to theft, robbery, and fraud, which, of course, the Seventh Commandment also prohibits (*CCC,* 2534). It forbids *greed* "and the desire to amass earthly goods without limit"; *avarice* "arising from a passion for riches and their attendant power" (*CCC,* 2536); and, especially, *envy,* "which can lead to the worst crimes" (*CCC,* 2538). As antidote, it recommends goodwill, humility, and "abandonment to the providence of God" (*CCC,* 2554).

II	I
Propensity: Acquisitiveness	Propensity: Expansiveness
Operation: Sensing	Operation: Intuiting
Fear: Incompetence	Fear: Constraint
III	IV
Propensity: Concentration	Propensity: Affiliativeness
Operation: Thinking	Operation: Feeling
Fear: Disarray	Fear: Abandonment

Figure 7.1. A Basic Quaternary
NOTE: See also Figure 3.1.

In its contemporary interpretation, the Tenth Commandment also maintains the Judeo-Christian "hostility to wealth." It "celebrates the joy of the poor, to whom the Kingdom already belongs" (*CCC*, 2546; Luke 6:20), and it reminds us that "the Lord grieves for the rich, because they find their consolation in the abundance of goods" (*CCC*, 2547; Luke 6:24).

Finally, the Tenth Commandment focuses Christian attention back on the Sermon on the Mount and advocates detachment from the things of the world: "Blessed are the poor in spirit." In its most sweeping interpretation, it forces back to mind that passage that has troubled theologians and the laity from the beginning: "Sell what you have and give to the poor."

REFLECTION

At the end of Chapter 4, I identified a pattern of cultural propensities—acquisitiveness, affiliativeness, concentration, and expansiveness—which centered in Jung's four psychological operations—sensing, feeling, thinking, and intuiting—and which led to four archetypal fears—incompetence, abandonment, disarray, and constraint. I now propose, on the basis of the dynamic tensions we encountered in our surveys of law, religion, and philosophy, that we arrange that information as a quaternary, the ancient fourfold structure that thinkers from Pythagoras to Schopenhauer (1974) have believed provides a particularly valid depiction of the universe. Figure 7.1 shows a basic quaternary.

II—*European Law*	I—*African Law*
Structure: Written formal laws	Structure: Oral customary laws
Goal: Preserve property	Goal: Preserve dignity
Punishment: Confiscation	Punishment: Humiliation
III—*Asian Law*	IV—*American Indian Law*
Structure: Written formal laws	Structure: Oral customary laws
Goal: Preserve social order	Goal: Preserve family harmony
Punishment: Shaming	Punishment: Excommunication

Figure 7.2. Ancient Laws in Quaternary
NOTE: See also Table 4.1.

An important structural implication of the quaternary is that diagonal elements exist in dialectic (contradictory) opposition to one another, for example, acquisitiveness/affiliativeness and expansiveness/concentration. Adjacent, nondiagonal elements are contrary but not contradictory, because they share some important characteristics. Thus European and Asian laws, because they share the quality of structuredness, are contrary systems, while European and American Indian approaches to law are contradictory (Figure 7.2). In a later chapter, we shall examine both psychoanalytic (thesis) and neurophysiological (antithesis) explanations for dialectical relationships—and we shall try to provide at least a step toward a synthesis.

For the present, it is enough to point out that (at least in my view) it is the "propensity toward expansiveness" that underlies the Quadrant I concern with free expression and individual dignity, on the one hand, and humiliation and fear of constraint, on the other. It is because of this propensity that Quadrant I people tend to use money and property in impulsive and flamboyant ways, and because of the opposite propensity, toward "concentration," that Quadrant III people are financially cautious, controlled, and responsible, if not downright stingy.

Similarly, it is the "propensity toward acquisitiveness" that drives Quadrant II people to achieve and compete and that motivates them to accumulate money and property as badges of success. And, last, it is the "propensity toward affiliation" that explains the Quadrant IV occupation with attractiveness and nurturance and that causes them to try to avoid anything that might suggest they are acquisitive rather than affiliative.

Finally, it is important to bear in mind the considerable variability within each of the quadrants. In the acquisition quadrant, for example, though all of the entries share what we have been calling European propensities, Protagoras, John Calvin, and Adam Smith were more materialistic than Plato, Luther, and Marx. In the expressive quadrant, though all share African propensities, the Tutsis and Zulus are more aggressive than the Hottentots and !Kung. As already indicated, the nature and origins of within-class variation are questions for another day.

After a short recapitulation, we will be ready to combine all this information—the form and substance of our survey of ancient law, philosophy, and religions—into a single framework (Chapter 8) that will serve as a moderator for our model of how people attach meanings to money (Chapter 9).

PART III

A BIOPSYCHOSOCIAL MODERATOR AND MODEL

In which I use inferences from the preceding chapters to create a biopsychosocial framework that describes different kinds of people, and to propose a model for how these kinds of people go about attaching different meanings to money and property.

Chapter 8

A Moderator—
Different Meanings
for Different People

RECAPITULATION I

Our chief goal so far has been to lay the foundation for a "moderator framework," a device to make sure our model recognizes the fact that money and property mean different things to different people. To this end, we surveyed the various attitudes toward money and property that have been manifested in the legal prescriptions, religious principles, and philosophical teachings of the diverse cultures during the earlier stages of their development. We did this, first, because these patterns of attitude are interesting in themselves, and second—and more important—because these patterns should help us identify a naturally occurring foundation on which to base the framework. The more closely the framework reflects what happens naturally, the more claim it has to validity.

The structure that has emerged from this survey comprises

1. An overall fourfold table that emphasizes between-group variation, with contradictory tension on the diagonals, contrary tension between the adjacent cells
2. A dialectic (if not a quaternary) within each of the quadrants of the overall table, to capture within-group variation
3. A general developmental dimension to account for changes over the life spans of individuals, families, and larger groups

The substance meshes neatly with the structure. With regard to law, it seems clear that some groups of people have established more informal bodies of law, that is, oral customary laws, while others have constructed more structured, written, formal codes. It also seems clear that the substance, or content, of these customs and laws is predictably different across the major early peoples of Earth, and fairly homogeneous within (1) European laws that protect property rights versus American Indian customs that maintain family harmony, and (2) Asian laws that effect social control versus African customs that guard individual dignity. It seems no less clear that the more structured and formal are the laws, the more severe will be the penalties for violating them. Whether the difference between informal and formal law is the result of different cognitive abilities, different preferences, or other factors, it is hard to doubt that whatever biopsychosocial structures and processes support written language in the individual are also at work in the preference of formal versus informal law on the cultural level, perhaps even in the emphasis on accumulation, affiliation, control, and expression. I shall soon propose that each of these emphases has a specific neurophysiological foundation on which social experience builds and with which it interacts.

In religion, too, the patterns are clear and distinct, and they are the same patterns we noticed in law. Early on, people seemed to attribute to their principal gods the attributes they valued most: mastery, symmetry, optimism, and unity. People who preferred mastery and symmetry seemed more to the toughminded side; those who preferred optimism and unity, more to the tenderminded. People who preferred mastery and optimism seemed more instrumental, active, energetic; those who preferred mysticism and symmetry seemed more contemplative. Later, religion seemed to reflect the temperament of the people, but in reverse, as though to rein in the natural excesses of each temperament. Where the temperament was aggressive and competitive, as among many European groups, law protected property, but religion advocated divestiture. Where the temperament was dramatic and flamboyant, as with many African peoples, the law protected dignity, but the religion emphasized how small humankind was in comparison to nature. Where the temperament leaned toward order and detail, as in Asia, the law forbade disorder, but the religion emphasized becoming immune to external control. And where the temperament was toward peace and emotional harmony, as in many American Indian tribes, the laws encouraged social unity, but the religion (spirituality) encouraged private emotional experience (e.g., the vision quest). This tempering quality of religion seems especially pronounced in the active, extraverted cultures, the ones whose excesses are more likely to be noticed.

As with law, then, religious differences appear clear-cut across the archetypal cultural groups. However, perhaps because religion reveals more intimate values than law, and perhaps because adherence is often more voluntary, there appears to be a greater degree of variation in religious tenet than in legal principle within the major groups. Some people created religions that emphasized interior experience, others external activity; some created religions that emphasized emotional processes, others, that emphasized reason. In Europe in particular we saw religious values toward money and property framed in dialectical form: thesis (e.g., wealth is evil), antithesis (wealth is good), synthesis (wealth is neutral). There may have been a degree of within-group variability in law or adherence to law, but it is not nearly so obvious as with religion.

Because religion in the less structured cultures serves the same purpose that philosophy serves in the more structured, namely, to articulate values and prescribe behavior, our examination of philosophy is limited to those localities in which philosophy per se flourished: Europe and Asia. Perhaps because philosophers are philosophers the world around, classical European (Greek) philosophy and classical Asian (Chinese) philosophy are remarkably parallel to one another. Even in the rarefied air of formal philosophy, though, we found the familiar dialectic: in Europe, Roman individualism versus Augustinian collectivism, synthesized in Thomism; in Asia, Legalism versus Taoism, synthesized in Confucianism. The consistency and extent of these patterns is enough to lead us to suspect that we have identified the kinds of naturally occurring phenomena on which we can safely build a moderator framework and a model.

The objective of the present chapter is to concentrate the foregoing themes into quaternary form, first as a fourfold figure of general temperament,[1] then in a series of fourfold figures depicting "financial temperament" on the individual, family, and cultural levels, and at different stages of development; to provide evidence that supports the validity of these figures. For convenience, I shall begin to refer to the total framework as the *Quaternary,* either general or financial; to the principal segments as the four *quadrants,* and to the dynamic structural and content relationships as *quadrant theory.*

My approach might qualify as something new in that it tries to synthesize selected aspects of the history of law, religion, and philosophy into a coherent framework for studying the meanings of money and property and to support that framework with a synthesis of modern neurophysiology, psychometrics, and psychoanalysis—a strange but exciting menagerie. In another sense, this approach will be something old and something borrowed, for it is fundamentally (with financial extensions) the structure proposed by Hippocrates and Galen, and kept alive by such scholars as Kant and Stewart (1887); more recently, Freud, Adler, and Jung; then Eysenck; and most recently Kagan, Zuckerman, Tellegen, and Cloninger. Adaptations are widely used in anthropological classification (e.g., Douglas, 1970), personnel management (e.g., Merrill & Reid, 1981), sales training (e.g., Cathcart & Alessandra, 1985), and marriage counseling (e.g., Olson, 1986). We shall need to spend some time tracing the highlights of this venerable history.

By way of overview, I propose that natural selection has resulted in neuroanatomical structures and neurochemical processes that cause people to see and experience and evaluate the world in predictably different ways. I propose that the two most basic dimensions that lie behind these differences are

Toughminded/tenderminded, after James (1890), which seems to be much the same dimension as that which people have traditionally called "masculine/feminine" (referring to disposition, not physiology) and "yang/yin"; and

Introverted/extraverted, after Jung (1923/1971), which seems to be the much the same as that which some researchers have recently called "inhibited/uninhibited."

I also suggest that, if we arrange these two dimensions as Cartesian coordinates—an X-axis crossing a Y-axis—the resulting quadrants are the very dimensions we identified in our survey of law, religion, and philosophy: acquisitive/affiliative and expansive/concentrated (Figure 3.1). That is, Toughminded Extraverts tend to be acquisitive, Tenderminded Introverts affiliative, and so forth.

After we examine neurophysiological, psychometric, and psychoanalytic data in support of these basic descriptions of temperament (personality) in general, we will examine financial temperament and supporting evidence, along with a developmental component to account for how meanings evolve over the life span.

Because the purpose of this chapter in particular is to stimulate academic research, some of the material will be a bit to the technical side. The general reader may prefer to skip forward to the discussion of financial temperament (p. 154).

I begin with a brief history of temperament in general.

TEMPERAMENT IN GENERAL

In about 450 B.C., the Greek philosopher Empedocles, building on the work of earlier cosmologists, concluded that the world was composed of four basic elements: fire, earth, air, and water. At roughly the same time, in the East,

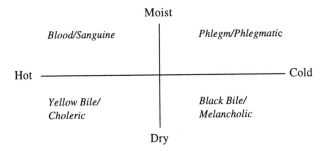

Figure 8.1. Galen's Primary Temperaments

the Vedic philosophers taught the same physics, with the addition of a harmonious central state, which they called ether (see Kagan, 1994, pp. 4-5, for elaboration). Fifty years later, Hippocrates prescribed a physiology of humors, a "humorology," in which the predominance of certain precious bodily fluids governed human behavior.

In the second century of the present era (175 A.D.), the Greek psychiatrist Galen elaborated on Empedocles' physics and Hippocrates' physiology to define a theory of human temperament that would endure until the nineteenth century—and find its own renaissance in the latter half of the 20th (e.g., Doyle, 1992d; Eysenck, 1944; Kagan, 1994). Juxtaposing various of the four elements, Hippocrates postulated two pairs of opposing qualities that governed temperament: hot/cold and moist/dry. Hot resulted from fire and air; dry, from fire and earth; moist, from water and air; and cold, from water and earth.

In the human sphere, Galen postulated a temperament connected with each of Hippocrates' humors (Figure 8.1). When the four qualities—moist/dry and hot/cold—were in balance, the four humors and their associated temperaments were also in balance, and the result was the ideal personality. If any given pair of different qualities predominated, the result was one of the four primary temperaments:

Moist and hot (blood) predominating—sanguine temperament

Cold and dry (black bile) predominating—melancholic temperament

Cold and moist (phlegm) predominating—phlegmatic temperament

Dry and hot (yellow bile, or choler) predominating—choleric temperament

The Greek contribution is important in several respects. It represents not only the first articulated Western conceptualization of human personality, and one that has endured in the same or similar form for more than two thousand years, but it specifies several important ideas that many later theorists adopted: the idea that personality is defined by a small number of stable qualities, that these qualities stand in opposition to one another, that contentment results from balancing those forces, and that both physiology and environment affect them. Indeed, the Greeks were more certain than we often seem to be that humans are biopsychosocial beings.

Over the centuries, Galen's formulation has proven remarkably durable. The astrologers, the best scientists of their time, maintained his quaternary through the Dark Ages into the Medieval period (Doyle, 1992d). Kant, in his *Anthropologie,* accepted the formulation, distinguishing between the "affective" temperaments (sanguine and melancholic) and the "active" ones (choleric and phlegmatic) and noting that the human will should be able to control the propensities. Bain, Stewart, and Wundt would bring the schema into the nineteenth century (Eysenck, 1953, p. 17; Kagan, 1994, p. 4; Kant, 1798/1974).

With the Enlightenment, however, temperament theory became embroiled in the freedom/determination controversy. The very thought of heritable propensities toward irascibility, melancholia, and so forth flew in the face of Enlightenment fascination with liberty, equality, and fraternity. Moreover, to give human genetics a toehold in society would be to admit eugenics, superordination, and the limitations of social programs, none of which is acceptable in politically "enlightened" circles (e.g., Herrnstein & Murray, 1994; Jensen, 1969).

Twentieth-century America's innocent confidence in its ability to right any wrong, repair any flaw, and control the uncontrollable nearly extinguished scientific interest in temperaments. Although Roback's (1931) efforts to balance freedom and determination regained for temperament theory a modicum of temporary scientific respectability, the zeitgeist made temperament the reluctant stepchild of one counterculture after another—hippies, druggies, drop-outs, cultists, New Agers. These latter connections did nothing to improve its standing in the eyes of the scientific community.

Kagan (1994, pp. 30-32) credits Diamond (1957) and Thomas and Chess (1977) with the modern renaissance of temperament, although it is Kagan himself who, along with Eysenck, deserves the bulk of the credit. Diamond explicitly applied Galen's formulation to the typing of American children— fearful, aggressive, impulsive, and apathetic—but he spoke before the culture was ready to listen. Thomas and Chess described (among other types) what Kagan recognized as his uninhibited (extraverted) and inhibited (introverted) children. Diamond, and Thomas and Chess, came by clinical observation to what Eysenck had come to by psychometric research, and Kagan would come to by biochemical research. Kagan not only recognized his types as part of the Greek system but provided a body of biochemical data to support his argument and deepen the meaning.

Not long after Thomas and Chess, Kagan (1994, p. 25) tells us, Olson and Morgan (1982), Henke (1990), Mills and Faure (1991), and others demonstrated that fear could be bred into animals, hence that there was a heritable aspect to timidity, a component of the phlegmatic temperament. More recently and considerably more important, Tellegen et al. (1988, esp. their Table 5; see also Lykken, Bouchard, McGue, & Tellegen, 1993, and Rushton, Fulker, Neale, Nias, & Eysenck, 1986) reported large heritability coefficients for many components of personality and temperament, including Tellegen's "superfactors," which I will argue are equivalent to the Galenic temperaments. As Kagan (1994, p. 27) observed with scientific understatement, "The combined effect of these studies has been to place the idea of temperament in a more favored position in interpretations of human behavior."

First-Level Dimensions

Having established the legitimacy of temperament as a foundation for a theory of personality, hence as a foundation for a theory of the meanings of money and property, we can now look more closely for evidence to validate those dimensions of temperament that I have called the most basic: Toughminded/Tenderminded and Introverted/Extraverted.

Toughminded/Tenderminded

The tough/tender dimension is supported by what strikes me as a reasonably persuasive confluence of neurophysiological, psychometric, and psychoanalytic research.[2] Neurophysiological research provides the foundation, the biological basis on which other experience can build. Psychometric research supplies the definition; it spells out the dimensions and subdimensions, and it describes their interrelations (see Eysenck, 1957, and Furnham & Lewis, 1986, p. 7, for predecessor structures). Finally, psychoanalytic research furnishes the elaboration; it suggests more and deeper interpretations that, when confirmed, help extend meaning. I suggest that there is more consistency across these three approaches to understanding personality than we generally believe.

Neurophysiological Support. Some of the most interesting neurophysiological research germane to these dimensions has explored the endocrinology of masculinity/femininity, or Toughmindedness/Tendermindedness. For example, Erhardt and Money (1967; see also Money & Erhardt, 1972), in their well-known study of "tomboyism,"[3] found that young women who had been exposed in utero to androgen, the male hormone, were not only more athletic and exhibited greater preference for team sports like neighborhood football and baseball but also exhibited more masculine interests—for functional rather than fashionable clothing, and for traditional boys' toys, guns, and trucks rather than dolls (Sloane, 1993, pp. 174-178). (For reflective essays on sex differences, see Short, 1994, and Balaban, 1994, both in Short & Balaban, 1994.)

More recently, Money (1978) and Reinisch and Sanders (1992) found that androgen[4] has even more influence than previously suspected. Not only did increasing amounts of androgen (in females as well as males) lead to progressively more pronounced male sex characteristics like pervasive body hair and deeper vocal pitch, and also to enhanced left-brain development in males and right-brain development in females, with consequent greater spatial ability in males and greater communicative ability in females, but—and this is what's really fascinating—the difference in amount of androgen correlated with differences in self-descriptions on personality questionnaires. In the presence of more androgen, both females and males reported not only greater feelings of aggressiveness but also more positive feelings of self worth and need achievement! Although we need to be careful not to oversimplify complex neurophysiological phenomena, these findings suggest a truly remarkable bridge between biology and psychology (Table 8.1a; e.g., Edelman, 1992). They offer strong support for the proposition that attitudes and values are grounded in the body, presumably including attitudes and values about money and property. For further support, see Reinisch, Rosenblum, and Sanders (1987, esp. Part V) and Rubinow and Schmidt (1996).

Psychometric Support. It was William James himself who coined the terms *toughminded* and *tenderminded* (1911, cited in Eysenck, 1953, pp. 228-229). Probably the most rigorous delineation of these concepts comes from the psychometricians, more specifically the factor analysts, whose goal is to

TABLE 8.1A Correlates of Low Versus High Androgen Levels in Humans

Low Androgen (femininity)	High Androgen (masculinity)
Inhibited left-brain development	Enhanced left-brain development
Greater communicative ability	Greater spatial ability
Greater verbal ability	Greater mathematical ability
Enhanced right-brain development	Inhibited right-brain development
Report low aggressiveness	Report high aggressiveness
Report low self-worth	Report high self-worth
Report low need achievement	Report high need achievement

SOURCE: Money (1978) and Reinisch and Sanders (1992).
NOTE: See also reviews by Baker (1987) and Halpern (1992) the thrust of which are to draw attention to environmental factors. Baker, in Baker, provides an interesting review of sensory differences: Women hear pure tones and feel bodily pressure more readily than men; men have sharper visual acuity than women. These perceptual skills may relate to cooperativeness and competitiveness.

construct theory and measurement instruments on the basis of what they call the underlying dimensions of a domain. They use highly sophisticated statistical techniques to sort descriptions into homogeneous categories,[5] or "factors." As mentioned earlier, Eysenck (e.g., 1944, 1991) and Cattell (1957) found a factor that included items that suggested idealism and political liberalism ("For" curing criminals and "against" the death penalty), and another that included items which indicated materialism, practicality, and political conservatism. Appropriating James's terms, Eysenck called these factors *toughmindedness* and *tendermindedness,* respectively (Table 8.1b). For a related distinction, see Bakan's (1966) "communal" versus "agentic."

As I have already indicated, this tough/tender factor seems essentially the same as that which other people have called yang/yin (Table 8.1c) or masculine/feminine (Table 8.1d; referring, I repeat, to disposition and not to physiology). In our own questionnaire study[6] of two large replicated national samples of the American adult population, we found a factor that reliably differentiates Tenderminded people from Toughminded. Not surprisingly, Tenderminded people disagreed more, and Toughminded people agreed more, with groups of questions that said men were smarter than women, better leaders, better at investing, and so forth (Table 8.1e). This factor seems perfectly consistent with Eysenck's and Cattell's factors, already cited. Thus the psychometricians have helped define the meaning of the tough/tender dimension. For an interesting corroboration from linguistics, see Tannen (e.g., 1989, 1990) and Gray (1993); with endocrinology, see Erhardt and

TABLE 8.1B Selected Terms From Eysenck's Factors

Tenderminded	Toughminded
Theoretical	Practical
Idealistic	Materialistic
Thinking (Philosopher)	Force (Soldier)
Believing (Priest)	Manipulation (Scientist)
"Against death penalty"	"For compulsory sterilization"
"Cure criminals"	"Flog criminals"

SOURCE: Eysenck (1953/1970, pp. 227-229).

TABLE 8.1C Terms That Differentiate Yin/Yang

Yin	Yang
Feminine	Masculine
Moist	Dry
Cold	Hot
Soft	Hard

Baker (1973). For similar corroboration from cognitive science, see Epstein (1994). For a multidisciplinary examination of masculinity/femininity, see Reinisch, Rosenblum, and Sanders (1987, p. 120).

Psychoanalytic Support. Psychoanalytic interpretations are potentially far more profound than most psychometric descriptions, but they are also much harder to validate; hence they must be taken with a grain of salt. Jung (1951/1971, chap. 6; see also Horney, 1967), for example, asserts that men and women have within them two dispositions, which he called Anima and Animus. Because (in psychoanalytic terms) Anima is more "Eros" than "Logos," more Love than Logic, Anima is oriented toward affiliation (and envelopment) while Animus is oriented more toward differentiation (and disintegration). In Jung's metaphorical view, Anima's weapon is her illusional quality and seductiveness; that of Animus, his sword—the sexual symbolism is clear. Anima wants to protect, nourish, and embrace; more

TABLE 8.1D Terms That Describe Gender Differences

Femininity		Masculinity
	Theoretical predictions (Brody, 1985, p. 24)	
Less	Guilt and anger	More
More	Envy and shame	Less
More	Depression and anxiety	Less
More	Feelings of vulnerability	Less
More	Alert to nonverbal cues	Less
More	Emotionally expressive	Less
Internalized	Direction of feelings	Externalized
	Empirical findings (Brody, 1985, p. 45)	
More	Report selves as sad	Less
More	Report selves as scared	Less
More	Articulate about feelings	Less
More	Emotionally expressive	Less
Internalized	Direction of feelings	Externalized
	Empirical findings (Halpern, 1992, chap. 3)	
Dependent	Field articulation	Independent
Higher	Verbal abilities	Lower
Lower	Quantitative abilities	Higher
Lower	Spatial abilities	Higher

SOURCE: Brody (1985) and Halpern (1992).

primitively, she wants even to seduce, envelop, and devour. Animus, correspondingly, wants to be protected, nourished, and embraced; in his deepest being, also to be seduced, enveloped, and devoured (Table 8.1f). In a later chapter, I shall propose that these primitive impulses add a surprising and quite interesting layer of interpretation to the meanings of money and property. As Professor Wells (personal communication) has been known to observe, for distinguishing among people this dimension is often "better than sex."

Introverted/Extraverted

The literature also provides neurophysiological, psychometric, and psychoanalytic support for Introverted/Extraverted, the other basic dimension of temperament.

TABLE 8.1E Terms From Our National Survey

Femininity	Masculinity
Disagree more	Agree more
Men better at investing than women	
Men smarter than women	
Men better leaders than women	
Police should use force necessary to maintain law and order	
Father should be boss in the house	
Too much fuss about animal rights	

SOURCE: From an unpublished study using data from the Life Styles Survey.

TABLE 8.1F Jung's Anima/Animus

Anima	Animus
More developed Eros (Affiliation)	Less developed Eros
Less developed Logos	More developed Logos
"Poison of Illusion & Seduction"	"Sword of Power"
Protecting	Hopes to be protected
Nourishing	Hopes to be nourished
Seductive	Hopes to be seduced
Enveloping	Hopes to be enveloped
Embracing	Hopes to be sucked in
Devouring	Hopes to be devoured

SOURCE: Jung (1951/1971, pp. 148-150).

Neurophysiological Support. Most of the neurophysiological research on Introverted/Extraverted concentrates on the limbic system, principally the hippocampus and amygdala, two adjacent clusters of neurons nestled deep in the center of the brain, blanketed by the cortex. Gray (1982), for example, proposed that people whose hippocampal systems are "more sensitive to aversive signals [are] thus likely to show an introverted personality and possibly disorders such as anxiety and depression." Kagan (1994) described categories that he called inhibited and uninhibited, and which he noted are highly similar to Introversion/Extraversion. He described the inhibited children in his studies as fearful or timid, slower to relax in new situations, and more reluctant to take risks of various sorts than uninhibited children. In addition, they often showed greater pupillary dilation, diminished recall,

TABLE 8.2A Characteristics of Inhibited/Introverted Children

---

1. Reluctance to initiate spontaneous comments with unfamiliar children or adults

2. Absence of spontaneous smiles with unfamiliar people

3. Relatively long time needed to relax in new situations

4. Impaired recall memory following stress

5. Reluctance to take risks and cautious behavior in situations requiring decisions

6. Interference to threatening words in the Stroop Procedure (a test of emotional reaction to stress)

7. Unusual fears and phobias (e.g., fear of swimming in oceans)

8. Large heart rate acceleration to stress and to a standing posture

9. Large rises in diastolic blood pressure to a standing posture

10. Large pupillary dilations to stress

11. High muscle tension

12. Greater cortical activation in the right frontal area

13. Atropic allergies (e.g., eczema and hay fever)

14. Light-blue eyes (in self and relatives)

15. Ectomorphic body build and narrow face

SOURCE: Kagan (1994, p. 165).

higher blood pressure under stress, increased muscle tension, and greater cortical activation in the right frontal area than uninhibited children. Like Gray, Kagan concluded that inhibited children are more sensitive to stimulation, and more readily upset, than uninhibited children, and that the inhibited children go to great lengths to control that stimulation. The behaviors they use to control stimulation are those that comprise what psychologists in general call "the introverted personality" (Table 8.2a). We will look more closely at the neural mechanisms later in this chapter.

Psychometric Support. Eysenck (e.g., 1944, 1991; see also Eysenck & Eysenck, 1964), Cattell (1957), and Goldberg and Rosolack (1994) identified Introversion factors defined by adjectives like "quiet," "withdrawn," "timid," "restrained," "fretful," and "moody," and Extraversion factors that included "gregarious," "spirited," "expressive," "playful," "energetic," and "flamboyant" (Tables 8.2b-8.2d). Despite the debate these days about what

TABLE 8.2B Eysenck's Introversion and Extraversion Factors

Introversion		Extraversion
High	Persistence	Low
High	Rigidity	Low
High	Subjectivity	Low
High	Shyness	Low
High	Irritability	Low
Low	Sociability	High
Low	Impulsiveness	High
Low	Activity	High
Low	Liveliness	High
Low	Excitability	High

SOURCE: Eysenck (1953/1970, p. 13, 1982, p. 7).

TABLE 8.2C Cattell's Introversion and Extraversion Factors

Introversion	Extraversion
Desurgency	Surgency
Depressed	Cheerful
Retiring	Responsive
Taciturn	Talkative
Submissiveness	Dominance
Unsure	Self-assertive
Modest	Boastful
Meek	Vigorous
Schizothymia	Cyclothemia
Obstructive	Easy-going
Rigid	Adaptable
Cautious	Impulsive
Threctia	Parmia
Withdrawn	Adventurous
Little interest in opposite sex	Great interest in opposite sex
Secretive	Frank

SOURCE: Cattell (1957, pp. 63-64) and Eysenck (1953/1970).

TABLE 8.2D Goldberg's Introversion and Extraversion Factors

Introversion	Extraversion
Quiet	Gregarious
Withdrawn	Spirited
Timid	Expressive
Restrained	Playful
Fretful	Energetic
Moody	Flamboyant

SOURCE: Goldberg and Rosolack (1994, Table 1.1).

TABLE 8.2E Terms From the National Survey Data That Differentiate Introversion and Extraversion

Introverts	Extraverts
Agree more	Disagree more
I am a homebody	
I would feel lost if I were alone in a foreign country	
Disagree more	Agree more
I want to be considered a leader	
I like to take chances	
I have more self-confidence than most	
I like to think I'm the life of the party	

SOURCE: From an unpublished study using data from the Life Styles Survey.

might be the basic dimensions of personality (e.g., Halverson, Kohnstamm, & Martin, 1994), there is consensus[7] that Introversion/Extraversion is one of them.

We found essentially the same results in our national samples (Table 8.2e). Introverts tended to agree more, and Extraverts to disagree more, with statements that describe safety, solitude, and modesty, while the opposite was the case with statements that describe risk-taking, leadership, and gregariousness.

TABLE 8.2F Jung's Conception of Introversion and Extraversion

Introversion	Extraversion
Concentrates libido	Expends self
Decisions based on subjective considerations	Decisions from objective considerations
Suppresses objectivity	Suppresses subjectivity
Gets overwhelmed by objects	Gets sucked into outside demands
Extreme sensitivity	Chronic fatigue
Frequently psychasthenic	Frequently hysteric
Novelty threatening; change upsetting	Exaggerated rapport
Low fertility	High defense
Monopoly of relationships	Multiplicity of relationships
Blake: "Devouring"	Blake: "Prolific"

SOURCE: Jung (1951/1971, pp. 188-196, 229-237).

Psychoanalytic Support. In the psychoanalytic arena,[8] Jung (1951/1971, pp. 188-196, 229-237) proposed that Introversion/Extraversion is one of the principal dimensions on which people vary. As we have already observed, the thrust of his formulation is that Introverts focus their energy inward[9] and make decisions according to subjective considerations, while Extraverts focus their energy outward and make decisions on more objective grounds. The downside of these orientations is that the Introvert suppresses the objective side of life; he or she becomes overwhelmed by external stimulation, is upset by novelty and change, and grows fatigued as a result of so much stimulation. The Extravert, on the other hand, suppresses subjectivity, gets "sucked into" outside demands, experiences an excessive rapport with other people that can grow to imitation and identification, and sometimes, as a result of his or her insensitivity, tends toward ruthless, even brutal, ways of coping with external stimulation. The most common neurosis in Introverts is psychaesthenia (depression); in Extraverts, hysteria (extreme denial). Introverts tend to focus their social energies on a very small number of relationships, Extraverts on large number. Finally, Introverts tend to produce relatively few offspring and to pay a great deal of attention to them; Extraverts produce many offspring and pay relatively little attention to them (Table 8.2f; see Jung, in Campbell, 1971, p. 180, and Rushton, 1995).

The theoretical benefit of these first-level dimensions is that they give our structure an epistemological foundation[10] grounded in basic human structure

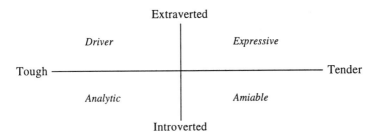

Figure 8.2. Cartesian Coordinates

and process. In particular, they give Tendermindedness, or femininity, a more prominent role than has often been the case in psychological theory. The practical benefit is that they allow us to get at second-level dimensions, which, as we shall see shortly, will connect neatly to the principal dimensions we identified in our survey of the legal, religious, and philosophical antecedents of the quaternary structure, as well as to additional bodies of philosophical and psychometric knowledge, and which therefore permit our framework to claim substantial construct validity (cf. Campbell & Fiske, 1959; Cronbach & Meehl, 1955).

Proposed Second-Level Dimensions

The second-level dimensions are simply the diagonal quadrants of the original fourfold table, or, more precisely, new coordinates that bisect the original coordinates (Figure 8.2). In geometric terms, the structure is rotated 45 degrees. For these dimensions, too, the literature provides confluent neurophysiological, psychometric, and psychoanalytic support. Because this literature often addresses pairs of dimensions simultaneously, so will we.

Neurophysiological Evidence for the Second-Level Dimensions

As early as 1824, Rostan (see Hall & Lindzey, 1957/1970, chap. 9) classified physiques according to the Greek temperaments: Digestive (melancholic), Muscular (choleric), Cerebral (phlegmatic), and Respiratory (sanguine). Viola (1909), Kretschmer (1921/1925), and, especially, Sheldon (1942, 1954) enjoyed a degree of respect for their explorations into temperament and bodily structure, but their work fell into disrepute[11] more, in my opinion, for political than for methodological reasons. However, recent and dramatic

TABLE 8.3A Simplified Neural Foundation for the Expressive/Analytic Dimension (after Gray, 1982, Cloninger, 1987, MacLean, 1990, Derryberry & Tucker, 1992, and Kagan, 1994)

Locus	Stimulus	Chemical Effect	Behavioral Effect	Temperament
Brainstem	High threat	High dopamine	Behavioral inhibition; passive avoidance, narrowing of attention and perception; convergent (narrowed) cognition; analgesic effect	**Analytic**
Brainstem	Low threat	Low dopamine	Behavioral activation; exploration, attention and perception remain expansive; cognition remains divergent; no analgesic effect	**Expressive**

advances in neurophysiology have provided not just a constitutional foundation but an explicitly psychobiological foundation for quadrant theory.

Expressive/Analytic. Derryberry and Tucker (1992, p. 331) describe a process in which the brainstem modulates the brain's response to threatening stimuli by controlling dopamine excretion (Table 8.3a). High threat results in high secretion, which causes a narrowing of perceptual focus onto the threatening object, as well as general analgesia, presumably in preparation for battle; low threat (low excretion) allows more expansive attention and more divergent cognitive associations.[12] The authors point out that manic patients manifest a particularly expansive style, while anxiety patients manifest a narrower style. This study seems to provide a good neural explanation for the divergent and cognitively flexible inclinations of Expressives versus the convergent and inflexible propensities of Analytics. In addition, Gray's (1982) description of what he calls Extraverts as "impulsive" and "distractible" seems to be a better description of Expressives in particular than of Extraverts in general. (See also Kagan, 1994, esp. p. 108.) Finally, Derryberry and Tucker propose that this same dopamine/brainstem mechanism affects cortical plasticity in infancy, which in turn may affect flexibility of learning in later life. Since plasticity and flexibility are important components of intuition, and, as we shall see later, because intuition is a distinguishing characteristic of the Expressive temperament, this mechanism may be particularly important in distinguishing between Expressives and Analytics.

TABLE 8.3B Simplified Neural Foundation for the Driver/Amiable Dimension (after Gray, 1982, Cloninger, 1987, MacLean, 1990, Derryberry & Tucker, 1992, and Kagan, 1994)

Exteroceptive Stimulation				
Locus	*Stimulus*	*Chemical Effect*	*Behavioral Effect*	*Temperament*
Anterior thalamic-cingulate system	Excitation	Increase endorphins and enkephalins	Increase interpersonal attachment	**Amiable**
Anterior thalamic-cingulate system	No excitation	Decrease endorphins and enkephalins	Decrease interpersonal attachment	**Driver**

Interoceptive Stimulation			
Locus	*Internal Cues*	*Self-Assessment*	*Temperament*
Limbic/cortical projections	+Affect +Energy	Self-report: Feel efficient, competent; willful and in charge	**Driver**
Limbic/cortical projections	−Affect −Energy	Self-report: Feel helpless, incompetent; not willful or in charge	**Amiable**

Driver/Amiable. MacLean (1990; in Derryberry & Tucker, 1992, p. 334) has similarly described a mechanism that provides a neural substrate for the aggressiveness/dependency that is characteristic of our Driver/Amiable dimension. In Table 8.3b, stimulating the anterior thalamic-cingulate system in the front-and-center part of the brain, just below and behind the frontal cortex, makes monkeys emit the same "separation cry" they use when removed from their children, and anesthetizing it disrupts maternal behavior. MacLean proposed that endorphins and enkephalins moderate this process, specifically that an increase in endorphins and enkephalins seems to reduce attachment, while a reduction (combined with excitation) seems to increase it. These are the same chemicals that produce the "endorphin high" that accompanies extensive exertion. These observations suggest that aggressors, anesthetized psychologically as well as physiologically by their higher level of endorphins, apparently feel less interpersonal attachment than people low on endorphins, and fewer of the Amiable inclinations in general.

Derryberry and Tucker (1992, p. 336) also provide a description of how circuits bridging the limbic and cortical regions modulate perception of interior states and result in self-evaluations that we associate with the Driver/Amiable temperament. If information from bodily state indicates positive affect and high energy, the person describes himself or herself as efficient and competent, but if the stimulation indicates negative affect and low energy, the self-evaluation is one of helplessness or incompetence. They note that other paralimbic activity will be interpreted as feelings of "will" and "intentionality," that is, the sense of being in charge of self.

The Quaternary. Cloninger (1986; Cloninger, Svrakic, & Przybeck, 1993) has proposed a model of temperament and character based on four stimulus-response operations that he asserts are "independently heritable, manifest early in life, and involve preconceptual biases in perceptual memory and habit formation" (Cloninger et al., 1993, p. 975):

Harm avoidance is "a heritable tendency to respond intensely to signals of aversive stimuli, thereby learning to inhibit behavior to avoid punishment, novelty, and frustrative nonreward." "Harm-avoiders" are pessimistic worriers, shy of strangers, and easily fatigued.

Novelty-seeking is "a heritable tendency toward intense exhilaration or excitement in response to novel stimuli or cues for potential rewards." Novelty-seekers are impulsive decision makers, respond extravagantly to reward cues, lose their tempers quickly, and actively try to avoid frustration.

Reward dependence is "a heritable tendency to respond intensely to signals of reward (particularly verbal signals of social approval, sentiment, and succor)" (Cloninger, 1987, pp. 574-575). Reward-dependent types are sentimental, attach readily to other people, and depend on the approval of other people.

Persistence is a heritable tendency toward "perseverance despite frustration and fatigue" (Cloninger et al., 1993, p. 978). Persistence[13] types are tenacious in the face of obstacles and discomfort.

Cloninger and associates describe their view of the neural and biochemical underpinnings for their model and extend it to second- and third-order factors for describing personality and personality disorders (e.g., Cloninger, 1987). In both observable characteristics and psychological operations, Cloninger's Harm-avoiders seem identical to Jung's Thinking types and Merrill and Reid's Analyticals; his Novelty-seekers, to Jung's Intuition types and Merrill and Reid's Expressives; his Reward-dependent types, to Jung's Feeling types and Merrill and Reid's Amiables; and his Persisters, to Jung's Sensing types, Merrill and Reid's Drivers.

It will not be hard, soon, to make some connections between these physiologically supported propensities toward competence/dependence and

TABLE 8.4A Cross-Tabulations: Extraverted/Toughminded and
Introverted/Tenderminded, to Produce Drivers and Amiables

Extraverted and Toughminded *(Drivers)*	*Introverted and Tenderminded* *(Amiables)*
[From Table 8.2a]:	
Extraverted/Uninhibited qualities	*Introverted/Inhibited qualities*
Adapt quickly to, and behave spontaneously in new situations	Reluctant to talk to strangers; shy; blushing
Gregarious and social, with fuller and more relaxed bodies	Slow to relax and warm to new situations
Optimistic, enthusiastic, and relatively uninfluenced by stress	Ectomorphic bodies, light-blue eyes, tense musculature
[From Table 8.1b]:	
Toughminded qualities	*Tenderminded qualities*
Practical	Theoretical
Materialistic	Idealistic
"Flog criminals"	"Cure criminals"
[From Table 8.1c]:	
Yang qualities	*Yin qualities*
Masculine, Dry, Hot, Hard	Feminine, Moist, Cold, Soft
[From Table 8.1d]:	
Masculine qualities	*Feminine qualities*
More anger and guilt	Less anger and guilt
Less envy and shame	More envy and shame
Externalize feelings	Internalize feelings
Less articulate with feelings	More articulate with feelings
Less sad, scared	More sad, scared
Less aware of cues	More aware of cues

expansiveness/concentration, on the one hand, and financial attitudes, values, and behaviors, on the other. But before we can do so confidently, we need to look more closely at the psychometric and psychoanalytic evidence for these dimensions.

Psychometric Evidence for the Second-Level Dimensions

Psychometric evidence concentrates on the patterns of relationship among variables and clusters of variables.

Psychometric Derivation. Tables 8.4a and 8.4b present the quadrants in the form of cross-tabulations of Toughminded/Tenderminded and Introverted/Extraverted. Toughminded Extraverts are, for example, spontaneous, gregarious,

TABLE 8.4B Cross-Tabulations: Extraverted/Tenderminded and
Introverted/Toughminded, to Produce Expressives and Analytics

Extraverted and Tenderminded (Expressives)	Introverted and Toughminded (Analytics)
[From Table 8.2a]:	
Extraverted/Uninhibited qualities	*Introverted/Inhibited qualities*
Adapt quickly to, and behave spontaneously in, new situations	Reluctant to talk to strangers; shy; blushing
Gregarious and social, with fuller and more relaxed bodies	Slow to relax and warm to new situations
Optimistic, enthusiastic, and relatively uninfluenced by stress	Ectomorphic bodies, light-blue eyes, tense musculature
[From Table 8.1b]:	
Tenderminded qualities	*Toughminded qualities*
Theoretical	Practical
Idealistic	Materialistic
[From Table 8.1c]:	
Yin qualities	*Yang qualities*
Feminine, Moist, Cold, Soft	Masculine, Dry, Hot, Hard
[From Table 8.1d]:	
Feminine qualities	*Masculine qualities*
Less anger and guilt	More anger and guilt
More envy and shame	Less envy and shame
Internalize feelings	Externalize feelings
More articulate with feelings	Less articulate with feelings
More sad, scared	Less sad, scared
More aware of cues	Less aware of cues

and optimistic, and also practical, materialistic, and politically conservative ("Flog criminals"). They agree more with statements like "I hate to lose even in friendly competition," "I am influential in my neighborhood," and "The car I drive is a reflection of who I am" (Table 8.5, top). Tenderminded Introverts, by way of contrast, are shy, slow to relax, slow to warm up in social situations, and also idealistic and politically liberal ("Cure criminals"); they disagree with the questionnaire statements to which the Toughminded Extraverts agreed. This dimension corresponds with Galen's choleric and melancholic temperaments (Kagan, 1994) and Merrill and Reid's (1981) Driver and Amiable categories.

The remaining cross-tabulations—Tenderminded/Extraverted and Toughminded/Introverted—produce what Galen would probably have called

TABLE 8.5 More Terms From Our National Survey

Amiables	*Drivers*
Agree less	Agree more

I hate to lose even in friendly competition.
I am influential in my neighborhood.
There should be a gun in every house.
I like the feeling of speed.
The car I drive is a reflection of who I am.
People recognize that I buy only the best.
We have more to spend on extras than most of our neighbors do.

Analytics	*Expressives*
Agree less	Agree more

I am interested in other cultures.
Couples should live together before getting married.
I am in favor of legalized abortion.

Agree more	Agree less

I have somewhat old-fashioned tastes and habits.
Changes in routine disturb me.
Everything is changing too fast.

SOURCE: From an unpublished study using data from the Life Styles Survey.

sanguine and phlegmatic and which Merrill and Reid (1981) did call Expressive and Analytical. Tenderminded Extraverts, or Expressives, are optimistic, enthusiastic, and relaxed; they behave spontaneously; and they adapt quickly to new social situations (Table 8.6b). They are also more idealistic, and politically liberal. They are interested in other cultures, believe that couples should live together before marriage, disagree that they have old-fashioned tastes and values, and disagree that changes in routine are disturbing. Toughminded Introverts, or Analytics, are tense, shy, and ectomorphic; reluctant to talk to strangers; and slow in warming to new situations. They are also more practical and materialistic, and politically conservative. In addition (Table 8.5, bottom) they are not particularly interested in other cultures, disagree that couples should live together before marriage, subscribe to old-fashioned tastes and values, and agree that changes in routine are disturbing. Thus the first-level dimensions lead directly to the second.

Basic Psychometric Dimensions of Personality. One of the livelier debates among factor analysts these days (if such debates be lively) focuses on the number of basic dimensions of personality. One group of researchers, led by

TABLE 8.6A Competing Factor Structures—As Originally Proposed

Goldberg/Costa-McCrae	Eysenck	Zuckerman	Tellegen
Extraversion	Extraversion	Extraversion	Emotionality
Agreeableness	Neuroticism	Agreeableness	Positive
Conscientiousness	Psychoticism	Aggression	Negative
Emotional stability		Sensation-seeking	
Intellect/Openness		Sensation-avoiding	

Hans Eysenck of the University of London, argues that there are three, and only three, basic dimensions (e.g., Eysenck, 1991); the other group, led by Lewis Goldberg at the University of Oregon, and Paul Costa and Robert McCrae at the National Institute on Aging, contends that there are five (e.g., Costa & McCrae, 1988, 1992; Goldberg, 1990). The literature also contains important papers by Tellegen (1985) and Zuckerman (1994), which appear to propose still other sets of factors—but which, as we shall see in a moment, provide the key to a synthesis.

Halverson, Kohnstamm, and Martin (1994) assert:

> Among personality psychologists, there is a rapidly growing consensus that the domain of individual differences in adulthood, as measured by rating scales and questionnaire items, is almost completely described by five broad factors. (p. 1)

Those bipolar factors and selected defining characteristics are (extracted from Goldberg & Rosolack, 1994, pp. 13-15):

Surgency (Extraversion)
  Gregarious, enthusiastic, expressive, energetic, impetuous
  versus
  Quiet, withdrawn, shy, inhibited, secretive, fretful, lethargic

Agreeableness
  Accommodating, considerate, amiable, obliging, generous, modest
  versus
  Fault-finding, combative, domineering, egocentric, irritable

Conscientiousness
  Exacting, orderly, reliable, perfectionistic, deliberate, thorough
  versus
  Scatterbrained, unpredictable, rash, absentminded, extravagant

TABLE 8.6B Competing Factor Structures—As Redefined

Goldberg/Costa-McCrae	Eysenck	Zuckerman	Tellegen	Galen	Jung	Freud
Level I						
Extraversion	Extraversion	Extraversion	Constraint	—	Extraversion	—
Level II						
(+) Agreeableness	(−) Neuroticism	Agreeableness	Low Positive Emotionality	Melancholic	Feeling	Oral
(−) Conscientiousness	(+) Psychoticism	Sensation-avoiding	Low Negative Emotionality	Phlegmatic	Thinking	Anal
(−) Agreeableness	(+) Neuroticism	Aggression	High Negative Emotionality	Choleric	Sensing	Phallic
(+) Conscientiousness	(−) Psychoticism	Sensation-seeking	High Positive Emotionality	Sanguine	Intuiting	Genital

145

Emotional Stability
    Passionless, unexcitable, unemotional
    versus
    Excitable, anxious, temperamental

Intellect (Openness to Experience)
    Contemplative, deep, artistic, smart, perceptive, unconventional
    versus
    Shallow, unimaginative, uncreative, imperceptive, dull

There is a large and growing body of data in support of the five-factor interpretation.[14]

In competition with the "Big Five" are Eysenck's "Giant Three" factors (e.g., 1953, 1991, 1994; traits excerpted from Goldberg & Rosolack, 1994, p. 17):

Extraversion
    Quiet, untalkative, unsociable, uncommunicative
    versus
    Social, sociable, extraverted, gregarious

Neuroticism
    Optimistic, assured, steady, confident
    versus
    Melancholic, doleful, self-pitying

Psychoticism
    Organized, punctual, prompt, neat, orderly
    versus
    Disorganized, devil-may-care, foolhardy, reckless

Eysenck (1994) argues that his three-factor model resides at a higher level of abstraction than the five-factor model, that, indeed, his Psychoticism factor subsumes the other model's Agreeableness and Conscientiousness and that his Extraversion factor subsumes Emotional Stability and Intellect. He also observes that further methodological argument is not likely to resolve the conflict—what will be necessary are external criteria and a testable network of hypotheses and observations to decide which set of factors best depicts reality. One reasonable external criterion (I propose) would be the Quaternary.

I suggest that both the Big Five and the Giant Three structures contain factors of different levels of abstraction and that making the two solutions more comparable in that respect will produce a factor structure isomorphic to the Quaternary and therefore supported by a great deal of research outside of psychometrics—in short, a structure that, yielding to a sports-metaphor temptation, I call the "Final Four".

Specifically, I see two levels of factors in both the Eysenck and the Goldberg/Costa-McCrae studies:

Level I—Introversion/Extraversion, the very inward/outward attitude that Jung postulated in his original typology. This attitude is manifested in the Extraversion factor in the three-factor model and in the Surgency, Emotional Stability, and Intellect factors in the five-factor model. Like tough/tender, this is a more sweeping, or "abstract," factor than the others, for which reason Jung (1923/1971, p. 178ff.) puts Introversion/Extraversion at a higher level than sensing, feeling, thinking, and intuiting.

Level II—The same four functions that Jung, Adler, and Freud described, manifested in the Psychoticism and Neuroticism factors of the three-factor model and in the Agreeableness and Conscientiousness factors of the five-factor model.

    A. *Driver/Amiable.* The Driver end of this bipolar factor is equivalent to Positive Neuroticism (assured, steady, confident) and Negative Agreeableness (combative, domineering, etc.). The Amiable end subsumes the traits of Negative Neuroticism in the three-factor model (melancholic, doleful, self-pitying) and of Positive Agreeableness in the five-factor model (accommodating, considerate, amiable, etc.).

    B. *Expressive/Analytic.* Similarly, the Analytic end of this continuum subsumes Positive Psychoticism from the three-factor model (organized, punctual, neat) and Positive Conscientiousness from the five-factor model (exacting, orderly, reliable, etc.). The Expressive end subsumes the inverse of phlegmatic-thinking, namely, Negative Psychoticism (disorganized, devil-may-care, etc.) and Negative Conscientiousness (scatterbrained, unpredictable, etc.).

Given this reformulation, I can now show how the Tellegen factors and Zuckerman categories are the same as the four factors (two bipolars) we have just described, and also the same as the four temperaments.

On the basis of extensive work in the psychometrics of personality, Tellegen (1985; see also Appendix B in Goldberg & Rosolack, 1994) proposed three "superfactors," which he calls Positive Emotionality, Negative Emotionality, and Constraint. If we remove, or "partial out," high and low constraint from Tellegen's structure exactly as we removed Introversion (High Constraint) and Extraversion (Low Constraint) from the Big Five and Giant Three, what remains is perfectly congruent with Galen's quaternary and our Final Four:

High Positive Emotionality—Sanguine—Divergent—Expressive

High Negative Emotionality—Choleric—Acquisitive—Driver

Low Positive Emotionality—Melancholic—Affiliative—Amiable

Low Negative Emotionality—Phlegmatic—Convergent—Analytic

Tellegen's (1982) Multidimensional Personality Questionnaire is a rigorous psychometric effort to measure these dimensions.

Zuckerman's (e.g., 1994) work strengthens this interpretation. He proposed a set of factors that he believed connected more reliably to a wider body of theory and data than either the Giant Three or the Big Five. In addition to the usual Introversion/Extraversion factor, which I have argued is of a different "sweep" than the rest, he found:

Aggression versus Agreeableness

Impulsive Sensation-seeking versus Sensation-avoidance

These, too, are precisely the same as the Quaternary. In the philosophical formulation, these two pairs are identical to choleric versus melancholic and sanguine versus phlegmatic; in the psychoanalytic formulation, to sensing versus feeling and intuiting versus thinking; and, in the psychometric interpretation just advanced, to Driver/Amiable and Expressive/Analytic. Thus contemporary psychometric research also supports the Quaternary as a moderator framework.[15]

Psychoanalytic Evidence for the Second-Level Dimensions

Hippocrates and Galen founded their theories on the unity of body and psyche. However, from early in the Christian era to late in the nineteenth century, that is, from after Galen to after Freud, the body was persona non grata in philosophical and psychological theory, and certainly in practice.

Not only was it the mere corruptible container for an immortal soul, but it was the medium through which the most detestable sins might be committed. Not until Freud's unveiling of the libido did the fear of things corporeal begin to diminish, and then not without a fight.

The Founders. Sigmund Freud (1856-1939) was probably the first biopsychosociologist of the modern era, perhaps the first since Galen. Among many original contributions, he postulated that libido, the erotic, pleasure-seeking drive that governs most human behavior, changes dramatically as the child progresses through a series of four psychosexual life stages[16] (Freud, 1920; Hall & Lindzey, 1957/1970, pp. 49-53; see also White, 1960, on "competence"). At the risk of seeming obsessed with the Quaternary, I suggest that these stages, too, correspond to the four temperaments:

Stage	Temperament	Description
Oral	Melancholic	Pleasure from oral incorporation or similar behaviors, like acquiring knowledge and owning things; oral aggressiveness sometimes takes the form of sarcasm or argumentativeness. Intimately tied to feelings of neediness and dependency.
Anal	Phlegmatic	Pleasure from anal retention or associated inclinations—stubborn, tidy, stingy; anal aggressiveness sometimes takes the form of cruelty and domination. Intimately tied to the inclination to avoid and withdraw.
Phallic	Choleric	Oedipal and related pleasures; fear of genital loss or absence. Deep repression of aggressive sexuality in boys results in harmless affection; milder repression in girls leads to ambivalence: affection and aggression.
Genital	Sanguine	Pleasure from social sexuality. Adult personality is decreasingly narcissistic, increasingly altruistic. All previous inclinations merge to define the adult personality.

Alfred Adler (1870-1937) moved from Vienna to Long Island in 1932. Given his interest in the American culture of the time, it is not surprising that, in place of Freud's libido, he proposed to substitute a "sense of inferiority"[17] as the primary motive. Man, he said, is "driven by an insatiable lust for power and domination in order to compensate for a concealed deep-seated feeling of inferiority" resulting from a lower place in the birth order, awareness of penile inferiority, experience of parental neglect, and other sources (Adler, 1956; Ansbacher, 1971; Hall & Lindzey, 1957/1970, p. 125).

Adler's later work centered in "life style," a construct he developed to include the individual's personality structure, life goal, and efforts to achieve that goal. He saw four themes permeating people's diverse life styles:

Getting—These people reduce feelings of inferiority by trying to buy love and affection

Useful—These reduce feelings of inferiority through efforts, often artificial, to make themselves useful, even subservient, to other people

Ruling—People of this style reduce feelings of inferiority through efforts to feel superior to other people

Avoiding—People of this life style reduce feelings of inferiority through the use of procrastination or other avoidance techniques

These themes correspond to the Amiable, Analytic, Driver, and Expressive propensities, respectively. Later we shall see how Poduska (1985, 1993) puts a financial interpretation on Adler's themes.

Like Freud and Adler, Carl Jung (1875-1961) insisted on a biological base for human personality. He found such a base for his central attitudes, Introversion and Extraversion:

There are in nature two fundamentally different modes of adaptation [r-strategy and K-strategy; see note 4 from Chapter 2] which ensure the continued existence of the living organism. The one consists in a high rate of fertility, with low powers of defence and short duration of life for the single individual; the other consists in equipping the individual with numerous means of self-preservation plus a low fertility rate. *This biological difference, it seems to me, is not merely analogous to, but the actual foundation of, our two psychological modes of adaptation.* (Jung, 1923/1971, p. 180, emphasis added)

Within each of these two attitudes, he described the four fundamental functions that we discussed in Chapter 4—sensing, feeling, thinking, and intuiting. Briefly put:

Feeling is the function that enables us to make judgments about beauty, ugliness, propriety, impropriety, good, evil, and so on more clearly than with other functions.

TABLE 8.7 The Core "Motifs of Four"

Elements	Water	Air	Earth	Fire
Temperaments	Melancholic	Phlegmatic	Choleric	Sanguine
Merrill-Reid styles	Amiable	Analytical	Driver	Expressive

TABLE 8.7A Quaternaries Employed by the Founders of Psychoanalysis

Freud's stages	Oral	Anal	Phallic	Genital
Adler's themes	Getting/ Pleasing	Useful/ Control	Ruling/ Superiority	Avoiding/ Comfort
Jung's operations	Feeling, Introverted	Thinking, Introverted	Sensing, Introverted	Intuiting, Introverted
	Feeling, Extraverted	Thinking, Extraverted	Sensing, Extraverted	Intuiting, Extraverted

TABLE 8.7B Quaternaries Employed by Later Psychoanalysts and Psychoanalytically Influenced Psychologists and Psychiatrists

Horney's neurotic needs	Compliant people need partners on whom they can depend	Detached people need partners from whom they can be distant	Aggressive people need partners whom they can exploit	Assertive people need partners who will admire them
Maslow's needs	Belonging	Security	Esteem via strength	Esteem via reputation
Peck's risks	Independence	Loss	Confrontation	Commitment
DSM-IV's diagnoses	Dysthymic, dependent, passive-aggressive	Schizoid/avoidant, obsessive-compulsive	Antisocial, paranoid	Manic, histrionic, narcissistic

TABLE 8.7C Efforts to Measure the Quaternaries

Murray's (TAT) categories	Oral Succorance: Thumb-sucking; passive-dependent; compulsive eating and drinking	Anal Retention: prudishness, need for cleanliness, retention of possessions	Oral Aggression: Gnawing, general aggressiveness	Anal Rejection: Need for disorder, autonomy, anal sexuality
Murray's (TAT) needs	Affiliation Succorance	Order Infavoidance	Acquisitiveness Dominance	Exhibition Autonomy
Atkinson/ McClelland's needs	Affiliation	Security	Achievement	Power
Myers-Briggs's types	Introverted-FP Extraverted-FJ Introverted-FJ Extraverted-FP	Introverted-TP Extraverted-TJ Introverted-TJ Extraverted-TP	Introverted-SJ Extraverted-SP Introverted-SJ Extraverted-SP	Introverted-NJ Extraverted-NP Introverted-NP Extraverted-NJ

Thinking is the function that enables people to make judgments about ideas, whether they come from outside the person (e.g., from teachers) or from inside (e.g., from hunches). Thinking, because it is a rational operation, is the polar opposite of feeling, which is an emotional operation.

Sensing is the function through which people perceive the world with greater intensity, greater realism, than through the other functions. It is the function of the pragmatist, the realist. Sensing, because its focus is practical reality, the here and now, is the polar opposite of intuiting.

Intuiting is the function through which people perceive more relations among things than through the other functions, "the widest range of possibilities." It is the function of the dreamer, the visionary. Because intuiting is a matter of vision, of flexibility of perception, it is the opposite of sensing.

Jung's typology has been enormously influential. Merrill and Reid (1981), Harrison and Bramson (1982), Martin and Martin (1982), Keirsey and Bates (1984), Cathcart and Alessandra (1985), Felton-Collins (1990), Alessandra and O'Connor (1990), and Williams (1996), among others, have proposed variations of his types for use in counseling, education, and business. Doyle (1992d) attached a characteristic fear to each of his operations—fear of isolation (feeling), fear of disarray (thinking), fear of incompetence (sensing), and fear of constraint (intuition)—along with particular financial motives and behaviors associated with those fears. And Myers, Briggs, and McCaulley used his work as the foundation for the Myers-Briggs Type Indicator (MBTI). Table 8.7a summarizes the founders' contributions. Beebe (1983) presents a collection of Jungian papers on money and associated "depth dimensions of physical existence."

Some Successors. Several very prominent of the more recent analysts and analytically oriented therapists described quaternaries of their own:[18] Karen Horney (1937) distinguished types of people in terms of four predominant "neurotic needs"; Abraham Maslow (1954) by levels on a "hierarchy of need"; and M. Scott Peck (1978) by a different "risk of love" for each type. In addition, the compilers of the *Diagnostic and Statistical Manual of Mental Disorders* (*DSM-IV;* American Psychiatric Association, 1994) classified personality disorders into an analogous quaternary—antisocial personality disorder, dependent personality disorder, narcissistic personality disorder, and obsessive-compulsive personality disorder—which appear to represent the extreme points of our second-level dimensions—Extreme Driver, Amiable, Expressive, and Analytic temperaments, respectively. See Table 8.7b.

Measurement. Finally, two efforts to measure psychoanalytic traits and states deserve mention (Table 8.7c). Henry Murray (1956) devised the Thematic Apperception Test (TAT)[19] to measure some of the psychological needs[20] identified in his extensive research. A projective series of standardized drawings qualitatively scored, the TAT is second in usage only to the Rorschach Ink Blots (Hall & Lindzey, 1957/1970, p. 197; see Murray, 1936, 1938; see also Sanford, 1936, 1937, cited in Atkinson, 1964, p. 222). Murray's theory and the TAT contributed directly to Atkinson and McClelland's studies of "need achievement" and "need affiliation," of which we shall make some use immediately below and much use in Chapter 10. And, as previously noted, Myers and Briggs (McCaulley, 1981; Myers, 1980; Myers & McCaulley, 1988) used Jung's theory of psychological types as the foundation for the MBTI,[21] a personality inventory widely used in counseling, education, and personnel management. The MBTI expresses its sixteen types through sets of four letters, for example, ENFP and ISTJ. ENFP means Extraverted/iNtuitive/Feeling/Perceiving, while ISTJ means Introverted/ Sensing/Thinking/Judging. The MBTI does not attempt to measure the unconscious events of which Jung spoke. Sadly, both the TAT and the MBTI have been of limited interest among researchers.

The convergence of these three areas of research—neurophysiology, psychometrics, and psychoanalysis—adds a considerable degree of validity to the Quaternary, and considerable definition to each of the quadrants that comprise it (Campbell & Fiske, 1959; Cronbach & Meehl, 1954). Our excursus into personality research has, perhaps at the cost of a few of those "dry and dusty academic moments" (p. 40), provided reasonable assurance that the Quaternary is a strong enough foundation for a view of temperament in general. Since financial behavior, like sexual and religious behavior, is a microcosm of behavior in general, we now turn to an analogous view of financial temperament.[22]

FINANCIAL TEMPERAMENT

Having established the Quaternary as a valid portrayal of the dimensions of personality in general, we can now extend it into the financial domain. First, we will consider four psychoanalytically oriented *financial* versions of the Quaternary—Fenichel (1935/1938), Fromm (1976), Adler/Poduska (Poduska, 1985), and Jung/Doyle (Doyle, 1992d)—and some psychoanalytic interpretations of selected quadrants, for additional validation. Finally, we shall explore a new series of financial quaternaries that I believe explain and expand on the existing ones.

Existing Financial Versions of the Quaternary

Fenichel (1935/1938), like Adam Smith (1753/1976) before and Heilbroner (1985) after, connects "the drive to amass wealth" with "the will to power" and "the will to possession." He describes the will to power as narcissistic, rooted in the gain and loss of regard,[23] the adult trying to regain the feeling of omnipotence he or she occasionally experienced as a child. To regain that feeling, the ego needs a "narcissistic supply" from the environment, much like an infant needs food. Money is such a supply:

> The original instinctual aim is not for riches, but to enjoy power and respect whether it be among one's fellow men or within oneself. It is a society in which power and respect are based upon the possession of money, that makes all of this need for power and respect a need for riches. (Fenichel, 1935/1938, p. 79)

In Fenichel's view, the will to possession, sharply distinct from the will to power, is the will to extend one's ego and protect it from threats that would diminish its boundaries. The desire for many possessions is therefore a symbolic effort to protect against this "ego shrinkage." As a therapist, Fenichel concentrates on various pattern of pathology:

> One thinks of cleptomaniacs [sic], or of the women who drain men of their resources, to whom money, which they are always striving to take away, symbolizes a whole series of introjected objects that have been withheld from them; or of depressive characters who from fear of starvation regard money as potential food.
> There are too those men to whom money signifies their potency, who experience any loss of money as a castration, or who are inclined, when in danger, to sacrifice money in a sort of "prophylactic self-castration."

There are, in addition, people who—according to their attitude of the moment toward taking, giving, or withholding—accumulate or spend money, or alternate between accumulation and spending quite impulsively, without regard for the real significance of money, and often to their own detriment (sometimes unconsciously desired). (Fenichel, 1935/1938, p. 84)

Thus Fenichel arrives at the same quaternary of which we have so often spoken. The "women who drain men" and who fear starvation are the Amiables; the men to whom "money signifies their potency" are the Drivers; the people who "alternate between accumulation and spending quite impulsively" are the Expressives; all in addition to the tidy, stubborn, and stingy characters of whom he originally spoke, that is, the Analytics.

Erich Fromm (1900-1980) reflected Freud in many respects but differed from him in some important ways. While Freud believed that character traits are unconscious sublimations of, or reactions against, the various forms of the sexual drive, Fromm, more like Sullivan (1953), saw them as the result of people's assimilation of and socialization into the world (Fromm, 1947, p. 57).

Fromm devoted much of his energy to the psychoanalytic examination of the roles money and property play in people's lives. In his famous study of character, he developed descriptions of four "non-productive orientations" that focus on the characteristic pathology of each type in the quaternary:

Receptive Orientation (Amiables). People of the receptive orientation feel that anything good that may happen to them must come from somebody else's strength. Thus

they are always in search of a "magic helper" [and are] indiscriminate in the choice of their love objects. . . . Since they cannot say "no," they love to say "yes" to everything and everybody, and the resulting paralysis of their critical abilities makes them increasingly dependent on others. . . . They tend to overcome anxiety and depression by eating or drinking. (Fromm, 1947, p. 63)

Hoarding Orientation (Analytics). People of the hoarding orientation find their security in saving and find spending a threat. Their hoarding encompasses not only money and property but thoughts, feelings, relationships, and even memories.

Orderliness signifies mastering the world outside by putting it, and keeping it, in its proper place in order to avoid the danger of intrusion. . . . These people tend to feel that they possess only a fixed quantity of strength, energy, or mental capacity, and that this stock is diminished or exhausted by us and can never be replenished. . . . Their highest values are order and security. . . . Mine is mine and yours is yours. (p. 67)

Exploitative Orientation (Drivers). People of the exploitative orientation enjoy taking things away from other people by force or cunning.

Things they can take away from others always seem better to them than anything they can produce themselves. They use and exploit anybody and anything from whom or from which they can squeeze something. . . . They feel attracted only to people whom they can take away from somebody else. . . . Since they are satisfied only with things they can take away from others, they tend to overrate what others have and underrate what is theirs. (p. 65)

Marketing Orientation (Expressives). People of the marketing orientation find identity not in reference to themselves and their powers but in the opinion others hold about them.

His prestige, status, success, the fact that he is known to others as being a certain person are a substitute for the genuine feeling of identity. . . . Thinking assumes the function of grasping things quickly so as to be able to manipulate them successfully. . . . The premise of the marketing orientation is emptiness. (pp. 73, 77-78)

Fromm's formulation reflects Nietzsche's master/slave division. For elaboration on this line of thought, see Fromm's debate with Ayn Rand on socialism versus capitalism (Branden, 1965/1966; Fromm, 1955; Rand, 1966). (For further provocative reading on the processes and effects of the marketing orientation, see McCracken, 1990, Ehrlich & Ehrlich, 1974, Rustow, 1980, and Galbraith, 1992.)

Adler's interest, as we have already discussed, was the drive to reduce feelings of inferiority. Poduska (1985, 1993; Kefir & Corsini, 1974; Kefir, in Poduska, 1985) postulated financial implications for Adler's four inferiority-reduction themes:

Getting—People of the getting theme try to reduce feelings of inferiority by trying to buy love and affection, with the result that they lend money freely, give generous gifts, and have a hard time refusing any request.

Useful—These people try to reduce their feelings of inferiority through efforts, often artificial, to make themselves useful to other people, even to the point of subservience. In their financial lives, they feign lack of resources, resist proposals passively, and avoid impulsive behaviors, all for the purpose of escaping demands and commitments and possible embarrassment.

Ruling—People characterized by the ruling theme try to reduce feelings of inferiority through a variety of efforts to feel superior to other people. In their financial life, this results in their trying to live beyond their means and efforts at one-upmanship.

Avoiding—People characterized by the avoiding theme try to reduce feelings of inferiority through the use of procrastination or other avoidance techniques, with the result that, in their financial lives, they leave much business unfinished and many problems unresolved.

Thus, to people of the ruling orientation, the presence of money means they are better than other people, the absence that they are worse; to people of the getting orientation, money means the capacity to buy the affection and love they may not otherwise deserve; to people of the avoiding orientation, it means the ability to shed responsibility; and to people of the useful orientation, it means a shield against embarrassment.

Elsewhere, in similar fashion, I attached financial implications to Jung's basic psychological functions, operationalized as Merrill and Reid's four social styles (adapted from Doyle, 1992d, p. 716). The result is an arrangement very similar to that which Poduska produced for Adler's themes:

Feeling (Amiables)—These people are sensitive, agreeable, and supportive but impulsive, undisciplined, and egotistical. In their financial lives they will tend to view money as unclean and harmful to relationships, and therefore avoid it. They will yield to authority but may be passive-aggressive.

Thinking (Analyticals)—These people are thorough, persistent, and exacting but indecisive, rigid, and picky. In their financial lives they will tend to overanalyze and delay decisions and implementation; they will prefer safety above all else.

Sensing (Drivers)—These people are realistic, independent, and decisive but severe, dominating, and pushy. In their financial lives they will be decisive and demanding; they will also tend to overextend themselves.

Intuiting (Expressives)—These people are intuitive, ambitious, and enthusiastic but impulsive, undisciplined, and egotistical. In their financial lives, they will tend to be optimistic and impetuous; they will enjoy the selling and "being sold."

There I also introduced the notion of *talisman.*

Further Financial Implications of Particular Quadrants

While Freud, Fenichel, Ferenczi, Adler (via Poduska), and Jung (via Doyle) described full-blown financial quaternaries, other analytic thinkers expanded the meaning—the validity—of various of the quadrants, especially the Analytic.

Analytic (Anal). Freud observed that many of his patients displayed the same set of behaviors: tidiness, stubbornness, and stinginess, the "neurotic triad." He also noted that, as children, these people had often tried to augment the pleasure of defecation by delay, gaining considerable control over their parents in the process, and that their parents often issued emphatic warnings that fecal products are filthy and dangerous. Freud concluded there was a connection between the kind of child who, on the one hand, takes physical pleasure in anal retention and psychological pleasure through controlling the people around him, and, on the other, the tidy/stubborn/stingy syndrome he saw in his practice.

In his study of cultures around the world, Freud also knew the story of the *Dukatenscheisser,* "The man who shat money." He knew of phrases in various languages equivalent to "stinking rich" and "filthy lucre." He knew "how the money which the devil gives to his paramour turns to excrement on his departure" (Freud, 1905/1976, pp. 76-77) and how Judas threw away the 30 pieces of silver, hanged himself, "and his bowels gushed out" (Matthew 27:3-10). Finally, as a Sinophile, he was probably familiar with the Chinese aphorism "The book is fragrant; money stinks." Thus he could generalize his connection of stinginess, feces, and the anal personality from his own patients to people in general.

Putting this all together, Freud theorized:

Wherever the archaic way of thinking has prevailed or still prevails, in the old civilisations, in myths, fairy-tales, superstition, in unconscious thinking, in dreams, and in neuroses, money has been brought into the closest connection with filth. (quoted in Ferenczi, 1914/1976, p. 82)

Wiseman (1974) observes that the analytic personality "finds money embarrassing and shameful, won't talk about it, and contrives to reduce it to the ultimate abstraction—numbers" (pp. 102-103). These are the misers, the collectors, the "bean-counters,"[24] who are more at home with order and efficiency, charts and figures, than with people; who exhibit "doggedness, perseverance, solidity, and conservativism" (p. 105), as well as parsimony.

Sandor Ferenczi (1914/1976) was in some ways more Freudian than Freud. He explained

> that children originally devote their interest without any inhibition to the process of defaecation, and that it affords them pleasure to hold back their stools. The excrementa thus held back are really the first "savings" of the growing being, and as such remain in a constant, unconscious interrelationship with every bodily activity or mental striving that has anything to do with collecting, hoarding, and saving. (p. 82)

Anal people see money as fundamentally dirty, yet, paradoxically, they try to hold on to it, because despite the corruption, retaining it gives them a feeling of pleasure and control.

Ernest Jones points out another characteristic frequently found in the anal personality—the sense of "self-righteousness" that comes from an overordered mind intent on imposing its particular will on the rest of the world (1948, pp. 413-414, cited in Wiseman, 1974, p. 125). This righteousness[25] is evident in certain social and religious movements throughout history, up to and including contemporary America.

Norman Brown (1959) expands on the foregoing interpretations. He accepts interest in money as a primary characteristic of the anal personality, but more than the earlier writers, he places interest in money on a foundation first of guilt, then, ultimately, of the death instinct.

To identify the underlying guilt, Brown turns to Nietzsche's *Genealogy of Morals* (1887/1974) as well as Freud's *Civilization and Its Discontents* (1930/1961). He notes that it was Nietzsche who connected "owe" (money) with "ought" (guilt) and postulated that "with the accumulation of culture (civilization) the sense of indebtedness to ancestors (guilt) increases, climaxing in Christianity as a theology of unpayable debt" (Brown, 1959, p. 267). He adds that Nietzsche also pointed out that the goddess of guilt and revenge, Tisiphone, is an anal character, "a person versed in the highest branches of arithmetic, and punctual in her habits."

Brown (pp. 268-269) sees guilt lurking behind both archaic man's giving and modern man's taking. Archaic *giving* is not to be romanticized, he insists; it is not genuine altruism but rather an attempt to assuage the guilt that rises from resenting one's ancestors for their role in inhibiting our full human potential for enjoyment (repression).

> The repression of full enjoyment in the present inevitably releases aggression against those ancestors out of love of whom the repression was instituted. Aggression against those simultaneously loved is guilt. And the more fully the debt to the past is paid, the more complete are its inroads on the enjoyment of life in the present; but then fresh quantities of aggression are released, bringing fresh quantities of guilt. (p. 268)

To extirpate this guilt, Brown proposes, archaic man gave the first gift. To extirpate the guilt of receiving that gift, another man gave back. From this reciprocity, this sharing of guilt, eventually grew the totemic brotherhood, the communion meal, and all the symbols thereof, including the communion wafer—money. (See Laum, 1924, 1929, and Desmonde, 1976, for a view of the origins of coins in communion liturgies.)

Brown suggests that both giving and taking thus impede the full enjoyment of which human beings are capable. Since whatever inhibits the potential for full enjoyment, inhibits Eros, the impediment must dwell in the realm opposite to Eros, that is, in the domain of Thanatos, the death instinct. In a nutshell, both giving and taking, the primary money processes, produce guilt and inhibit eroticism. Hence money rests on a psychology of guilt, which in turn rests on a psychology of death, and therefore efforts to find enjoyment through money are destined to failure. This emphasis on death is not inconsistent with the neurophysiology of the fear mechanism.

Brown's analysis sheds light especially on the oral/Amiable type. Despite the anal title of his essay ("Filthy Lucre"), his discussion concentrates less on money as a foul but pleasurable product of human existence, more on it as a source of guilt and remorse initiated in early acts of receiving and possessing, and still manifest in Amiable people's distress in the presence of money. As the anal character is motivated by the drive to avoid bodily corruption, the oral character is motivated by the drive to avoid corruption of the soul. In the terminology of the Quaternary, the former is the Tough-minded motive, the latter the Tenderminded.

Amiable (Oral). Other psychoanalytic authors were equally emphatic about the oral nature of money. Melanie Klein (1957) provides an oral foundation on which Wiseman (1974, pp. 47-48) builds. She proposes that fear of death is the fundamental motive and that hunger is the child's first threat of death. Being fed on demand is good; being fed too slowly, too late, or too little is evil. Thus children learn that the "good breast" is the source of everything good, the bad breast the source of all deprivation. In "the fantasy of the inexhaustible breast," Wiseman (p. 49) sees the connection of Klein's theory with money. It is hard not also to see the formation of the oral personality:

> In these early vain yearnings . . . , I suggest we can see the beginnings of the desire for limitless riches. . . . If what has been sought under the guise of making a fortune is really an "inexhaustible breast" such as the baby's earliest wishful imaginings had conceived of, then it is obvious that all the money in the world cannot provide it. . . . Only in the psyche can we find something that comes closer [to the inexhaustible source]: a bountiful and loving internal object created out of the imago of the mother. (Wiseman, 1974, p. 49)

For the oral personality, then, money and property signify the disappointment that the infant experiences when it discovers that its yearnings for food and affection are in vain. Money for the oral (Amiable) character is that fundamental evil that stands between us and what is really important in life, indeed, between us and life itself.

Analytic/Expressive (Anal/Genital). Karl Abraham (1917/1976, p. 101) connects anxious spending to the desire to free self from the anal fixation. In the case of a woman who was extremely dependent and anxious (and in similar cases), he noticed

> the tendency to buy many objects at random, articles that were for the most part valueless and only desired at the moment. . . . Buying objects which have only a momentary value, and passing quickly from one object to another, are symbolic gratifications of a repressed desire—that of transferring the libido in rapid succession to an unlimited number of objects. The allusion to prostitution is unmistakable in this connection; for there, too, money is the means of obtaining transitory and easily changed relationships.

Amiable/Driver (Oral/Phallic). Social psychologists McClelland (1961) and Atkinson (1964) concentrated on the role of two of Murray's motives in individual and national economic growth and decline. These seem to represent the Driver and Amiable quadrants, respectively:

Need achievement—"Concern over performing well in relation to a standard of excellence (i.e., pride in skillful performance)" (Atkinson, 1964, p. 225).

Need affiliation—"Concern over establishing, maintaining, and restoring positive relations with others" (i.e., "friendship") (Atkinson 1964, p. 227; see also McClelland, 1961, p. 160).

People with high need achievement scores on Murray's TAT—Drivers—are not necessarily smarter or swifter or in any other way "better" than other people. They are different only in that, when presented with a challenge, they throw themselves at it wholeheartedly. More often than people with lower need achievement, they come from the middle class, volunteer for challenging activities, participate more in community activities, resist social pressure, and choose experts rather than friends as working partners (McClelland, 1961, pp. 43-44). They are the people whose temperament leads to economic advancement, the people who are temperamentally inclined to become the movers and shakers of the world.

McClelland observes that people with high need affiliation scores— Amiables—are approval-seekers who report feelings of liking and the desire to be liked or forgiven more often than people with low scores, and to "select faces rather than neutral stimuli in a perceptual task." They are also considered likely to succeed by peers, and they choose friends rather than experts as working partners. The central theme is a "concern in fantasy and in action for warm, close relationships with other people" (McClelland, 1961, pp. 160-161). People high in need affiliation tend to be low in need achievement ($r = -.46$, $p < .01$; reported in McClelland, 1961, p. 166).

Thus a number of psychoanalysts and psychoanalytically oriented researchers have provided theories, and even measuring instruments, that add depth to the Quaternary ("content validity"; American Psychological Association, 1966).

NEW FINANCIAL QUATERNARIES

In this section, I present a series of fourfold figures that describe what I take to be the fundamental traits of financial temperament on the individual, family, and cultural levels. These quaternaries, together with all of the

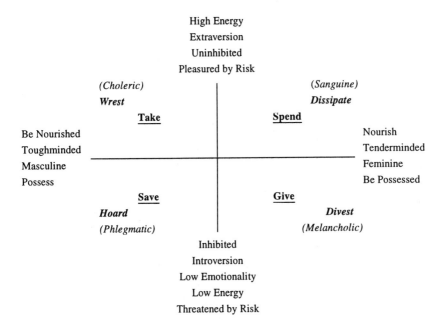

High Energy
Extraversion
Uninhibited
Pleasured by Risk

(Choleric)   *(Sanguine)*
Wrest   **Dissipate**

Take   **Spend**

Be Nourished   Nourish
Toughminded   Tenderminded
Masculine   Feminine
Possess   Be Possessed

Save   **Give**
Hoard   **Divest**
(Phlegmatic)   *(Melancholic)*

Inhibited
Introversion
Low Emotionality
Low Energy
Threatened by Risk

Figure 8.3. The Financial Quaternary—Individual Level
SOURCE: Copyright © 1997 Kenneth O. Doyle. Used by permission.

inferred meaning we have accumulated so far about the four propensities, comprise the conceptual framework toward which we have been working— the moderator that will compel us to take note of the fact that money and property mean different things to different kinds of people.

Individual Level

Way back in Chapter 4, I proposed that the basic human motive is fear and that we all use money and property as talismans to protect ourselves symbolically from the particular fear that is characteristic of our temperament.

In Figure 8.3, I propose that the fundamental fear-reducing financial activities are give/take (need/have) and save/spend, such that Amiables deal with their fear of abandonment mainly by giving, Drivers manage their fear of incompetence by taking, Analytics control their fear of disorder by saving, and Expressives cope with their fear of constraint by spending. Amiable giving is, approximately as Brown suggested above, not true altruism but rather giving to receive, a manifestation of neediness. As always in the

Quaternary, the diagonals are in contradictory tension, the adjacent cells in contrary.

Figure 8.3 also depicts three grades of behavior: (1) At the very center, where the crosshairs meet, the entirely balanced ideal personality described by Galen, Jung, and many others; (2) one step out from the center, normal propensities toward giving and taking, and saving and spending; and (3) one step further out, excessive or dysfunctional propensities toward divesting and wresting, and hoarding and dissipating. The reasons for this intensification range from neural strengthening (Edelman, 1987; see also p. 173 in Chapter 9) to efforts to cope with progressively stronger fear (p. 187) to the more familiar social and cultural influences.

The behaviors in the Tenderminded quadrants (spending and giving) Jung (1923/1971, pp. 148-151) associates with the "Anima," that is, inclined to nourish, to be possessed, and so forth, even to devour. Those in the Toughminded quadrants (taking and saving) he describes as just the opposite, associated with the "Animus," that is, inclined to possess and to be nourished, as well as to be devoured. Similarly, the behaviors in the Uninhibited quadrants (taking and spending) are characterized by more energy, emotionality, and attraction to risk than their opposing behaviors (saving and giving).

Beneath the surface quaternary is what Jung might call the "shadow" quaternary, a recognition of the realm of the unconscious. The *Shadow Quaternary* is a mirror image of the *Surface Quaternary:* the more intense the surface behavior, the more intense the hidden opposite propensity. The Shadow Quaternary specifies, for example, that the hardest-driving Drivers are covering up an extremely intense fear of their softer, Amiable qualities, and the most amiable Amiables are repressing their frightening (to them) inclinations toward the ruthlessness of the extreme Driver. Nearer to the crosshairs, in the area of normal propensity, repression (if any) is considerably less. Thus a person can be motivated mostly by surface propensities: I can give or take, save or spend, merely because it feels true or good or beautiful to do so.

This is the basic *Financial Quaternary,* from the structure and dynamics of which the remaining quaternaries derive.

Family Level

Families can be characterized in the same way as individuals (Figure 8.4): Amiable families are emotionally needy, exhibit a propensity toward dependence; Drivers families are acquisitive, with a propensity toward inde-

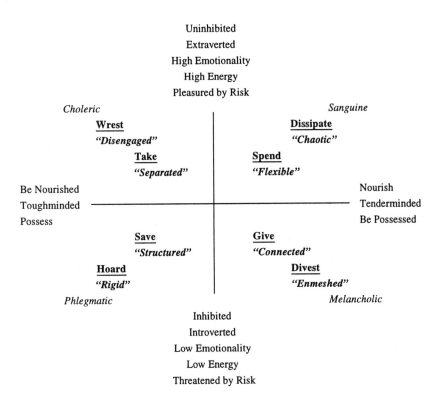

Uninhibited
Extraverted
High Emotionality
High Energy
Pleasured by Risk

Choleric   *Sanguine*

Wrest   **Dissipate**
"Disengaged"   *"Chaotic"*

     Take   **Spend**
     "Separated"   *"Flexible"*

Be Nourished   Nourish
Toughminded   Tenderminded
Possess   Be Possessed

     Save   **Give**
     "Structured"   *"Connected"*

Hoard   **Divest**
"Rigid"   *"Enmeshed"*

Phlegmatic   *Melancholic*

Inhibited
Introverted
Low Emotionality
Low Energy
Threatened by Risk

Figure 8.4. The Financial Quaternary—Family Level
SOURCE: Copyright © 1997 Kenneth O. Doyle. Used by permission.
NOTE: Quoted terms are from Olson (1986).

pendence; Analytic families are retentive, inclined toward frugality and regulation; and Expressive families are emotive, inclined toward emotion, even dishevelment. Thus the underlying fears in families are the same as in the individual—abandonment, incompetence, disarray, and constraint. Also, as with individuals, the more intense the fear, the more intense the behaviors the families use to cope with those fears: divesting, wresting, hoarding, and dissipating. The financial propensity of the family is a function of its general temperament, which may be more than the temperament of the individual members, and is a microcosm of its general attitudes, values, and behavior. Finally, there is a *Shadow Family Quaternary* that manifests itself most vividly in extreme, dysfunctional cases, for example, the Analytic family releasing pressure through a brief spending spree.

Olson (1986) provides much indirect support for the principal parts of this proposal, through his analogous circumplex model of family functioning. On one dimension, his "separate" and "disengaged" families—see the quoted terms in Figure 8.4—are moderate and extreme Drivers, respectively; his "connected" and "enmeshed" families, moderate and extreme Amiables. On the other dimension, his "structured" and "rigid" families are Analytics; his "flexible" and "chaotic" ones, Expressives. Overall, the circumplex model is a perfect reflection of the Surface Quaternary on the family level. In fact, Olson's assessment instruments address financial compatibility, though in only a very general way. For evaluation of Olson's model and measurements, see Green, Harris, Forte, and Robinson (1991); for reply and revisions, see Olson (1991).

Families are, of course, more complex than individuals. The involvement of additional people, whether spouse or children or extended members, raises interesting problems, not the least of which have to do with communicating values and building intimacy. With regard to communicating values, I suggest that family members, adults as well as children, "internalize" those financial values that reflect their personal propensities, while they will fail to internalize those that are contrary or, especially, contradictory to those propensities. Small discrepancies may produce a degree of tension (dissonance), which should produce growth; larger discrepancies will produce conflict, and the weaker members will eventually either separate themselves from, or be separated from, the stronger. On the other hand, money and property create the opportunity for better family relationships, in that they are a vehicle through which people can learn about each other, come to understand and respect one another, and grow in intimacy. Different types of people will have different definitions of, and capacities for, intimacy, however. Mild intimacy, of the "exchange of hostages" sort, is probably within the reach of any combination of types; intense intimacy, or empathy, in which one person truly "feels with" another, may be limited to people of the same type. In general, family members will use money and property to relate with one another according to the principles specified in the basic Financial Quaternary.

Cultural Level

Figure 8.5 describes the Financial Quaternary at the cultural level. The structure and dynamics of the *Cultural Financial Quaternary* are the same as on the individual and family levels; the propensities, the dialectics, the

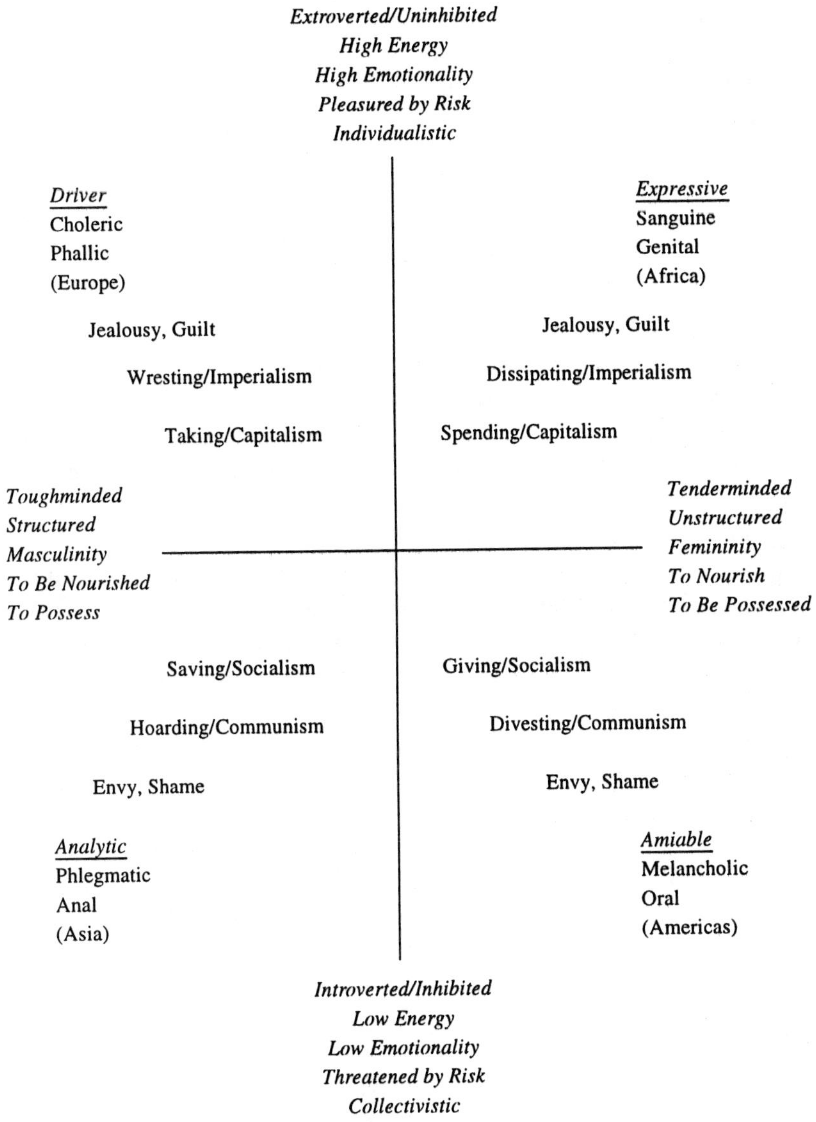

Extroverted/Uninhibited
High Energy
High Emotionality
Pleasured by Risk
Individualistic

Driver
Choleric
Phallic
(Europe)

Expressive
Sanguine
Genital
(Africa)

Jealousy, Guilt   Jealousy, Guilt

Wresting/Imperialism   Dissipating/Imperialism

Taking/Capitalism   Spending/Capitalism

Toughminded   *Tenderminded*
Structured   *Unstructured*
Masculinity —————————————— *Femininity*
To Be Nourished   *To Nourish*
To Possess   *To Be Possessed*

Saving/Socialism   Giving/Socialism

Hoarding/Communism   Divesting/Communism

Envy, Shame   Envy, Shame

Analytic
Phlegmatic
Anal
(Asia)

Amiable
Melancholic
Oral
(Americas)

Introverted/Inhibited
Low Energy
Low Emotionality
Threatened by Risk
Collectivistic

Figure 8.5. The Financial Quaternary—Sociocultural Level

SOURCE: Copyright © 1997 Kenneth O. Doyle. Used by permission.

fears and the ways of dealing with the fears, both on the surface and in the shadow, are all the same.

Douglas's grid/group schema provides support for our application of the Quartenary on the sociocultural level. In her system, strong "grid," in which material things are valued, wealth and pomp are justified, and there is no guilt associated with spending, seems like a sociocultural specification of the Extraversion pole; weak grid, in which spiritual joys are valued and asceticism advanced, looks like our Introversion pole. At the same time, her low "group" condition, in which the individual is elevated over the collective, seems consistent with our Toughminded, or Masculine, pole, her high group condition, with our Tenderminded, or Feminine, pole. Accordingly, her four quadrants seem compatible with ours.

Following Weber's (1934/1976, pp. 13-31) lead, I suggest that saving and giving on the cultural level produce the different varieties of socialism—the Toughminded Asian version that focuses on calculated equivalencies and retention, and the more "melancholic" American Indian version that emphasizes community—while taking and spending produce both disciplined, combative European capitalism and free-wheeling, flamboyant African capitalism.[26] In parallel fashion but more intensely, hoarding and divesting create varieties of communism, while wresting and dissipating produce different kinds of imperialism.

Capitalism arises from feelings of jealousy—the Toughminded variety from the need to possess to be nourished, the opposite Tenderminded version from the need to *be* possessed *to* nourish. Because both versions involve narcissistic activity, both produce feelings of guilt. In contrast, socialism rises from envy, which in turn rises from the desire to be taken care of, to be safe, to minimize risk. Because they imply powerlessness, both the Toughminded control version and the Tenderminded dependency version of socialism produce feelings of shame. I suggest, then, that the chief social and economic philosophies of world history—capitalism and socialism—flow directly from the jealousy and envy that we first noted among the earliest humans, and, more deeply, from the underlying biopsychosocial propensities described in the Quaternary. The most controversial corollary of this proposal is that capitalism and socialism are rooted in, hence partially influenced by, heritable biological structures and processes.

The fact that capitalism of whichever sort is fundamentally competitive implies a propensity toward differentiation, while socialism's anticompetitive nature indicates a propensity toward "equivalencing," the minimizing of differences among people. This contrast suggests a difference in how people perceive and think about the world, capitalists emphasizing differences ("sharpening," after Bartlett, 1932), socialists emphasizing similarities ("leveling"). (See also Holzman, 1954.) Sharpeners are also more likely to employ structured cognitive processes than Levelers, and to be comfortable with risk. Thus capitalism is likely to fare best where the majority of influential people are skilled at differentiation, employ structure, and not only accept but enjoy risk. Absent any of these qualities, capitalism is likely to be less successful, socialism more.

Finally, I suggest that the same phenomena that produce philosophical and social systems also produce systems of ethics. Our systems of ethics, I maintain, are more a function of how different kinds of individuals, families, and cultures perceive and (therefore) value the world than the result of cool deductive or inductive reasoning. Because of this intimate connection with ethics, the struggle between capitalism and socialism quickly dons the vestments of morality and religion. People of the opposing viewpoints accuse each other of one deadly sin, either envy or jealousy,[27] while they themselves commit the other. Because Extraversion is active, Extraverted sin results in guilt; because Introversion is passive, interior, Introverted sin results in shame. As fear increases and behavior intensifies, people try to defend themselves first by redoubling their characteristic arguments, perhaps with voices raised, then by either attacking (Extraverts) or avoiding (Introverts). At some point, the intensity becomes such that the opposite, repressed propensity breaks out of the shadow, as when a Driver struggling heroically to ward off threats of incompetence breaks down for a moment and sobs, or an Amiable protecting the welfare of her children metamorphoses into a tigress.[28] Because socialistic teachings are more Tenderminded, attacks from the left are likely to be more personal; because capitalistic teachings are Toughminded, attacks from the right are likely to be more pragmatic and to sound more insensitive. For compatible analyses from another angle, see Rand (1943/1963, 1957, 1966) versus Fromm (1955, 1956, 1959, 1976) and Gilder (1981) versus Heilbroner (1985). Branden (1965/1966) examines the Rand/Fromm debate from a Randic perspective. Tawney (1920), Galbraith (1958), Looft (1971), and Lasche (1978) examine a culture they consider in extremis.

To summarize, these three figures show the connection between the four propensities (two pair) and a wide range of financial phenomena in individuals, families, and cultures. We will complete the moderator framework by adding a developmental component, and then turn to the process through which people give meaning to money and property.

THE DEVELOPMENTAL VANTAGE

I suggested previously that a moderator framework for the meanings of money and property ought to contain a developmental component, to account for differences in the meanings we attach to money at different stages of our lives (e.g., Furnham, 1984). Breger's (1974) synthesis of the work of the major developmental theorists—Erikson (1950, 1959), Piaget (1952), Loevinger (1976), and Kohlberg (1984)—suggests three important adult life stages that will serve at least for illustration. In the first, which I call the "discovery" stage, the person has become intellectually and emotionally ready for intimacy with another. At this stage, money and property serve as media through which people send and receive information by which they can evaluate other people and be themselves evaluated. Relating this developmental stage to the basic Financial Quaternary suggests that this information can be about much more than economic status; it can communicate the values and attitudes, even the conflicts and fears, that are delineated in the Quaternary. Given sufficient insight, it can even communicate some of the profound intimacy of the Shadow Quaternary.

Breger's second stage I call the "modeling" stage. The adult has reached the degree of intellectual and emotional maturity that she or he can begin to pass on to other people, particularly younger people, the wisdom and experience accumulated over the years. At this stage, money and property become media through which life lessons are communicated from one generation to the next: what is pleasurable, what is valuable, what is life-threatening. Connecting this stage with the basic Financial Quaternary leads one to consider different lessons for the different types of people, different quadrants. The more mentally healthy and satisfied the adult, the more balanced the lesson is likely to be; the more disappointed, frustrated, or bitter the adult, the more imbalanced the lesson, disproportionately limited to the values and attitudes associated with a particular quadrant. We might expect to see this pattern of increasing temperance in the satisfied family as well, and decreasing temperance in the dissatisfied or frustrated family.

Breger's third and final stage I call the "evaluation" stage. Here the adult, in contemplation of death, has begun to review the totality of his or her own life. In the satisfied personality, growing temperance has diminished the differences among the quadrants further still, making perspective a hallmark of the evaluation. The frustrated personality will dwell on the fear characteristic of his or her type, occasionally, when the fear is most keen, revealing the shadow.

These stages of individual development (and parallel stages for family and cultural development; see Doyle, 1992d) can be crossed with the Quaternary to add a third axis: Driver/Amiable by Expressive/Analytic by stages of development. Thus the meanings of money and property can be examined not only in quadrant terms but in terms of the evolving meanings of each propensity over the life span.

To summarize this chapter: I first made an important distinction between very sweeping first-level dimensions (Introversion/Extraversion and Tough- and Tendermindedness) and more specific second-level ones (Driver/Amiable and Expressive/Analytic). This distinction allowed us to support our conceptual framework with a new synthesis of quaternary research in neurophysiology, psychometrics, and psychoanalysis. I then introduced the idea of "financial temperament" as a microcosm of general temperament, accumulating psychoanalytic thought about the meanings of money and property for people of each of the four temperaments. I proposed quaternary frameworks for financial temperament on the individual, family, and cultural levels, adding, finally, a developmental component to show how the meanings of money and property change over time.

The chief purpose of this framework is to help us build a model for how people of the various temperaments go about attaching meanings to money and property. To that model we now turn.

Chapter 9

A Model—The Process of
Attributing Meanings
to Money and Property

This chapter proposes a model that describes how the various kinds of people go about attaching their particular meanings to money and property. In the preceding chapters I argued that biological, psychological, and sociocultural influences have combined to produce the four types of individuals, families, and cultures (two dimensions) that are represented in the fourfold figures at the end of Chapter 8. I now propose that meanings are governed by those very same biopsychosocial forces.[1] The same neuronal structures and processes, psychological dynamics, and cultural influences that together have made Europeans systematically different from Asians, Danes different from Italians, and *Romani* different from *Siciliani* have laid the foundation for the different meanings we associate with the world in general and money and property in particular.

NEUROSCIENCE AND COGNITIVE SCIENCE

Before we examine the model itself, we need to consider a handful of processes and structures that are essential to this model. The processes are natural selection, cultural selection, and neuronal-group selection. These processes are important because they work together to establish the neuroanatomical structures that transmit and receive the neurochemicals that make the various kinds of people different from one another and then enable them to perceive and value the world in their distinctive ways.

Natural selection, as always, means the evolutionary process through which characteristics that strengthen the species are retained while those that weaken it are gradually eliminated. According to this principle, individuals

173

with more desirable characteristics are more likely to mate and produce offspring than are organisms with less desirable characteristics. I propose that natural selection operates on the temperament level too, to support the survival and refinement of people within the various types. In cultural selection, I envision an analogous process through which cultures retain those traits and operations that are most consistent with the biologically encoded survival values that help the group maintain and refine its essential character. Thus, in any culture, "mainstream" individuals are more likely to find mates and procreate than are other members. For example, an Analytic culture will gradually purify itself of elements that are inconsistent with the essential order-and-control character of the culture, at least until it reaches the point of excess that Nietzsche warned about, and begins to reverse course.

Neuronal-group selection is a more difficult concept and requires additional explanation. While Edelman (1992, chap. 9) properly cautions that his theory of neuronal-group selection remains subject to further research, he also provides considerable evidence that supports the validity of his model (especially his pp. 94-99).

According to Edelman's model, in the first stages of the neuronal-group selection process, groups of neurons in a given part of the brain compete with one another for an active role in a particular brain function. Those that experience the most activity grow, "musclelike," and become established in the region. Within these branches, the synapses of the most active groups of neurons themselves become strengthened. The process results in circuits common to all members of the species, as well as circuits unique to the individual organism.

The patterns of stronger and weaker synapses constitute "maps" that are connected to one another through dense and complex neural-pathway networks, somewhat like the fields of rods and cones inside the human eye. Different maps sense different aspects of the stimulation for a given system (e.g., color, size, shape, and so forth for the visual system). The massive signaling from one map or set of maps to another ("reentry") organizes sensations into perceptions. This organizing involves not only current stimulation but also data from earlier maps stored in cortical memory.

Encoded in each organism are "survival triggers," evolutionary ranges of behavior patterns—too much, too little—necessary for the species' survival, such as particular heart and respiration rates, patterns of sexual activity, and, most important for our purposes, biochemical function. Among the known survival values encoded in the brainstem/limbic system are those that specify the limits for too much or too little oxygen, too much or too little light, and so forth. I extend this line of thinking to propose that these structures also contain encoded limits for too much or too little agitation (Analytics vs. Expressives), and too much or too little dependence, closeness, or nurturance (Drivers vs. Amiables). It is this last information, agitation and nurturance, that, I propose, fundamentally distinguishes our various kinds of people, the people of the different temperaments.

The three structures that are particularly germane to our model are the three parts of what MacLean (1990) has described as the "triune brain":[2] the brainstem, the limbic system, and the neocortex. The brainstem, or "reptilian brain" (cf. Coyle & Molliver, 1987, cited in Franklin, 1987), developed first in the history of species, and it still appears first in human fetal development. It regulates the body's autonomic, endocrine, and motor activities, which include blood pressure, respiration, reflexive muscle response ("freezing"), as well as the production of epinephrine, norepinephrine, dopamine, and other chemicals, the crucial importance of which, for our purposes, we have already noted (Tables 8.3a and 8.3b).

The limbic system, comprising principally the amygdala and hippocampus, follows the brainstem phylogenically and ontogenically. More differentiated than the brainstem, that is, more capable of sophisticated interpretation, this "mammalian brain" provides "greater sensitivity to emotional signals in the environment, more flexible emotional responses, and a greater capacity for learning" (Derryberry & Tucker, 1992). It is generally viewed as the center of emotional response, particularly fear. For a vivid depiction of the brainstem's response to fear, see LeDoux (1994).

Most recent in development, and enormously sophisticated, the neocortex is the exclusively "human brain." It provides sharper perception outside and inside the body, "more finely tuned emotional responses, and enhanced cognitive capabilities related to anticipation and planning" (Derryberry & Tucker, 1992).

As these consecutive brains evolved, there also developed arrays of "descending connections" between the neocortex and the more primitive levels, and "ascending connections" from the brainstem upward. The descending connections allow cortical cognition to affect emotion in the limbic system and brainstem; the ascending connections allow "reptilian" and "mammalian" perceptions to influence cognition, memory, attention, and other higher functions (e.g., Blaney, 1986; Weiner, 1985; both cited in Derryberry & Tucker, 1992). In general, brainstem processes are quick, reflexive, and "rough-hewn," geared toward instantaneous protection in the face of threat, while neocortical processes are refined and considered, that is, "fine-tuned," for optimal processing of complex experiences. Gray (1982), Zuckerman (1994), and others caution against oversimplification and rash conclusion, especially with regard to any one-to-one correspondence between brain processes and behavior.

With this information in hand, we can now proceed to the model.

OVERVIEW

The joint effort of natural selection and cultural selection leads to the establishment of survival values and cultural values that ensure the evolution not only of the species but also of the various temperaments. These general values, whether inherited through encoding in our neurons or learned from immediate experience or through media of whatever sorts, also apply to money and property. Threats against these values produce fear, which is the foundation for meaning. By associating physiological feelings with social experience, people learn that money and property can be used in ways that reduce those fears. By "behaving-in-context," people learn even more complex social rules, all nevertheless rooted in fear. Therefore, the basic meaning of money and property is protection, and money and property are talismans against the fears characteristic of the various temperaments.

Figure 9.1 provides an overview of the model. In Figure 9.1, the lowest row of cubes represents the biological contribution to the meanings of money and property, the highest row represents the sociocultural contribution, and the center row represents the combined effect, that is, the whole person.

Each complete cube is a stack of fourfold tables, the layers of each corresponding to the levels of the brain on which meaning can occur—the brainstem, the midbrain, and the neocortex. The crossed lines are the temperament coordinates, Driver/Amiable and Expressive/Analytic on the cultural and psychological levels, and the analogous too much/too little agitation and too much/too little nurture on the biological level.

The first column of cubes represents biocultural history, the effects of natural selection and cultural development. The second column represents the biological and cultural "survival values" that history has encoded in our genes and implanted in our minds.

The next three columns—the whole-person cubes—represent, first, the individual's memories on each of the three levels of meaning, with special attention to fears and talismans; second, the processing center, comprising the three levels of the brain; and, third, sensations and perceptions, which

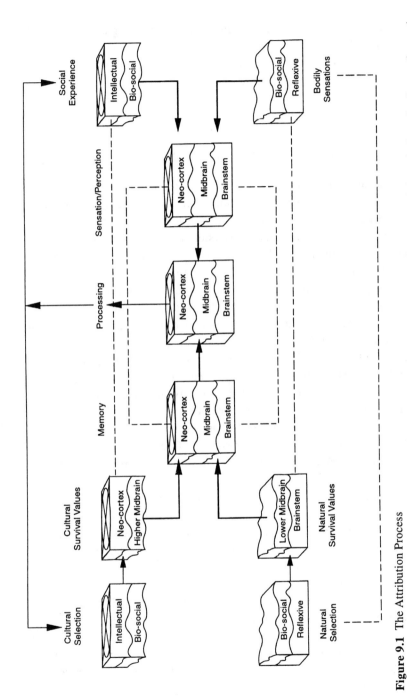

Figure 9.1 The Attribution Process

NOTE: Meaning is created in the Processing Center. In this overview, solid lines describe the flow of biopsychosocial stimulation to the Processing Center and out again. Dashed lines identify major interactions. The Quaternary moderates activity throughout the process.

177

the processing center associates with memories, with biological and cultural values, and with social experience and bodily sensation to create meaning.

The last column in the figure completes the process, representing the first step in the reiteration of the process.

The rest of this chapter will concentrate on each of the components of the overview, column by column.

BIOLOGICAL AND CULTURAL FOUNDATION

Natural selection provides the foundation for the model. Tables 9.1a-9.1d reminds us that, as a result of the natural selection process, two different first-level neuroanatomical structures have evolved, one that governs the propensity toward Introversion/Extraversion, another that governs the propensity toward Toughmindedness/Tendermindedness. As we observed in Chapter 8, cross-tabulating those two propensities produces four neurophysiological types of people, Extraverted/Toughminded Drivers, Introverted/ Tenderminded Amiables, and so forth. The validity of the biological quaternary is supported by a small but persuasive body of neurophysiological research (Edelman 1992).

Cultural selection builds on this foundation. Rooted in natural selection, cultural selection has produced analogous pairs of psychological and sociocultural propensities, the first toward acquisitiveness/affiliativeness on the individual level, and competition/cooperation on the family and societal levels; the second toward divergence/convergence on the individual level, conflict/exchange on the family and societal. Chapter 8 showed that these propositions are consistent with much psychometric and psychoanalytic research.

In Figure 9.1, the lower cubes represent the four quadrants from the biological perspective, showing how natural selection has prepared the organism to stipulate survival values that promote the survival and improvement of the species. The upper cubes represent the parallel contribution from cultural selection. The middle row, the complete cubes, involves stacking the upper cubes on top of the lower.

Table 9.1a reminds us of the array of neurophysiological, psychometric, and psychoanalytic research that supports the use of the Quaternary as a moderator framework for our model. In addition, it highlights the biological, psychological, and social results of natural selection and cultural selection— individual, family, and cultural propensities and values that emanate from this dual evolutionary process.

TABLE 9.1A Natural Selection and Cultural Selection

OVERVIEW: The joint effort of natural selection and cultural selection leads to the establishment of survival values and cultural values specific to our temperaments, threats against which trigger biological and social fear reactions. Through social experience paired with bodily experience we learn that particular temperament-linked uses of money and property will reduce the fear and protect against further threat. Therefore, the basic meaning of money and property is protection, and money and property are talismans against the fears characteristic of the various temperaments. Here, natural selection and cultural selection together produce sets of neuroanatomical structures and processes that produce four propensities (two dimensions), which in turn distinguish individuals, families, and cultures.

	Drivers	*Amiables*	*Expressives*	*Analytics*
Galen	Cholerics	Melancholics	Sanguines	Phlegmatics
Natural selection				
Neurophysiology, first level; e.g., Kagan, Money	Uninhibited/ masculine	Inhibited/ feminine	Uninhibited/ feminine	Inhibited/ masculine
Neurophysiology, second level; e.g., Cloninger	Increased endorphins	Decreased endorphins	Low dopamine	High dopamine
Cultural selection				
Psychometrics; e.g., Tellegen	High emotion, negative	Low emotion, positive	High emotion, positive	Low emotion, negative
Psychoanalysis; e.g., Freud	Phallic	Oral	Genital	Anal
Families; e.g., Olson	Acquisitive, separate, disengaged	Affiliative, connected, enmeshed	Divergent, flexible, chaotic	Convergent, structured, rigid
Social economies: e.g., Brinkerhoff and White	Competition	Cooperation	Conflict	Exchange

BIOLOGICAL AND CULTURAL VALUES

However sophisticated we as a species have become, we still share with lower forms of life an enormously powerful and instinctive motive to preserve ourselves and our species, to pass our DNA from one generation to the next. Associated with that drive for self-perpetuation are signals encoded in our genes that warn of threat against survival—too hot, too cold, too wet, too dry, too bright, too dark. Similarly encoded, it seems reasonable to propose,

TABLE 9.1B Establishment of Survival Values and Cultural Values

Here, through usage, the four propensities evolve into operations and skills that cause the various kinds of people to perceive and (therefore) to value aspects of the world differently. The results incline individuals and groups toward particular behaviors,, in general and with regard to money and property.

	Drivers	Amiables	Expressives	Analytics
Survival values	Too much nurturance	Too little nurturance	Too little stimulation	Too much stimulation
Operations and skills				
Operations (Jung)	Sensing: Sees empirical/ physical attributes most clearly	Feeling: Sees evaluative, emotive attributes most clearly	Intuiting: Sees a diverse potential most clearly	Thinking: Sees connections and relationships most clearly
Skills	Emphasizes differences: Seeks higher place in achievement hierarchy. Accumulates tangibles.	Emphasizes equivalence: Actively diminishes differences among people seen as vulnerable. Accumulates relationships.	Emphasizes differences: Seeks higher place in admiration hierarchy. Entertains; acts extravagantly; resists detail and structure.	Emphasizes equivalence: Acknowledges but doesn't seek to participate in hierarchies. Seeks detail, order, intricacy.
Values (Cloninger)	Persistence: Perseveres in face of resistance, rebuff	Reward dependence: Responds warmly to social approval, etc.	Novelty-seeking: Responds enthusiastically to novelty	Harm avoidance: Avoids punishment, novelty, disappointment

Results

	Competence: Acquisitiveness, determination, and appreciation of risk	Attraction: Self-effacement, modesty, and aversion to risk	Freedom: Impulsivity, extravagance, and appreciation of risk	Security: Caution, restraint, and aversion to risk
Values, individual	Competence: Acquisitiveness, determination, and appreciation of risk	Attraction: Self-effacement, modesty, and aversion to risk	Freedom: Impulsivity, extravagance, and appreciation of risk	Security: Caution, restraint, and aversion to risk
Values, group	Achieving individuals; competitive economies. Disdains emotions. Rewards personal success, punishes wimpishness. Tough capitalism and imperialism	Affiliative individuals; cooperative economies. Resents accumulation. Rewards group cooperation, punishes initiative. Tender socialism and communism	Divergent individuals; conflict economies. Disdains limitation. Rewards individuality, punishes conformity. Tender capitalism and imperialism	Convergent individuals; exchange economies. Resents stand-outs. Rewards group conformity, punishes risk-taking. Tough socialism and communism
Typical financial behavior	To take (have)	To give (need)	To let go	To hold on
More intense financial behavior	To wrest	To divest	To dissipate	To hoard
Motive and consequence	Impersonal jealousy and guilt	Personal envy and shame	Personal jealousy and guilt	Impersonal envy and shame

TABLE 9.1C Fears and Talismans as the Foundation for Meaning

The fears triggered by threats against the biological and cultural values, and the talismans we create to protect ourselves against them, comprise the foundation for meaning.

	Drivers	*Amiables*	*Expressives*	*Analytics*
Propensity	Achievement	Affiliation	Divergence	Convergence
Brainstem fear	Too much nurturance	Too little nurturance	Too little stimulation	Too much stimulation
Midbrain fear	Incompetence	Abandonment	Constraint	Disarray
Neocortical fear	Fear of losing the badges of success	Fear of contamination by money and property	Fear of not having enough money to do something	Fear of mistakes and embarrassment in financial matters
Shadow fear (repressed)	Desire to be taken care of	Desire to dominate	Desire to control	Desire to run wild

TABLE 9.1D Fears and Talismans Vary Over the Life Span

The fears and talismans change in accidentals but not essentials over the life span.

	Drivers	Amiables	Expressives	Analytics
Discovery stage	I'll be rejected because I'm too weak.	. . . because I'm too strong.	. . . because I'm nothing special.	. . . because I'm irresponsible.
Modeling stage	I'll have no achievements to pass on.	. . . no affection to pass on.	. . . no distinctiveness to pass on.	. . . no security to pass on.
Evaluation stage	Overall, a life without accomplishment.	Overall, a life without family, friends.	Overall, a life without vigor, vitality.	Overall, a life of prodigality.
Money/property as talisman	Against incompetence	Against abandonment	Against constraint	Against disarray

are softer alarms that signal other threats, the efforts to avoid which have established the four temperaments.

The key to understanding how these softer signals may have established the temperaments is a postulated extension of Edelman's theory of neuronal-group selection. This extension proposes that natural selection has embedded in our neurons survival values—triggers—that stimulate patterns of behavior that correspond to the four types: behavior patterns that indicate a preference for less nurturance, because they find nurturing or being nurtured aversive (Driver); other behavior that seeks more nurturance (Amiable); behavior that shows a preference for more agitation or stimulation (Expressive); and behavior that shows a preference for less (Analytic). The extended theory specifies that, through usage, these behaviors evolve into skills that cause the various types of people to perceive different aspects of the environment more clearly. That which people see most clearly, they value most highly, and they interact with the world according to those values. Through social experience we learn sets of cultural values that are consistent with those biological values.

To be more specific, low nurturance sets the stage for Jung's "sensing" operation. In the absence of distractions and discomforts that rise from too much nurturance, the sensing operation gives Drivers an especially keen ability to concentrate on the empirical world, to make distinctions on the basis of easily quantifiable empirical factors, and to emphasize differences among people, especially in terms of their place in a hierarchy of achievement. Overall, those skills lead Drivers to place high value in *competence*. Extended into the world of money and property, competence supports "taking" or "having," or, in more extreme form, "wresting." The skills of differentiation and ranking, and taking and wresting, incline Drivers to create and maintain competitive economies like capitalism and even economic imperialism. In those economies, the fact of ownership leads to jealousy— the concern that someone might take one's property away—and the fact of ownership-plus-jealousy leads to guilt.

The opposite survival value, high nurturance, inclines Amiables in just the opposite direction. High nurturance sets the stage for the "feeling" operation, which makes Amiables see the emotional features of the world more vividly, the hue and shade and saturation of people's moods and motives. Overall, the feeling operation leads Amiables to place high value in *affiliation*. Extended to money and property, affiliation becomes "to give"; in more intense form, "to divest." Feeling skills also incline Amiables to try to minimize competition, differences, hierarchies, and other things that might make people feel bad, and pushes them to create cooperative economies like socialism and even communism. The absence of property leads naturally to envy; envy combined with neediness produces shame.

On the other dimension, the high-stimulation condition lays the groundwork for Jung's "intuiting" operation, the hallmark of which is perception of a very wide range of possibilities, whatever the topic. The intuiting operation, like the sensing operation, causes people to emphasize differentiation, but because of the propensity toward Tendermindedness (low androgen, etc.), it establishes a warm and fuzzy hierarchy of admiration or recognition rather than a hard and prickly hierarchy of competition. This operation also inclines people to seek stimulation through lively and extravagant behavior, surrounding themselves with vivid colors and sounds, and in other ways that enliven the senses. Overall, the intuiting operation leads Expressives to place high value on ingenuity, creativity, and *freedom*. Extended to money and property, the intuiting operation becomes "to spend," even "to dissipate." In the economic realm, the search for stimulation that characterizes people of this type leads them to create economies built largely on conflict, a freewheeling, even chaotic, form of capitalism that contrasts with the more disciplined capitalism of the Driver culture. As with Drivers, ownership produces jealousy, which in turn leads to guilt, but jealousy and guilt of a more emotional sort.

In contrast, the absence of stimulation creates a fertile climate for Jung's "thinking" operation, which finds stimulation distracting, counterproductive, and upsetting. The thinking operation enables people to see and appreciate order and structure and detail and motivates them to behave in ways that maintain an ordered and structured life style. Overall, the thinking operation leads Analytics to place high value on control and *security*. It inclines them to create socialistic or even communistic economies that recognize differences but make sure everyone gets his or her fair share so nobody gets upset: To each according to his need, from each according to his ability. In contrast to Amiable socialism and communism, which are built on kinship and need, Analytic socialism and communism are built on exchange and equity. The limits or absence of ownership leads (again) to envy, which leads to shame, but envy and shame of a more impersonal, dispassionate sort than with Amiables.

To summarize, biological survival values received from natural selection and reinforced by cultural selection, and cultural values taught by cultural selection and rooted in natural selection, incline the organism toward operations and skills particular to its temperament, and these temperaments cause the various kinds of people to perceive and evaluate the world in their own ways, and to value the different aspects of the world accordingly. The most important information in Tables 9.1b and 9.1c is the contrast between Driver values of low affiliation, high differentiation, and high persistence in the face of difficulty versus Amiable values of high affiliation, low differentiation, and high dependence on stronger people, and the contrast between Expressive values of high stimulation, high differentiation, as well as extravagance, novelty, sensuality, and conflict versus Analytic values of low stimulation, low differentiation, and a high need to avoid embarrassment punishment or other harm. Figure 9.1, second column, locates this information in the overall process of creating meaning.

ATTRIBUTION OF MEANINGS

Attribution of meaning is a complex process that correlates the biological and sociocultural survival values of which we have just spoken with brainstem/midbrain/cortical memories of personal experiences and with new stimulation filtered through the sensing, feeling, thinking, and intuiting operations. Most prominent among these bits of information are our particular fears and the corresponding talismans. In Figure 9.1, the attribution process comprises the three center cubes: memory, sensation/perception, and processing.

Memory

We learn primarily from direct experience in social interaction, secondarily from "mediated" experiences—television, movies, magazines, textbooks, and so forth—in both cases pairing social messages filtered through the four operations with bodily sensations characteristic of our temperament. We store those impressions in memory.

Memory is only partly cortical (linguistic). The brainstem and midbrain store not only survival values but "memories" of past behavior patterns in the form of stronger neuronal pathways. They also store prelinguistic traces of previous experience, especially traumatic experience. Because unconscious drives are so primitive and so difficult to access, some authors suspect that shadow values are also stored in the brainstem (see Edelman, 1990).

In the financial world, cortical memories comprise everything the individual has learned intellectually about money and property through both personal experience and media. Brainstem and midbrain memories include anything that results in triggering the too-much or too-little stimulation or nurturance alarms, and any networks of association that we have come to connect with those stimuli.

Especially important are those memories that we have learned to call "threats," or, more loosely, "fears," because natural selection has made the response to threat the most powerful in any organism's repertoire. Threats are stimuli that trigger the survival alarms to produce fear. They are either primary threats, frightening in themselves, like a raging fire or a snarling beast, or secondary, learned threats, those that sound the alarm indirectly, through their association with primary threats.

Most of the frightening stimuli related to money and property are secondary, learned from personal experience and through media. Some we have learned so well that they seem "nearly primary," for example, that rich people will try to oppress poor people and that wealth will taint us and contaminate our relationships. Others are somewhat less clear and distinct, like images of what it was like to live during the Great Depression or to experience eviction, bankruptcy, or job loss. Learned memories also include impressions of what it is like to be the subject or object of envy or jealousy and to experience shame or guilt.

Though we also store memories of positive experiences, the experiences that produce the strongest memories are the frightening ones, especially for younger children. An Amiable child will learn something about the meanings of money from the story of St. Francis of Assisi, for she will respect that holy man, but she will learn more from reading how the Chinese and Roman emperors oppressed their peasants, the feudal lords their serfs, or the robber barons their employees, for she will identify with the victims of the oppression and share their fear. Similarly, a teenage Driver will learn something about what's important to himself by observing a successful entrepreneur, but much more from watching someone who is down and out, and a dowager Expressive will find some confirmation of her values from visiting with her friends at the country club, much more from watching the bag lady in the park. In each of these cases the latter stimulus is frightening—the peasants, the down-and-out, the bag lady—because it personifies the most-feared loss.

Some of the strongest fears associated with money and property derive from those motives we observed early in the history of humankind—jealousy and envy. Perhaps recalling the archaic days when our ancestors all squatted for dinner around a fresh mastodon carcass, we can sense with alacrity that someone wants to take away something we have or that someone has something we don't. Through social experience, we gradually learn to extend our acquisitive or possessive reaction from a morsel of mastodon to more and more aspects of money and property.

The basic process through which stimuli become threats is through association with anxious bodily states. The more frightening the early image and the more vivid the bodily state, the more deeply the match penetrates into the lower parts of our brains, and the more permanent and influential the fright becomes.

Also stored in memory are images of our talismans. Talismans are symbols—charms—that we believe will protect us from threat. They include prayer, sex, work, recreation, book-learning, exercise, and many others, as well as money and property. Beneath the surface, all talismans mean the same thing for the same type of person, but the meaning varies across the types. For example, the meaning of sex, the meaning of prayer, and the meaning of money are different for the Driver than for the Amiable, Expressive, or Analytic, yet sex, prayer, and money all mean the essentially the same thing for the Driver, all united by an element of conquering, and, occasionally, when unconscious needs reach the surface, an element of being conquered.

Money and property in general take on talismanic attributes early in life and maintain them for the duration, though the specifics may change, for example, from a bright, shiny Schwinn to a bright, shiny Saab, and the sensitivities may vary from childhood to adulthood to old age. The process through which we create talismans is parallel to the way we construct fears: social information paired with experienced or anticipated bodily state, but in this case the bodily state is relief. The more powerful and permanent the fear, the more powerful and permanent must be the talisman that wards it off.

The power of the talisman to relieve fear is continually strengthened and shaped, and occasionally challenged, by social experience. On top of my natural propensities and responding to their own, my parents, relatives, and friends teach me about threats and fears, snakes and separation, and show me how to be afraid. They encourage some fears and discourage others. They teach confidence as well, but the primitive fear message is always the stronger. My school, my temple, and the other institutions of which I am respectful teach their own agenda of things to be feared, and all manner of media flash all kinds of messages before my eyes. In short, my social circle (as well as my instincts) tell me what to fear, how deeply to fear it, and how to deal with it.

Sensation/Perception

New stimulation in this context includes whatever we receive through our senses, as well as whatever we imagine we might receive, along with any selectivity or coloration stemming from past experience, including the shadow. The individual sees, hears, feels, smells, or tastes this information, and passes signals into the brain, directly to each of the three levels and simultaneously through the midbrain to the other levels. The most important proposition here (already noted) is that, as a result of natural selection and cultural selection, different kinds of people perceive the various aspects of the world more clearly, as a function of their temperament: While everyone sees the panoply, Drivers see most vividly the empirical features, Amiables the evaluative, emotive features, Expressives the breadth of possibility, and Analytics the detail.

Processing

The Biological Side of Meaning

The process of attaching meaning to money and property is essentially the process of connecting sensations and perceptions about money and property to fears, talismans, and other memories, and to body signals. The correlation process begins deep in the midbrain. There, to ensure the survival of our species, nature and culture have worked together to create a "fear center," with extensions down into the brainstem and up into the neocortex, and back again. This fear center is the cornerstone of meaning.

In the midbrain, the amygdala and hippocampus correlate biological signals from inside the body with social messages from outside. The brainstem adds urgency and emotional coloring to those messages, to the extent that they connect with networks that ultimately ring the survival alarms. Slightly slower, the cortex attaches linguistic interpretation—names and labels—to the match. For example, the cortex may label as "anxiety" the state surrounding the discovery in the morning mail of an unexpected envelope bearing the IRS logo, coupled with some particular bodily uneasiness, a complex of physiological signals including, perhaps, a dry mouth, trembling hand, uneasy stomach, and subtler signs. In addition, the midbrain processes repressed memories (shadow) that periodically find expression, such as when the organism is experiencing prolonged or especially severe stress.

The brainstem's emotional coloring is mainly a matter of reflexive fear, with "loud alarum bells" that sound whenever stimulation falls outside the biologically encoded survival values, whether to signal a shortage of oxygen, an excess of heat, or too much or too little stimulation or nurturance. Meaning of this sort is necessarily prelinguistic, limited to gross sensations of good or bad, pleasant or unpleasant, safe or not safe, which the brainstem sends to the midbrain for correlation with the rest of the elements.

On the cortical level, the complex back-and-forth signaling among neuronal patterns in the neocortex establishes higher consciousness, the last word (so to speak) in *Homo sapiens sapiens*. It is at this level that we become fully able to think symbolically, to connect money and property with fears and talismans, and—*sapiens*—to reflect on the connection.

The neocortex creates categorizations of social messages and experiences that the amygdala and hippocampus correlate with our perceptions of our biological side, that is, bodily states and evolutionary values. The social experiences and the physiological signals (I hypothesize) evolve over the life span and vary in their relative influence, social experiences more influential in youth, physiological signals more potent as we grow older. The midbrain structures interact with the linguistic centers of the cortex (Wernicke's and Broca's areas) to create the capacity to interpret self and world in symbolic terms so that we can reflect on them. This reflection creates an "explosion of meaning"[3] through which we understand ourselves, other people, and the cosmos (see also Csikszentmihalyi & Rochberg-Halton, 1981; Mithen, 1996).

Edelman (1992) asserts[4] that neuroscience, for all its complexity, provides a necessary but not sufficient explanation for the construction of meaning. The higher-order consciousness he describes accounts for only the most basic forms of human mental activity. At this point, he hands the baton to psychologists interested in the cognitive science study of speech and meaning,[5] mentioning Jerome Bruner by name (Edelman, 1992, p. 175; see also Bruner, 1990, p. 34).

The Social Side of Meaning

The establishment of meaning is a social process that begins to take shape even earlier than speech (Bruner, 1990, p. 71). The giving mother, the providing father, the "taking" sibling, the deceiving neighbor—all these people in all their roles, and others, help broaden and deepen the child's understanding of herself and the world of money and property. She learns meaning best as she learns speech best, by doing-in-context, learning not just what sounds to use but the subtle rules for how to use them. *Naming* gives meaning to the bodily sensation and to the behaviors that express that sensation. Sensation adds meaning to the message, and they both add meaning to individual-in-group identity. These early experiments with self-description—"You give, I receive"—grow into more complex and realistic narratives and eventually into what Bruner calls full "autobiographies" through which the infant, then the child, then the adult learns (and teaches others) about herself in relation to her world.

Among the feelings about which the infant learns are some that will become fundamentally important for understanding the meanings of money. It is a small step from independence and aggressiveness to acquisitiveness, from affiliation and passivity to effacement, and so forth, and not a much larger step from those to the fundamental financial behaviors: to take, to give, to spend, and to save. Thus infants will begin to attach meaning to some acts and feelings relevant to the meanings of money and property as early as the first year of life. Freud's notion of personality arrested at oral or anal stages seems complementary.

By extension, the child's whole complex of behavior gets connected with the whole complex of bodily sensations and social values, and meaning deepens and spreads and evolves to the point that it may come to represent the culture of a family, a clan, or an entire people.

The labels the child attaches to her functions, intentions, and feelings not only name them but also station them in her developing value system. Beginning with rough-hewn notions of pleasure or pain, good or evil, too much or too little stimulation, and so forth, and progressing into Bruner's subtle and fecund autobiographies, she builds a personal theory of value that tells her that something is good and life-sustaining and compatible, or evil and threatening and incompatible, for her particular type in these particular circumstances.

The Quaternary is as powerful a moderator on the social side of meaning as on the biological. Expressives reason, imitate, hope, and imagine, they build their theories of life and their theories of morality, all in accordance with the survival values buried deep in their brains and in a world (partly of their own construction) bursting with variety and possibility. Everything is shaded by that propensity toward intuitive perception; everything derives from the need for stimulation. Similarly, Amiables, Drivers, and Analytics all carry out their cortical processing in the light of their biological propensities and basic psychological operations. It is this relativity that accounts for the widespread conflict about money and property; it is the moral dimension[6] that accounts for the intensity.

People of any given temperament honor the values and behaviors that distinguish their temperament from others, and they disdain (and, yes, fear) the values and behaviors characteristic of other temperaments, particularly the one diametrically opposed (e.g., Fiske & Taylor, 1991, pp. 80-81). The more closely one clings to the values and behaviors of one's own temperament, the more threatening the opposing qualities become, for they imply the loss of the world one knows best and, unconsciously, the loss of important parts of oneself. Ironically, the stronger the fear the more tightly we cling to our values and behaviors, and the more tightly we cling the more frightened we become, in a kind of "spiral of fear" that tends to become more and more extreme (see Noelle-Neumann, 1984, for an analogous spiral). We will talk more about extreme behavior in Chapter 10.

The Expanding Network

As the explosion of meaning continues, our network of social information, bodily sensation, and existing meaning expands in two directions: first across life stages, second, from the inner self into the environment. Of life stages we have already spoken (p. 170). It is sufficient only to add that each new life stage (Table 9.1d) creates an opportunity for us to discover new meaning by observing how money and property fit into our efforts to find ourselves through close relationships with other people (discovery stage), share ourselves with the upcoming generation (modeling stage), and reflect on our life experience (evaluation stage).

Expansion into the environment runs parallel to the extension of self, the complement to Fenichel's (1935/1938) "ego shrinkage," and has its roots also in scientific psychology and existential philosophy. For example, James observed, in *Principles* (1890), that "between what a man calls me and what he simply calls mine the line is difficult to draw," and Sartre, in *Being and Nothingness,* maintained that to acquire and lose possessions is to enlarge and diminish the sense of self.

George Herbert Mead (1934, p. 154; see also p. 12 in Chapter 1) maintained that the meaning we attribute to objects reflects back to add meaning to our selves. The external objects comprise the "generalized other," which is the origin of self-consciousness and identity. In a similar vein, Csikszentmihalyi and Rochberg-Halton (1981, p. 38ff.) show how, through the dialectical processes of differentiation and integration, we use money and property to distinguish our selves, families, and worlds from others and, at the same time, to integrate self, family, and cosmos into a unified whole (Csikszentmihalyi, 1964; Teillard de Chardin, 1959). Thus what we own (and what we don't) extends from the deepest center of personality to the farthest reaches to which our creativity can take us, and back again. More recently, Csikszentmihalyi (e.g., 1990, 1996, 1997; see also Buber, 1958/1966) advocates cultivation of a "flow" between self and environment such that we periodically lose track of the difference.[7]

As further support for the connection between self and possessions, Belk (1988, see also Belk, 1989; Belk, Bahn, & Mayer, 1982; but see Cohen, 1989, for an opposing view) points to the diminishment we feel when objects we treasure are lost or stolen. He cites Rosenblatt's (Rosenblatt, Walsh, & Jackson, 1979) suggestion that victims of theft or casualty go through the same series of emotions as people who have lost a loved one, as well as his own finding that, after anger and rage, burglary victims most commonly reported "feelings of invasion and violation." He also cites literature on ancient property (burial) rituals as well as efforts to replenish self after loss. Belk's notion of possessions is far-ranging, from hair to public monuments to the moon, and his data suggest quite a straightforward gradation in the degree of closeness we perceive in particular classes of possessions.[8] One study of adult perceptions (Prelinger, 1955) suggests that personal possessions are next in closeness to attributes like age and occupation, literally just as close as perspiration. Dittmar (1992; see also Wells & Prensky, 1996, chap. 6) provides a thorough review of related literature, and Boulding (1971-1985) leads us to parallel thoughts about group dynamics.[9]

The Quaternary moderates these phenomena as well. If our perceptual structures and social values lead us to perceive particular parts of the environment with added clarity and to value them more, then our perceptions of the generalized other perceiving us, our experience of flow, and our interpretations of what we own and what we don't should reflect those differences. There will be in each a shading toward mastery or being mastered, toward expression or control. Fundamentally, there will be in each a shading of the talisman.

ILLUSTRATIONS

To illustrate the explosion of meaning that results from the establishment and expansion of higher consciousness; to show the association with temperament, brain processes, and life stage; and to connect all of those with money and property, I will devote the rest of this chapter to some hypothetical descriptions of youthful Expressives, Analytics, Drivers, and Amiables in early encounter with self and society. To control tedium, I won't reiterate all the information for each type; rather I will talk mostly about one type—Expressives—and then present abbreviated descriptions of the other types.

Expressives

From time to time, as a result of their biology interacting with the environment, Expressives experience a vague but growing restlessness that itches to be satisfied, especially when they have been quiet or alone for a while, or when they encounter a situation heavy with rules and regulation, the feeling that they are in a box from which they need to escape, *now*. This feeling of being boxed in is exacerbated by the Expressive perceptual apparatus, which is highly flexible and designed to scan the whole environment in search of the greater amounts of stimulation required to produce the excitement they crave. The more confining the box, the more intense the need for stimulation.

At some point, the lack of stimulation trips the "not-enough-stimulation" trigger that natural selection and cultural selection have embedded in Expressive memories. This in turn impedes the production of dopamine and other agents of excitation in the brain and throughout the body and produces a state similar to sexual restlessness, close, perhaps, to what Freud meant by libido. It is this boxed-in feeling of which Expressives are afraid, exactly as a gregarious prison inmate might fear solitary confinement.

To quiet those alarms, these "sanguine" individuals—Galen's term—engage in all manner of "novelty-seeking" behavior—Cloninger's—that brings in excitement from the outside. Optimistic, enthusiastic, and attracted to diversity, they search out different and interesting people, places, and things in which to immerse themselves, and they present themselves in different and interesting ways to attract similar people. Indeed, they sometimes lose themselves in the stimulation for which they so desperately search. When their behavior becomes extreme, it may be classified as narcissistic, hypomanic, or histrionic. It contains an element of chaos.

Spousal and family relationships among Expressives are flexible, if not chaotic, marked by wide swings of emotion and attachment. Business relationships may be superficial, owing to the tendency to lose track of the real self in the flamboyant swirl. Business activities often center in sales and entertainment.

When enough of them gather together, the society or culture they form is easily visible for vitality—and even for conflict, because these lively individualists not only don't fear but actually enjoy competing with one another. The competition is different from Driver competition, however, in that Expressive competition is softer, more for entertainment and recognition—to scratch that itch—than to vanquish opponents. As a group, Expressives admire unusual behavior and appearance, flout rules and regulations, promote sensuality and sensuousness, and reward distinctiveness with recognition.

In the arena of money and property, Expressives just do what comes naturally: They look for what's different and interesting: zany clothes, flashy cars, unusual investments—something that not only fills the eye but makes for a good story when they get together with their friends (or anyone else who will listen). In particular, they avoid anything that constrains, like budgets. Their basic inclination is "to let go": hence they spend, even dissipate. But their dissipation has a narcissistic, jealous quality—they spend to identify themselves, to create an image. In short, money and property are vehicles through which they can *express* themselves, instruments to keep their fear of constraint under control.

If the behavior that finally turns off the Expressive's alarm is something people call "exuberance," if the people in her (or his) life (directly and through media) describe exuberant people in positive terms, and if she comes to appreciate exuberant behavior because it takes away the boxed-in feeling and makes her feel free, the young Expressive will come to understand not only what exuberance is all about but what she is all about and what her world is all about. If people call that stimulation "generosity," one of the financial versions of exuberance, and make it clear that generosity is a respected quality in their world, she will understand more about her identity, and theirs, and the match between the two. In this case, she will feel "in sync" with her world.

If her teachers, then her employers, her spouse and her friends, her children and then her grandchildren react positively to her natural efforts to find stimulation, she will develop progressively deeper and more intricate, and more satisfying, networks of meaning that expand as she passes through the successive life stages—how money and property help define who she is and fit into the way she relates with people, how they connect with her efforts to share self with the upcoming generation, and how they fall into perspective when she looks back to evaluate her life.

On the other hand, she may find herself in contrary or, worse, contradictory surroundings, where people label her search for stimulation "impetuosity" and tell her they don't respect impetuous people, and where they call the ways she approaches money and property "prodigal" and tell her that they disdain prodigal daughters (as well as sons). In this circumstance, she will learn something different about herself and her connection with society. She will feel quashed; she will feel "marginalized," boxed in again; and, at least to some extent, she will feel betrayed and depressed, and she will either confront the society or withdraw from it, more likely the former, even as it shuns her and tries to force her to conform.

From the combination of quieted alarms, satisfaction of their stimulation-hungry perceptual mechanisms, admiring messages from people they respect, and the absence of that awful boxed-in feeling, Expressives learn that the colorful use of money and property has the power to reduce their anxiety. Hence money and property colorfully used are talismans against the fear of constraint.

Analytics

In contrast, the people we are calling Analytics have come to associate certain feelings of physiological tension with social signals and personal observations involving *too much* stimulation. If Expressive perception (low dopamine, etc.) is plastic and designed to scan the whole environment, Analytic perception (high dopamine, etc.) is designed to concentrate on narrow swatches. If Expressives can't tolerate the thought of being boxed in, Analytics can't bear feeling "at loose ends." Indeed, when too much stimulation triggers their survival alarms, Analytics will experience an uneasy sense that they're not on top of their affairs, that they need to do something to get life back under control. Tense, shy, and ectomorphic—the "lean and hungry look" that troubled Caesar—Analytics are not so fun as Expressives, but far more steady and dependable.

Analytics learn that they can keep their too-much-stimulation alarm from ringing by engaging in a pattern of behaviors that involve high structure, low risk, and the avoidance of people, places, and things they are likely to find too exciting or upsetting. As individuals, they learn that they can maintain this "phlegmatic" state by keeping their affairs under control, for example, by living within their means, avoiding risk, keeping close track of income and outflow, and purchasing insurance and other guaranteed financial products. Tidy, stubborn, stingy (Freud), often righteous (Jones), and fundamentally inclined "to hold on," they save and they hoard. But, because they still feel impoverished, they envy the money and property of others.

Family relationships among Analytics are likely to be rather structured, even rigid, as they apply their concentration skills to intimate relationships. Business relationships are likely to be based on careful attention to who receives which benefits at what costs, so nobody has grounds to be upset. No one is likely to accuse Analytics of keeping too loose a rein on their finances—classic occupations are programmer, accountant, and actuary.

In social settings, Analytics will find that large crowds make them uneasy, flashy clothes put them off, and loud people offend them, so they try to maintain a composed life style. They submit to intricate social rules that reduce uncertainty, devise exchange economies that ward off conflict, and coin aphorisms like "The nail that stands up gets pounded down." The greater their discomfort, the more likely it is that they will also find their attention narrowed, their musculature rigid, their stomachs queasy and that they will experience a general desire to flee the situation. The more tense they become, the more able they also become to perceive degrees of order and structure and the more likely to place greater value on those attributes.

If the behavior that finally turns off the alarm is something people call "responsible" or "dependable," the Analytic will understand more about himself (or herself) and his place in the world. If people call his behavior "thrifty," he will feel better about himself and more confirmed (and safe) in his attitudes. But if people call him "cheap" or "rigid," he will feel not only affronted—and misunderstood—but embarrassed and put off. Depending on how the people in his life react to his natural tendency toward avoiding stimulation, he will either grow more comfortable with the meaning of money and property in his life or more uncomfortable. Occasionally during the uncomfortable times, he may discover in himself a surprising yearning to drop all his responsibilities and simply let himself go. This shadow motive will be short-lived, however, and he will soon return to his more controlled condition.

The main message the Analytic learns from correlating social experience with how he feels is that money and property cautiously employed have the power to reduce threat—they are talismans against his fear of too much stimulation, his fear of disarray.

Driver

If Expressive and Analytic perceptual systems represent different ends of a continuum of agitation or stimulation, Driver and Amiable systems vary along a continuum of independence/dependence, mastery/helplessness, or, in a word, "nurturance." The Driver system is designed to distinguish the harder elements of the environment from the softer, paternity from maternity, the material, empirical world from the world of feelings or ideas. Drivers have natural and social alarms that sound under conditions of excessive nurturance, producing endorphins and enkephalins, which anesthetize the organism generally (probably in preparation for battle) and specifically reduce feelings of interpersonal sensitivity and attachment. In social terms, Drivers find nurturance cloying, and they recoil from it like a little boy might recoil from Aunt Tillie's smothering kisses—a reminder, in psychoanalytic terms, of their repressed fear of their own infantile helplessness and need to be nourished.

Because they find it so unpleasant, Drivers behave in ways that keep helplessness at bay. They take, and they wrest. As individuals, they buy, compete, exploit; they accumulate tangible "badges" of their achievement and independence. In their families, they keep emotional if not physical distance from spouse and children, and they teach their offspring to be competitive, tough, and jealous of their status and their perquisites. In business relationships, they win through intimidation, and they take pleasure in the "kill." Representative occupations include entrepreneur, corporate raider, and litigator.

When enough Drivers gather to form a society or culture, they reward aggressive behavior and punish wimpishness, using some form of accumulation as the principal reward, and some form of confiscation as the principal punishment. They establish hierarchies based on accomplishment, and they quickly assign individuals and groups to levels in those hierarchies. In short, in all their roles and circumstances, throughout the course of life, they behave in ways that make them feel masterful.

It's the same with money and property: If you do something that makes Drivers feel weak, they will, like the little boy, resist; weaker, recoil; if you do something that allows them to prove themselves, they will seize the opportunity. Every task Drivers take on teaches them about self and society, because it provides the opportunity to match feelings of too much nurturance to social descriptions of their behavior. If people describe his (or her) style as "courageous" and "successful," he will connect those words with the feelings and understand more about himself and his place in society; if they describe his style as "overbearing" or "ruthless," he may understand still more. He may very well take pleasure even in those latter labels. As he balances courage and ruthlessness at the successive life stages, he makes broader and deeper connections between his feelings, his observations of self, and the social messages that come from the people around him.

Anything that Drivers use to protect themselves against too much nurturance—against signs of weakness or incompetence—is a talisman. Thus I maintain that Drivers use the accumulation of money and property as a talisman against the "fear of incompetence."

Amiables

In the same way that Drivers recoil at too much nurturance, Amiables wither at too little. The Amiable will go to bed with her (or his) mate, hoping that, tonight, she will experience the affection she's always wanting, but sensing deep down that somehow what she gets won't be enough, perhaps quantitatively, more likely qualitatively, to convince her that she's lovable. This bereft feeling trips the too-little-nurturance trigger, which reduces the endorphin/enkephalin flow, which in turn produces greater feelings of dependence and helplessness, and an increased inclination to perceive the emotional side of life. The Amiable is especially skilled at noticing any signs in others that they may be feeling as empty and dependent as she.

When Amiables experience warmth and emotional closeness, they feel full and complete, as though they could and would do anything for this person, like a mother feels she would give up her life to protect her child. If the Driver feels emasculated by too much nurturance, the Amiable feels stripped of her maternity, eviscerated, by too little, as though her very self has been ripped out and thrown on the ground. In the realm of money and property, the Amiable feels (as did many of the early Christians) that any superfluity is evil and that the corrupting qualities of this "root of all evil" will taint them and make them unlovable.

The Amiable survival alarm sounds at anything that threatens nurturance—harsh words, competitive activities, and social differentiation weigh them down with an abiding melancholy, especially when children and other vulnerable persons are involved. Because almost every facet of the material world can imply social differentiation, Amiable individuals generally disdain materialism, and they build up a resentment toward those who own more then they "should." Because of the interaction of their perceptual mechanisms and their social values, they minimize differences among people ("leveling"). On occasion, their rage at the oppressiveness of rich may take on a remarkably oppressive quality itself ("shadow").

Amiable families also disdain money. They tend to live modestly and to disregard the world of investment and accumulation. They generally operate under the fear that any substantial presence of money and property will intrude upon the relationships among the members. They are unlikely to accumulate any significant wealth, perhaps not even adequate wealth, unless one or the other spouse (or some outsider, like an employer) takes on the responsibility, in which event the followers will become even more dependent.

Amiable cultures reward redistribution of wealth, so that no one feels left out—except possibly the unworthy rich. They devise religions that condemn material interests, establish systems of taxation that punish financial success, and create Robin Hood economies that "take from and rich and give to the poor." They practice a softer kind of introversion than the Analytics (low androgen), though surely one that values personal relationships over personal possessions. Amiables thrive in these Amiable cultures, but sometimes the webwork of sensitivities and sensibilities has the effect of paralyzing the family or community.

When the Amiable pairs her melancholy feelings with social labels like "sensitive" and "caring," she learns about herself, likes what she learns, and redoubles her efforts to nourish (and be nourished). When she pairs those feelings with labels like "syrupy" and "desperate," and "manipulative," she feels rejected and even more depressed. As she encounters the series of life stages, she discovers new meanings for money and property as symbols in self-identification, in relationships with others, and in her search for lifelong perspective.

Amiables fear anything that might make someone feel bad, for making someone feel bad threatens nurturance and affiliation. They have come to pair feelings of anxiety with social experiences in which one person, especially a vulnerable person, has been oppressed, defeated, or even "one upped" by another, and to associate reduction of anxiety with the absence of money and property. They have learned that avoiding the accumulation of money and property is a talisman that controls their "fear of abandonment."

The next, and final, chapter will describe a range of uses to which this kind of information can be applied.

PART IV

ELABORATION

In which I discuss applications and implications,
and contemplate where to go from here.

Chapter 10

Applications and Implications

All that remains is to address potentially the most difficult question of all: Of what value to society is this examination of the social meanings of money and property? Because concern about money and property penetrates into nearly every corner of the world, and because conflict in the name of wealth or poverty seems almost that widespread, the list of practical applications and speculative implications is virtually endless. I will describe a handful of these, but first I should review my main proposals in some detail.

RECAPITULATION II

In the first part of this book, I began to spell out what I mean by "a psychology of money and property," describing it as the study of meanings beyond those traditionally associated with Economic man. I suggested that meaning was not just social, and not just psychological, but *biopsychosocial,* the result of the brain's interpretation of bodily responses to social experience.

In the second part, I proposed that through natural selection and cultural selection the early peoples of the Earth gradually separated themselves into four prototypical cultures, one of which came to predominate on each of the four major continents and still today (with growing variability) characterizes the descendants of those earliest peoples. I offered evidence for this notion from the predominant cultural constructions of archaic Europe, Asia, Africa, and the Americas, especially the laws, religious teachings, and philosophical principles of those ancient times. And I noted a pattern in the interplay of these "propensities," namely, that Asian and African values occupied opposite ends of one continuum, European and indigenous American values the opposing poles of another.

In the third part, I argued that the reason those values fall into these patterns is that the four archetypal peoples (two dimensions) evolved subtly different neural structures, which, combined with cultural influences, led to different ways of seeing, valuing, and interacting with the world. These differences in values defined fears particular to the four cultures, and the desire to protect ourselves against these fears prompted our ancestors to search for talismans wherever they could. Among the many possible talismans, money and property were, and are, especially popular.

I arranged this information in a fourfold framework, the Quaternary, similar to that which Hippocrates and Galen had employed in the West, the Ajurvedic philosophers in the East. I proposed a general temperament quaternary and financial temperament quaternaries, all analogous, for each of three levels of observation—individual, family, and sociocultural. In technical psychological terms, I called the two dimensions acquisition/affiliation and divergence/convergence; in more popular terms, Driver/Amiable and Expressive/Analytic; and, in financial terms, take/give and spend/save. I supported the Quaternary with confluent research findings from neurophysiology, psychometrics, and psychoanalysis and proposed it as a "grand moderator" for a biopsychosocial model of the process through which people attribute meaning to money and property, to remind us that money and property mean different things to different kinds of people at different times in their lives.

According to this model, natural selection has embedded in our neurons, and cultural selection in our memories, sensitivities—"survival triggers"— that provide the foundation for each of the four types. Analytics are threatened by too much stimulation (i.e., "disarray"), Expressives by too little ("constraint"); Drivers are threatened by too much nurturance ("incompetence"), Amiables by too little ("abandonment"). By matching bodily sensations with social messages, people learn that using money and property in some ways creates a threat, in other ways leads to a reduction in threat. Thus they learn that fears are the foundation for meaning and that money and property are talismans against those fears. From this beginning people have built enormously complex networks of meaning.

Against this summary, we can now explore some possible uses for this work.

APPLICATIONS AND IMPLICATIONS

Sales and Advertising

Four-part structures have been widely used in sales for many years (e.g., Alessandra & O'Connor, 1990; Doyle & Houk, 1990; Merrill & Reid, 1981;

Driver: The Conquering Self	*Expressive: The Unfettered Self*
Signs: Buys quality. Tends to over-extend. Enjoys risk. Competitive.	*Signs:* Generous. Spends freely, even impulsively. Takes undue risk.
Financial propensities: To take, wrest.	*Financial propensities:* To spend, dissipate.
Visible image: "I'm a winner!"	*Visible image:* "Look, I'm special!"
Fear: Being judged incompetent.	*Fear:* Being constrained, boring/bored.
Persuaded by: Pragmatics—bottom line.	*Persuaded by:* Testimonials, charisma.
Talisman: Buys "badges of accomplishment," e.g., Armani suits, Lexus autos.	*Talisman:* Buys to be admired, noticed—drama, flamboyance, extravagance.
Analytic: The Managed Self	*Amiable: The Affiliating Self*
Signs: Dependable, systematic. Saves a lot. Likes bargains. Avoids risk. Indecisive.	*Signs:* Cooperative, giving, compliant. Financially passive, even dependent.
Financial propensities: To save, hoard.	*Financial propensities:* To give, divest.
Visible image: "I'm steady."	*Visible image:* "I'm wholesome."
Fear: Losing control.	*Fear:* Isolation, not being taken care of.
Persuaded by: Data and logic.	*Persuaded by:* Warm relating.
Talisman: Buys security, e.g., insurance, treasury securities.	*Talisman:* Disdains symbols of accomplishment; uses money to attract, nourish.

Figure 10.1. The Quaternary in Sales and Advertising

Wilson Learning Corporation, 1984). Sales personnel are trained to estimate a prospect's temperament ("social style") on the basis of a variety of verbal and physical cues, then to gear the pitch to it. Figure 10.1 provides the kind of information used in this process: identification signs, financial propensities, projected images, characteristic fears, keys to persuasion, and talismans.

In the hands of a skilled salesperson, the Quaternary can be a useful tool for quickly sizing up and persuading a client. The task becomes more complicated when the salesperson must deal with two or more prospects at the same time, for example, business partners or husband and wife, who seem seldom to share the same temperament. Generally, the best the salesperson can do is either alternate the approach between the two prospects or direct most of the pitch at the (presumed) decision maker, at great risk of offending the other prospect and losing the sale.

Using the Quaternary in advertising is markedly more difficult than using it in sales, because the advertiser doesn't have the luxury of sizing up only one or two prospects at a time. Indeed, some advertising and marketing professionals have argued that the heterogeneity of media audiences makes it impossible to direct a message to one type without offending the others, particularly the polar opposite. On the other hand, Saab, America Online, and other companies have sponsored ads that seem to appeal to two or more types simultaneously.

In contrast to traditional mass media advertising, however, *interactive* advertising (e.g., Wells, 1995) provides an excellent opportunity to test the effectiveness of the Quaternary. It would be a simple matter to offer Driver, Amiable, Expressive, and Analytic options on an early screen, followed by different branches for the different types of people, along with a variety of intent-to-purchase outcome measures. One could even prepare a short test or questionnaire to help people choose among the temperaments. Because advertising is a "blunt instrument" and message production expensive, it is questionable whether further breakdown of the typology would prove cost-effective, for example, to secondary types.

Another application of quadrant theory in sales and advertising would be to help understand the psychological connotations of the products them-selves. Gossage (1967) and Dichter (1971) advocate the psychoanalytic study of psychological implications. Inglis (1972) and Packard (1957) pro-vide lively critiques of advertising. After the fashion of the FCB grid (e.g., Ratchford, 1987), the quadrants can help identify the characteristics of the product, so the different characteristics may be matched to the different target audiences. While the FCB grid and similar "perceptual mapping" approaches (see Davis, 1997, chap. 18) assign a product to a category to help specify a message, the Quaternary additionally invites a different product message for each personality type (Figure 10.?). For cellular phones, for example, the pitch to Drivers might be that the phones help you stay on top of business; to Amiables, that they keep you in touch with your family; to Expressives, that they signify "a certain cachet"; to Analytics, that they ensure safety at an affordable price.

In comparison to traditional market research, the Quaternary framework has some disadvantages and some advantages. Its principal disadvantage is that it collects much less detailed information, so it may not give the creative staff as much to work with in devising messages to reach the target audience. On the other hand, if we are willing to go forward on the basis of content validity and clinical inference, the Quaternary provides an enormous amount of information that should be useful to the creative staff. Additionally, it is cheaper than traditional market research, and often easier to understand. In the best of worlds, advertising and marketing researchers could use the

Driver: To Prove Competence	*Expressive: To Express Individuality*
Investments: Growth stocks for profit	*Investments:* Go-go stocks for pizzazz
Cell phone: Keep on top of business	*Cell phone:* Sex appeal, self-esteem
Life insurance: Profitable, reduces estate tax	*Life insurance:* Worth way more than average
Political candidate: Law and order	*Political candidate:* "I *am* somebody!"
Analytic: To Assure Security	*Amiable: To Nourish Relationships*
Investments: Treasury bills for return/safety	*Investments:* Bank accounts, to avoid evil
Cell phone: "This deal can't be beat"	*Cell phone:* Keep your family safe
Life insurance: Protection plus a conservative investment	*Life insurance:* You can't replace love, but you can make sure they're taken care of
Political candidate: Stop wasteful spending	*Political candidate:* "I feel your pain"

Figure 10.2. The Quaternary and Product Characteristics

Quaternary to organize the campaign and give it psychological depth, employing traditional market research to flesh out their inferences.

In comparison to traditional research, the Quaternary *model* makes matters at once more simple and more complex. It sharpens our search for salient signs, but it requires us to build parallel models for the different types of people. Most researchers and practitioners assume that different people see the world the same way but are conditioned to react differently to it. Quadrant theory asserts that people actually perceive the world differently, through especially keen sensing, feeling, intuiting, or thinking capabilities. To the extent this is true, we will, in the spirit of Sol Worth (Worth & Adair, 1972), have to build different models to describe how the various kinds of people perceive sales and advertising stimulation—not just what stimuli they prefer and how they arrive at that preference, but how those operations and preferences incline them toward buying.

Personnel Compensation

Thirty years ago, Opsahl and Dunnette (1966, p. 118) urged greater attention to the symbolism of money in personnel management, especially compensation. Lawler (1971, 1990) concentrated on instrumentality, arguing that pay takes on greater meaning as it leads to more valued outcomes and that the greater the meaning it carries, the more it should affect on-the-job performance. Thierry (1984, 1992) expanded on Lawler's work, proposing that pay is important to the extent that it communicates something germane to the worker's self-concept (1992, p. 701). He also proposed that a compensation system must attend to what pay says about the worker's relative position with regard to other workers, to the level of control workers feel they have when they are paid in terms of their effects on other people, and to the meaning of the goods that workers can purchase with the money they are paid.

The quadrants connect with and build on Thierry's theory in a number of ways. First, as a framework, they describe four archetypal self-concepts with which pay may "communicate," what we might call, following Thierry's lead, the Masterful Self (Driver), the Affiliating Self (Amiable), the Unfettered Self (Expressive), and the Managed Self (Analytic). Second, as in sales and advertising, the quadrants suggest that we may need different theories (subtheories) of compensation for the different worker temperaments: a theory for the worker who is attracted by the opportunity to compete for relative position versus the one who is put off by competition (Driver vs. Amiable); a theory for the worker who enjoys trying to persuade other people versus one that hates it (Expressive vs. Analytic); and, of course, the four dimensions of the theory for the meanings of the goods that workers purchase with their pay. Indeed, if managers and supervisors could discern an employee's temperament, they could, like the salespeople above, make some educated guesses as to what's likely to motivate that employee. The chances seem good that managers who use the total compensation package to communicate type-linked messages to employees will have better results than managers who simply deliver paychecks. The same line of thinking applies to vocational and educational counseling.

Cross-Cultural Communications

In her enormously popular books on spousal communication, Tannen (e.g., 1990; see also Gray, 1993) describes the male and female worlds as different cultures and tries to decode the communications from one to the other. In similar fashion, Kochman (1981) tries to bridge the gap between African American and European American cultures by demonstrating how the people in one group often misunderstand the behavior of the people in the other group. Many of the stylistic differences that Tannen, Kochman, and others have observed are specific instances of the patterns of which quadrant theory speaks.

Indeed, I'm inclined to believe that money conflicts[1] among cultural groups—occupational groups, geographical groups, political groups, ethnic groups, as well as gender and race groups—can be better understood through the Quaternary than through more conventional methods of analysis. For example, salespeople and accountants are often at odds with regard to mutual clients. If we think of the salespeople and accountants as representatives of opposing cultures, the sales culture largely Expressive and the accounting culture largely Analytic, we understand more about the different people and how to approach them. The tensions between the Korean and Black residents of South Central Los Angeles are another example of the Analytic-Expressive cultural dialectic. Finally, capitalists and socialists the world over are easier to understand if we think of their mutual opposition as yet another instance of the tension between risk preference and risk aversion. Heilbroner (1985) describes capitalists in similar (if more politically charged) terms.

According to quadrant theory, the first step toward doing business, engaging in politics, or building personal relationships across these cultures would be, as it is in sales and advertising, to assess temperament on the basis of the Quaternary. Once temperament is tentatively identified, the theory suggests how people of that type are likely to think, feel, and behave about money and property; with whom they are likely to conflict and for what reasons; what fears they probably harbor; and to which kind of approach they are likely to warm. On the individual level—this particular prospect, supplier, boss, employee, or negotiator—the rest of the process is just like one-on-one sales; on the group level—getting different groups to buy the same product or follow the same leader—the process is just like advertising.

Self-Understanding and Psychological Assessment

The Delphic oracle surely understood that to "know thyself" is one of the most demanding tasks a person can undertake. The better we know ourselves, the better decisions we are likely to make about the role of money and property in our lives, and, conversely, the better we read the messages our financial behaviors send us, the better we will understand ourselves in general.

One approach to self-understanding is through psychometric assessment on the individual, family, and societal levels. On the individual level, assessment instruments based on (or consistent with) the Quaternary could be useful in personnel management (e.g., to estimate how to reward and compensate employees), in vocational/educational advising (e.g., to identify careers that clients will probably find more consistent with their financial values), and in personal financial counseling (e.g., to infer values, attitudes, and motives, and to hypothesize underlying psychodynamics, all for the purpose of making more informed saving and spending decisions). The Myers-Briggs Type Indicator (Myers & McCaulley, 1988) is the most widely used Quaternary instrument, though it is not explicit about money and property. Quadrant theory could help extend the usefulness of the Myers-Briggs Type Indicator further into the financial counseling domain (e.g., Anastasi, 1992; Brock, 1994; Doyle, 1991). It could also expand the inventory's theoretical foundation. The appendix in this book presents an annotated bibliography of good books on the psychology of money and property, many of the self-help genre.

On the family level, assessment instruments could be useful in identifying similarities and differences in how different members of the family think, feel, and behave about money and property. Such assessments could be especially useful in marriage and family counseling, in marriage "renewal," and in premarital counseling, to say nothing of family financial counseling and planning (cf. Doyle & Houk, 1990; Feldman, 1976; Garman, 1997, chaps. 7, 12; Garman & Forgue, 1997, chap. 5; van Arsdale, 1982). Olson's (1986) circumplex model of family relations is a Quaternary model, as is the "exit-voice-loyalty-neglect," or EVLN,[2] model of Rusbult, Johnson, and Morrow (1986). As with the Myers-Briggs Type Indicator, the Quaternary can add foundation to these models and measures.

Finally, on the societal level, assessment instruments could help provide insights for improving cross-cultural communication with regard to money and property, and deeper understanding about the meaning of wealth and poverty across and within cultures and subcultures to inform policy decisions. Douglas (1970) provides a schema consistent with our Quaternary, her well-known "grid/group classification." I envision the Quaternary used to "map" societies on the quadrants, not unlike the mapping of consumer products or messages (Doyle, 1992c; see also Adams, 1994; Cooper, 1976; Rapoport, 1969). In these cases, quadrant theory would invite more attention than other systems to the fears, pleasures, and unconscious processes that influence interpersonal and intergroup relations. Benedict (1934) and Hall (1959) provide alternative sociocultural classification schemas.

Regardless of level of analysis, assessment in terms of the Quaternary is more explicitly dialectical than conventional assessment. Because the foundation of the Quaternary framework is a crossed pair of bipolar continua, the types and attributes we observe are always in tension with contrary or contradictory ones, whether conscious or unconscious. Accordingly, quadrant theory contemplates not just "need achievement," as McClelland (1961) did, but need achievement in tension with "need affiliation";[3] not just a yearning for freedom, but such an inclination in opposition to a deep-seated fear of constraint. Attending to this dynamism reduces our amazement at, for example, the youthful anarchist who turns stockbroker, or the banker who sells all he has and becomes a social worker in Appalachia. It leads us to expect that, in intimate relationships, opposites will attract (and then drive each other crazy) and that, under the pressure of divorce, for example, the nurturant partner will, at least for the moment, become the aggressor, while the masterful one becomes the victim. These dynamics require more difficult classification decisions, but they add a bit more realism to the assessment. Quadrant theory requires us to envision individuals and groups not as static collections of traits but as dynamic systems of attributes-in-tension.

Money and Intimacy

Few if any aspects of intimate relationships occasion so much misunderstanding and conflict as money (Blood & Wolfe, 1960; Blumstein & Schwartz, 1983; Katz, 1993). If I lack sufficient insight to recognize that my buying habits are efforts at one-upmanship intended to protect myself from deep-seated feelings of incompetence and inferiority and that for those reasons I'm driven not merely to keep up with the Joneses but actually to out-spend them, I simply won't understand what my spouse means when she complains about my "materialism." At the same time, if she can't see that the gifts she gives her friends and family go way beyond normal affection, she won't understand it when people criticize her for overspending, and she won't recognize her desperate need for affection, or how her neediness clashes with my own. She will see her behavior as sensitive and generous, but others will see it as trying "to buy love." Without attending to the talismanic meanings of money and property, she and I will continue to snipe at one another about our surface behavior, never getting to the real issues. Worse still, we will fail to take advantage of the opportunity for intimacy—for deeper understanding, respect, trust, and mutual self-revelation—that conflicts about money and property can facilitate.

Money and property often make their appearance early in the evolution of intimacy, generally in an effort to win the attention, affection, or respect of the other person; as incentive or compensation for one kind of service or another, not infrequently sexual; to state (or misrepresent) one's assets, fears, values, and aspirations; or even to bully other people or elicit pity from them. By examining themselves in terms of the symbolic meanings associated with the quadrants, the partners can use money and property to discover more about themselves and each other for the purpose of helping to foster intimacy.

At the other extreme, when intimacy fails couples often separate. Participants and observers will surely agree that the adversarial dissolution process—divorce, American style—not only strips away people's defenses in public but also invites all manner of confusion and dysfunction at a time when people are particularly angry, vulnerable, and frightened. Money is both sword and shield in this combat, both weapon and talisman. Behind and beneath its economic value, money in divorce means security to people whose security is acutely threatened; affiliation to people whose family life is being ripped apart; achievement to people who view themselves as having failed, at least at marriage; and dignity to people who feel awash in humiliation. No wonder people battle to the death over a ratty old desk or an aging lawnmower. To make matters worse, the principals are generally represented by people of Driver temperament, with their own psychological needs to satisfy, problems to resolve, and fears against which to defend. Clients can become pawns in a game in which lawyers struggle to work through their own neurotic fears.

Psychopathology and Misbehavior

Quadrant theory suggests that people tend toward excesses that are consistent with their financial temperaments: Drivers become more rapacious, Amiables more needy, Expressives more prodigal, and Analytics more niggardly. Thus money and property are not just media through which people express themselves but tools (as Aristotle recognized) that can bring out the worst in us, perhaps more readily than the best.

Some individual misbehaviors seem clearly aligned with particular temperaments: hoarding with the Analytic temperament, for example, and overspending with the Expressive. Indeed, the *meaning of the misbehavior* seems as related to temperament as does the meaning of money and property—the physiological state combined with the social message (Faber, 1992; O'Guinn & Faber, 1989). In the case of problematic gaming, for example, quadrant theory says that Drivers gamble to demonstrate their mastery of the game; hence we ought to find them playing blackjack or betting on horses more often than participating in chance games like roulette, slots, or bingo. Expressives should prefer games that involve an admiring crowd; craps, perhaps, or even the beloved three-card monte. Amiables and Analytics seem less likely to gamble, for they should view gambling as a threat to soul or savings; if they do play, Amiables might do so to numb their loneliness (e.g., through the rhythm of the slots or the din of the crowd), Analytics—least likely gamblers of all—to test a "system" that is supposed to shift the odds in their favor. In the Quaternary, extreme behavior is misbehavior, and it comes from biology, culture, and the repressed drives of the shadow. Quadrant theory leads us to view financial misbehaviors as no less talismanic than other financial behaviors: People engage in misbehavior to protect themselves against threat.

This interpretation is implicit in the *DSM-IV* (American Psychiatric Association, 1994) classification of personality disorders,[4] in which some of the diagnostic criteria are explicitly financial (Table 10.1). This connection between financial behaviors and diagnostic signs provides the opportunity to extend the validity of the Quaternary by expanding the core constructs to equate extreme behavior with personality disorders and correlating those with clinical evaluations and with personality inventories such as the Minnesota Multiphasic Personality Inventory (MMPI; Hathaway & McKinley, 1951; MMPI-2; Butcher, 1990) and the California Psychological Inventory (CPI; Gough, 1957). If the connections are confirmed, quadrant theory could help clinicians make more dynamic diagnoses (e.g., involving dialectical relationships), and perhaps more efficient or reliable diagnoses (because financial behavior is so readily observable). The same patterns exist on the family and sociocultural levels, where excess to the point of "running amok" is equivalent to individual personality disorder (e.g., China's Cultural Revolution).

Interpreting the Entitlement Debates

Quadrant theory asserts that temperament governs social and political attitudes and values. When Conservatives argue that we need to "privatize" health care, they are protesting much more than "Liberal tax-and-spend policies." They are protesting other people's inability to see the social world through capitalist eyes; they are exhorting people to take care of themselves, to stand up and "fight and take risks." What they are saying on a deeper level is that to rely on the collective would be to admit to the deep-down fear that they are incompetent, unable to cope with life's demands, too frightened to

TABLE 10.1 Financial Misbehavior in Quaternary

Financial	Driver	Amiable	Expressive	Analytic
Temperament	Choleric	Melancholic	Sanguine	Phlegmatic
Financial	Taking (having)	Giving (needing)	Spending	Saving
Propensity	Wresting	Divesting	Dissipating	Hoarding

Individual level (DSM-IV)

Personality	Borderline	Dependent	Hysteric	Obsessive/
Disorders	Antisocial		Narcissistic	compulsive
	Conduct Disorder			Avoidant
	Histrionic			Schizoid
				Schizotypal
				Paranoid
Selected	Aggressiveness,	Clingy; wants	Unrestrained	Hoarding,
DSM-IV	confrontative	others to take	buying sprees;	niggardly,
diagnostic	theft, e.g.,	care of one;	foolish business	obsessed
criteria, with	armed robbery,	desperate for	investments;	with detail
money/property	mugging;	nurturance;	fantasies	and rules,
emphasis	bullying	needs reassurance	of plenty	avoidant

Family level (Olson)

Dysfunction	Rigidly	Chaotically	Chaotically	Rigidly
	disengaged	enmeshed	disengaged	enmeshed

Societal level

Propensity	Wresting	Divesting	Dissipating	Hoarding
Economic	Structured	Unstructured	Unstructured	Structured
philosophy	imperialism	communism	imperialism	communism
Dysfunction	Acquisition	Affiliation	Freedom	Control run
	run amok	run amok	run amok	amok

take care of themselves and their families. When, at the same time, Liberals argue for "socialized medicine," "national health care," or, most recently, "managed health care," they are arguing for more than compassion, nurturance, and "lovingkindness"—they are saying that the task is too big and the risks are too frightening to face all alone. More deeply still, they are saying that they have nothing, and, having nothing, they deserve what others have. (For a compatible analysis, see Gilder, 1981, chaps. 5 and 6, and Heilbroner,

1985. For essays on envy and jealousy, see van den Haag, 1975, and Salovey, 1991.)

Liberal observers will interpret Conservative efforts to limit entitlement programs as threats against the vulnerable members of society. Because to threaten the vulnerable is the ultimate sin, Liberals will unleash their most fearsome weapons—attacks based on their own highest values. They will accuse the Conservatives of trying to cast widows out into the cold, pull the rug out from under the disabled, and rip the last morsels of bread from the mouths of starving children. Their rage is the stronger because they identify with the vulnerable and therefore feel under personal attack. At the same time, Conservatives will interpret Liberal attempts to build solidarity by redistributing wealth as nothing less than a declaration of war, and, like Liberals, they will unsheathe their sharpest weapons. They will say that the Liberals are thieves and extortionists, that they want to support lazy and deceitful people at the expense of the beleaguered middle-class worker, that Liberals are nothing more than communists out to destroy the American way of life. Conservatives and Liberals alike will focus on the people for whom they have the least respect, the people least like themselves: for the Conservatives, those who have been unable or unwilling to compete in the marketplace, for example, welfare recipients; for the Liberals, those who have accumulated money through "evil" means, that is, most businessmen. The ancient debate about individual versus communal property still stirs up the deepest fears and elicits the most vicious defenses.

Retirement Saving and Investing

Temperament also governs how much, and in what manner, people save for retirement.[5] As Merrill and Reid (1981) and others have pointed out, Analytics can be expected to save more systematically than other types, but they can also be expected to put their money into excessively conservative instruments like insured savings accounts, leaving themselves vulnerable to inflation. Drivers can also be expected to save more than Amiables and Expressives, but Drivers are also more likely to raid their retirement accounts for opportunities that seem more important or profitable in the present moment. Amiables are not likely to save effectively unless or until they discover that there is no one around to take care of them. In a relationship, they will submit to their partner's plan; on their own, they will be excessively cautious. Finally, Expressives are likely to invest sporadically, but they are just as likely to withdraw the money impulsively and to take excessive risk for the sheer pleasure of the ride and the joy of describing (and exaggerating) their experiences to others.

Quadrant theory suggests that, if government agencies, banks, insurance companies, and investment houses are serious about encouraging people to rely less on Social Security retirement benefits, they will need to send more refined messages to different market segments, that is, to people of the different types: to Amiables, messages that make self-reliance sound attractive ("Don't be a burden on your children."); to Drivers, messages about staying on top of things in the future as well as now; to Analytics, about inflation risk; and, finally, to Expressives, messages about future freedom and dignity—combined with an automatic investment program (e.g., Doyle, 1991-1998, 1992a). The key is to touch on the different fears, without unduly stoking them, and without offending one type of person while trying to reach the others.

The Worthy and the Unworthy

In the background of many economic debates lurks the distinction between the "worthy" and "unworthy" poor and, for that matter, the worthy and unworthy rich. Capitalists (in quadrant terms) fight especially hard to keep from having to give money and property to the unworthy poor; socialists fight especially hard to strip money and property from the unworthy rich.

Quadrant theory can help us understand worthiness. The most worthy are those who are most like us, whoever we are; the least worthy, those least like us. To tough-minded capitalists, poverty of most sorts is a badge of incompetence. To them, I hypothesize, the worthy poor are those who are fundamentally strong, though perhaps temporarily down on their luck, and who, in behavior as well as words, express appreciation for any help they receive—in other words, those who admit that they are capitalists at heart and acknowledge their debt to other capitalists who are higher up the ladder. The unworthy poor are those who come across as shiftless ("lazy bums") and dishonest ("welfare cheats"), whether or not they have much control over those attributes in themselves, and who are also unappreciative, that is, who refuse to kowtow. A curious remnant from Puritan days, the unworthy poor seem also to be viewed as sexually promiscuous.

The unworthy rich (to socialists) are those who come across as arrogant, miserly, and hard-hearted, who put business before family, and, perhaps worst of all, who are tainted by connections with organized capitalism, that is, the corporate world. Another reflection of the inclination to insult others in terms that would insult us and to project our greatest anxieties onto others, the unworthy rich (Drivers) are widely considered, or hoped to be, sexless and isolated, two of the deepest Amiable fears. The worthy rich are just the opposite—modest, generous, warm, sensitive, and so forth—in other words, nearly as tenderhearted and nonthreatening as socialists see themselves. It is as though the worthy poor became impoverished through some cosmic accident, and the worthy rich became wealthy through some fiscal virgin birth.

Our definitions of unworthiness always come down to *that which threatens us,* where the threat is that which is different, particularly that which is, in Quaternary terms, contradictory. Because people of various races and ethnic groups tend also to be of systematically different temperaments, the perceptions, values, and behavioral styles of contrary and contradictory racial groups can be expected to grate on each other. It follows, then, that we will tend to view rich and poor people who belong to racial and ethnic groups other than our own as unworthy and assume that their wealth is undeserved, their poverty just and proper, no matter which racial or ethnic group we belong to. Thus to Whites the wealthy Black must be a drug dealer or equivalent, and, to Blacks, the wealthy White must have made his money "off the backs of the poor."

As we have already seen, capitalists see the world vertically, as a ladder on which everybody competes for his or her rightful place; socialists see the world horizontally, as a commune or utopian community in which to stand out is sinful, and where one's responsibility is to give according to one's means, to take according to one's need. Fear leads voters to translate abstract social uncertainty and vague economic dissatisfaction into whatever concrete fears they themselves finds more upsetting—the fear of being pushed off the capitalist ladder or the fear of being expelled from the socialist commune. Because people's responses to fear are swift and sure, fund-raising and vote-gathering efforts that blend emotional arguments with rational ones (e.g., Shah, Domke, & Wackman, 1996) should be more effective than conventional, wholly rational approaches, and campaigns that go straight to fear should be more effective still: "It's the economy, stupid!"

"The Wealth of Nations"

As we have already seen, Nietzsche (1887/1974) and McClelland (1961) and Atkinson (1964) spelled out dialectical, ebb-and-flow theories of societal evolution. Nietzsche observed that minorities throughout history have had a way of causing disdain for the majority's values, with the result that the majority is eventually overthrown, the old minority becomes the new majority, and the cycle begins again.

McClelland described a pattern in which increasing need achievement in a given culture predicts economic success two or three generations later, and that very success then leads to decreasing need achievement and subsequent economic decline.[6] He measured need achievement in cultures by counting entrepreneurial references in the society's literature; he measured it in individuals through stories told in response to Thematic Apperception Test (TAT) pictures. He confirmed his theory in classical Greece, pre-Incan Peru, Spain in the Late Middle Ages, and England prior to the Industrial Revolution.

McClelland found a dramatic increase in signs of need achievement in Russian children's readers from 1925 to 1950, and he attributed the change to the new political ideology that stressed individual achievement over passive dependence on authoritarian forces beyond the individual's control (1961, p. 413). He generalized his prediction to China on the basis of similarities of Communist Party literature in the two countries (pp. 412, 423). Fifty years before the fact, his data predicted an increase in capitalistic activity in both countries beginning two to three generations after 1940-1950, that is, in the 1990s and beyond. Current events seem to confirm that prediction.

In the light of that remarkable fact, McClelland's American data are troubling. Also on the basis of children's readers, he observed a sharp and steady increase in need achievement in the United States from about 1830 to 1890, then a steep and steady drop until the 1950s. The rise to 1890 would predict increasing economic development into the 1940-1950s; the fall of need achievement into the 1950s would predict economic decline early in the twenty-first century. The accuracy of this prediction remains to be seen.

Because quadrant theory's Driver/Amiable dimension is equivalent to McClelland's need achievement/need affiliation categories, replicating McClelland's approach with the quadrants could extend his important work to countries in which he did not collect data, particularly Asian and African countries. In addition, the Expressive/Analytic dimension could add additional foundation to the prediction, again particularly in Asia and Africa and especially in reference to dictatorships, anarchy, and political stability (cf. McClelland, 1961, pp. 168-169, 203).

The addition of the Expressive/Analytic dimension would be especially timely because of the dramatic political and economic development expected in Asia during the twenty-first century, and, it is hoped, also in Africa.[7] One of the most interesting situations is the reaffiliation of Hong Kong with the People's Republic of China, for this reunion juxtaposes China's archetypically Asian political system with Hong Kong's largely European (British) business style. This test of the ability of socialism and capitalism to live together—"one country, two systems"—will be of great interest to Asia in general, Taiwan in particular, and it should be of significant interest throughout the world. For a fresh analysis of "the changeover," see Lee (1998, in press).

McClelland did not collect data in Hong Kong or the People's Republic. Quadrant theory, however, would suggest guarded optimism, for the Analytic propensity of the People's Republic and the Driver propensity of Hong Kong are united by a common Toughmindedness; they are contrary, not contradictory, and similar in attributes likely to support a market economy. On one level, the issue will be whether Beijing's Analytics will be able to let Hong Kong's Drivers receive and enjoy the rewards capitalists need to maintain and even build their momentum, and whether Hong Kong's irascible Drivers can maintain a respectful posture toward Beijing when the inevitable tensions arise. On a deeper level, Hong Kong's future will also be influenced by the envy that many people on the mainland seem to feel toward Hong Kong, and the jealousy Hong Kong can be expected to feel toward its privileges. In collision, these two emotions could result in an internecine Cold War that could jeopardize both systems.[8] The biggest danger seems to be that Beijing, despite the best of intentions, might fail to give Hong Kong the freedom it requires to function as a world-class risk-taking, reward-enjoying economy. It would be especially interesting to compare this kind of prediction with a politically more sophisticated prediction (e.g., Huntington, 1996, p. 245).

Economic Theory

Consistent with Katona's (1951) emphasis on identifying individual and group differences in economic phenomena, quadrant theory argues that researchers trying to understand why people spend, save, borrow, and so forth need to look separately at various "markets" defined by temperament. Indeed, it would suggest that modern economics has provided an elegant theory of the Driver quadrant, just as Freud provided an elegant theory of the Analytic. What motivates Analytic markets (like the accounting and computer industries) should be very different from what motivates Expressive, Amiable, or Driver markets, and how Driver markets—for example, Wall

Street traders—will react to predictions of prosperity or recession ought to be very different from how Amiable, Expressive, or Analytic markets will react. Just as quadrant theory proposes that we might need a distinct theory of perception for each of the four propensities (or at least the two dimensions), it proposes that we might need different theories of consumption, saving, and investing for each. Burggraf (1997) makes exactly this point in reference to "the feminine economy." In addition, the dynamics of the quadrant model may help explain cycles of economic change and the behavior of groups under stress.

Scitovsky (1992, e.g., p. iv) extended the utility model to include not just the relieving or forestalling of discomfort—Hawtrey's (1925) "defensive" variables—but the active pursuit of pleasure—the "creative" variables. He challenged conventional economic theory by demonstrating (as the Epicurean Greeks had maintained) that "more" or "better" does not necessarily mean an increase in pleasure and that welfare or happiness does not automatically increase if consumption rises or becomes more uniform. Drawing especially on Hebb and Berlyne, he distinguished between high-arousal and low-arousal people—he quotes Eysenck on Extraversion and Introversion—and observed that economic models concentrate on the latter, neglect the former. Quadrant theory employs essentially the same foundation, but with the advantage of recent advances in neuroscience, and builds on it a more complex psychology.

As indicated above, Herrnstein (1990; Prelec & Herrnstein, 1991; Rachlin & Laibson, 1997; see also Leibenstein, 1996) underscores the utility model's inability to explain such common misbehaviors as drinking too much and spending money foolishly. He proposed the matching law as an equally rigorous but more psychologically satisfying alternative to utility theory. Quadrant theory is more compatible with the matching law than with rational choice theory, for an essential part of quadrant theory is the identification of the powerful "irrational" drives that govern human behavior. Quadrant theory, however, is not so general as the matching law (or rational choice theory). Its role in the debate between economists and analytic psychologists is to remind theorists in both camps that "individual differences do, in fact, exist" and that theories born in either laboratory need to mature in the real world.

This narrowness in formal utility theory should become increasingly a problem as the economic world becomes more cross-national and cross-cultural, for theories that work in the majority of European and European American markets will probably not work so well in Asian, African, and

American Indian markets, or in others that share those diverse propensities. Even within the European American world, conventional economic models should not work so well outside the Driver subcells. The less Puritan the attitude of an individual or a group, the less valid utility theory is likely to be.

The subjectivity of most psychological measures is another reason for the distance that stands between economics and psychology. Although it would be something worse than inconvenient to measure the production and utilization of dopamine, norepinephrine, androgen, and the like on representative samples of the world's population, such measures on a limited, experimental basis might provide the combination of objectivity and differentiation that could bring the two disciplines closer together, the kind of objectivity for which Scitovsky looked to Hebb and Berlyne. If neurophysiological variables, singly or in combination, or in concert with other variables, were found to predict giving, taking, saving, and spending, the benefit to both disciplines would be immeasurable. Furthermore, as relationships involving these chemicals, the dimensions of temperament, and individual and group financial behavior under various circumstances and at different life stages become better understood, quadrant theory and the matching law, perhaps even rational choice theory, might begin to fit together. In the meantime, subjective temperament measures—questionnaires and, say, the TAT— validated experimentally against biochemistry after the fashion of Reinisch and Sanders (1992) may be enough to intrigue the more adventurous of the experimental psychologists and analytic economists, that is, the low-dopamine types.

A CLOSING WORD ON RESEARCH

It's important to bear in mind, as I cautioned at the beginning, that this is a book intended more to stimulate research than report it. The musings, assertions, suggestions, proposals, and (in their Sunday best) *hypotheses* presented here are only that—not demonstrated fact—until independent researchers are satisfied that the framework and model are reliable and valid foundations for interpreting the meanings people associate with money and property and that the inferences we draw are themselves dependable and meaningful.

High on the agenda is the formal validation of the principal hypothetical constructs—Driver, Amiable, Expressive, and Analytic types, a.k.a. the acquisition/affiliation dimension, rooted in too little versus too much nurturance, and the divergence/convergence dimension rooted in too little versus too much stimulation. I have tried to lay the foundation for research of that sort by providing a large number of four-part figures and tables, across which researchers can simply accumulate characteristics for each construct until a working definition emerges. This is traditional cross-disciplinary construct validation, and Cronbach and Meehl (1955) and Campbell and Fiske (1959) are still the primary guides. Elsewhere, I have described the propensities the various social science disciplines display in cross-disciplinary effort (Doyle, 1992b).

Validation research needs to pay at least as much attention to process as to structure, despite our inclination to equate psychological science with the study of covariance. Although it will be tempting (for example) to concentrate on testing the "Final Four" Quaternary structure against the Big Three and Giant Five (p. 146 in Chapter 8), researchers should direct the majority of their attention to studying the ways the different kinds of people connect meaning to money, using the Quaternary as moderator. Studying differences in the structure and function of the mechanisms of perception will surely be exceptionally demanding, and potentially of enormous benefit. Determining the biological origins of the values specified in the matching law will be no less arduous, and no less profitable.

The nearly complete disregard of the unconscious has not been one of scientific psychology's greatest achievements. Murray's TAT, so productive four decades ago, still seems more likely to get at unconscious (semiconscious) phenomena than contemporary questionnaires and surveys (see Atkinson, 1964; McClelland, 1961; Murray, 1938). The interface between Edelman's (1992) neurophysiology, Bruner's (1990) cognitive psychology, Cloninger's (1987) psychiatry, and Tellegen's (1985) and Zuckerman's (1994) psychometrics looks most promising in this regard. Csikszentmihalyi's notion of "flow" (e.g., 1996, 1997) may provide an additional mechanism for connecting the individual and the environment.

Another need is for collaboration between researchers in the Academy and people truly experienced with money and property, whether at home, at work, at play, or on Capitol Hill and Wall Street. Outside of business schools and a few other applied locations, many academics are at least publicly contemptuous of money and property; with perhaps even fewer exceptions, businesspeople are equally disdainful of academic rites and rituals. Mutual disinterest, distrust, and disrespect have deprived both worlds of the fruits of the other's labors.

The study of the psychological meanings of money and property seems like an especially good place for occasional efforts at breaking out of the confines of single-discipline research programs, no matter how hard university administrative structures and departmental traditions try to discourage it. Research programs need neurophysiology and neurochemistry to identify the biological bases, psychometrics to quantify and articulate the constructs, and psychoanalysis and depth psychology to suggest more penetrating hypotheses and interpretations. Even more exciting, I think, would be the occasional program that incorporates the humanities into the empiricist mix, serious and popular fictional literature[9] from around the world, as well as law, religion, and philosophy. Shell (1982) offers penetrating insights into the isomorphism of economic and literary cognition, DiGaetani (1994) provides a nice collection of literary studies of the meanings of money, and Jackson (1995) organizes excerpts from a wide range of Western literature into a thesaurus of the imagination.

But it's the novelists and short story writers who can remind us of the juicier, more complete creature we set out to study, who can flesh out who we are with regard to money and property, how we relate to one another, and how we connect with the world around us. For example, Willa Cather (1905/1941), in *Paul's Case,* writes of the Expressive (and, by opposition, of the Analytic):

> His chief greediness lay in his ears and eyes, and his excesses were not offensive ones. . . . He had never lied for pleasure, even at school; but to make himself noticed and admired, to assert his difference from other Cordelia Street boys. (p. 66)

And Chekhov (1925/1941), in *The Darling,* tells us more about the Amiable (and the Driver):

> Oh, how she loved him! Not one of her other ties had been so deep. Never before had she given herself so completely, so disinterestedly, so cheerfully as now that her maternal instincts were all aroused. For this boy, who was not hers, for the dimples in his cheeks and for his big cap, she would have given her life, given it with joy and with tears of rapture. Why? Ah, indeed, why? (p. 246)

Finally, Steinbeck (1939) and John Donne (1624/1971) tell us about being a part of it all:

> If a man owns a little property that property is him, it's part of him and it's like him. If he owns property only so he can walk on it and handle it and be sad

when it isn't doing well, and feel fine when the rain falls on it, that property is him, and in some way he's bigger because he owns it. (*The Grapes of Wrath,* p. 39)

No man is an island, entire of itself; every man is a piece of the continent, a part of the main. . . . Any man's death diminishes me because I am involved in mankind, and therefore never send to know for whom the bell tolls; it tolls for thee. (*Meditation XVII,* 1623)

Notes

CHAPTER 1

1. **Willing to give up.** Whether or not we objectively have a surplus may be less important than whether or not we *feel* we have a surplus. See O'Guinn and Wells (1989) on "subjective discretionary income."

2. **Exchange our produce.** This situation comprises what economists call the "double coincidence of wants," a circumstance the rarity of which alone was enough that money had to be invented. See Newlyn (1971), cited in Crump (1981, p. 53).

3. **Go home happy.** Economists generally view the exchange as "self-liquidating," that is, with no lasting connection between the exchanging parties, social or otherwise. Other social scientists view this assumption as generally unrealistic. See Crump (1981, p. 54).

4. **Barter.** For thoughtful discussions on barter, see Humphrey and Hugh-Jones (1992), Sahlins (1972), Gregory (1997), and Lauterbach (1954).

5. **Portable, durable, etc.** These are the classic qualities of money. For elaboration, see Burstein (1963) and Galbraith (1975).

6. **Coins.** For essays on coins in primarily Western history, see Casson and Price (1981) and Porteus (1969). For essays on coins in Eastern history, see Glathe (1939) and Coole (1936). And for a Jungian interpretation of coins, see Lockhart (1983). For a recent and especially readable history of money, see Weatherford (1997); see also Williams (1998). For the classic histories of money, see Del Mar (1885/1968), Hepburn (1903), Quiggin (1949), and Angell (1929).

7. **Creates new money.** Part of the magic of banking is the creation of new money. For a discussion of this function, see Galbraith (1975, chap. 3). Good histories of banking include Knox (1969), Green (1989), and Piergiovanni (1993).

8. **Plastic card form.** Weatherford (1997) includes a particularly interesting discussion on the history of credit and debit cards, as well as checking and Internet banking. Sloan and Stovall (1993) and Fang (1997) provide broader histories of communication technology, within the context of which these innovations occurred.

9. **Occasional trysts.** As early as 1914, Wesley Mitchell, whom Schumpeter described as "the grand old man of economics" (quoted in Zelizer, 1994, p. 10), called for more association between economics and psychology, to bring passion and human variability into economic equations.

10. **More the utilitarian.** Alfred Marshall, whom Scitovsky called "the most distinguished British economist of the turn of the century," criticized Jevons and others for too much emphasis on the "lowest instincts of humanity" (Marshall, 1930, pp. 88-90). Scitovsky himself (1986, p. 187) called Jevons "the most abstract and formalistic economist of his time."

Marshall challenged the theory of consumption, the linchpin of scientific economics, arguing that "although it is man's wants in the earliest stages of his development that give rise to his activities, yet afterwards each new step upwards is to be regarded as the development of new activities giving rise to new wants, rather than of new wants giving rise to new activities" (Marshall, 1930, pp. 89-90; quoted in Scitovsky, 1986, p. 187).

11. **Welfare.** Welfare in this context refers not to assistance, or the "dole," but to the common weal, or "happiness." Happiness, sadly, has been largely neglected by social scientists in general, until very recently. For standard critiques of welfare economics, see Parsons and Smelser (1956, pp. 30-32) and Schumpeter (1954/1994, pp. 1069-1073). For studies of happiness, see, for example, Lykken and Tellegen (1996), Emmons (1986), Deiner (1994), and, of course, Aristotle.

12. **Diminishing marginal utilities.** The concept behind the utility equation, the consumption function, and diminishing marginal utilities originated with Jeremy Bentham but was formalized by John Maynard Keynes (1936, p. 96). The essence is that the more we earn, the more we will spend or save, but as our incomes grow our spending or savings increases less with each successive occasion. The psychologist's quarrel with this principle is that, at best, it describes some mythical average consumer, masking the interesting fact that some kinds of people will spend more than their incomes increase, and others will spend far less, for psychological rather than economic reasons.

In addition, although most goods do have "decreasing marginal utility," that is, people want a little less with each successive purchase, some items, like salted nuts and addictive drugs, have "increasing marginal utility," at least for a while. Money and property probably fall into the former category for some people (e.g., Drivers), the latter for others (e.g., Analytics).

13. **Objectively and efficiently.** An interesting side question is, What phenomena of nature and nurture have sorted these people into these two camps?

14. **General and comparative theory.** Harris, 1974, p. vii.

CHAPTER 2

1. **Born in Africa.** As anyone knows who monitors the *New York Times, U.S. News & World Report,* and other national media, discoveries about the origins of humans seem to be appearing nearly every month, so it would be wise to consider my account quite tentative. Traditional assumptions about serial relationships among humanid, humanoid, and human species seem especially vulnerable. Fortunately, my goal here is only to lay the groundwork for a plausible account of biopsychosocial differentiation (natural selection and cultural selection), so it is not essential to know, for example, whether *Homo erectus* sired Peking man and Neanderthal man, simply preceded them in time, or even lived contemporaneously with them. For elaboration, see Rushton (1995).

Similarly, some anthropologists have taken issue with the conventional view that "life was hard for *Homo Erectus* (e.g., Lee & DeVore, 1968, and Harris, 1977, p. x).

Cattell (e.g., 1948) emphasized the importance of studying how group "personality," which he called "syntality," influences individual personality. He proposed describing syntality with the same rigor, and perhaps the same dimensions, with which one tries to describe individual personality.

2. **Envy and jealousy.** Envy and jealousy have received relatively little attention from social scientists, perhaps because they exude a quasi-religious quality. For thoughtful discussions, see Klein (1957), Cancian (1965), and Salovey (1991). Nancy Friday (1983) provides a more popular account.

3. **In due time.** DNA research, by matching the known rate of mutation to the number of mutations from one population to another, can describe the speed and direction of the branching of genetic trees. Some studies indicate that the first anatomically modern humans appeared in Africa roughly 200,000 years ago, that from this population a distinct non-African population broke off about 100,000 years ago, and that this latter population split into Mongoloid (Asian) and Caucasoid (European) subpopulations about 40,000 years ago (Cann, Stoneking, & Wilson, 1987; Gibbons, 1991; Stringer & Andrews, 1988; Vigilant, Stoneking, Harpending, Hawkes, & Wilson, 1991). Other studies, for example, Wilson and Cann (1992), suggest that the mutations rates are slower than generally assumed, hence that the first modern humans date to as much as 850,000 years ago, the subsequent population separations proportionally more distant. To compound the complexity, McNeill (1979) and others argue that the pace of cultural development is so much faster than that of biological evolution that "the variables that change human conduct through time do not seem to be related in any calculable way to biological variations among different human populations" (p. 8).

4. **Fewer offspring.** MacArthur and Wilson (1967) and others distinguished "r-strategy" and "K-strategy" populations, on the basis of their sociobiological integration with the environment. r-strategy populations produce a large number of offspring and provide little parental care to any of them; K-strategy populations produce few offspring and provide a great deal of care. Rushton (1995), amid great controversy, has extended this line of thinking to intraspecies research, specifically the human races. Jung (1923/1971, pp. 180-181) described these strategies as "not merely analogous to, but the actual foundation of, our two psychological modes of adaptation," that is, introversion and extraversion. One could see in the risk-taking competitiveness of capitalism a reflection of r-strategy, as opposed to the K-strategy (socialistic) use of nurture to minimize risk.

5. **Spared for exchange.** It is impossible, of course, to date the first use of money, but Del Mar (1885/1968, pp. 15-17) assures us that states with established commerce necessarily employed some form of money. Contrary to other authors, he argues that money preceded the alphabet, noting that the earliest writings, like the Vedic poems and the Code of Manu, all allude to money, but there is not a word of writing on the earliest coins. He further argues that money came in use before the pastoral stage ended, pointing out the pastoral names for early money, like *pecus/pecunia*. Most commentators agree that the international character of Phoenician trade encouraged the invention of both the phonic alphabet and coins (Albright, 1961, pp. 452-453; Freedman, 1961, pp. 288-289).

6. **First in the West.** Although we now describe the area that was Mesopotamia as the "Middle East," it is culturally more Western than Eastern, so I take the liberty of claiming Sumer for the West. Quiggin (1949, p. 271) faced the same issue and came to the same conclusion. The Smithsonian curators are apparently of the same view, in that they begin their history of the West with Mesopotamia.

7. **Medicine.** Garrison (1929) tells us that the Babylonians produced the first theory of bodily fluids, or "humerology," long before Hippocrates.

8. **Games of chance.** Gaming has a long history. Painted pebbles found in the Pyrenees may suggest that Mesolithic people engaged in games of chance. The earliest known dice or board games trace to Ur (2600 B.C.), the Indus Valley (2000 B.C.), and Egypt (1900-1800 B.C.). Religion has uniformly condemned gambling, either as an affront to Divine Providence or an addictive distraction from the pursuit of virtue. But see Job 1:6-12 for God's implied wager with Satan that Job will remain blameless and upright. Social scientists are in general agreement that the excitement involved in gambling is reinforcing, perhaps habituating, perhaps even addicting. For deeper interpretation, see Culin (1907/1992), Geertz (1971, 1973, pp. 412-453), and Hiltebeitel (1987). Geertz's interpretation centers in "deep play," which is similar to Csikszentmihalyi's (1996, 1997) "flow."

9. **Disks or rings.** It's curious that these early pre-coins should be circular (with center hole) rather than square or rectangular, for the latter would have been easier to make. It's additionally curious that contemporary consumer research indicates that people prefer package designs based on the circle to those of any other shape. A psychoanalyst might suggest that a hole-in-circle has a sexual connotation, which, if true, could help explain its popularity. Sometimes, however, a pre-coin is just a pre-coin.

10. **Gilgamesh.** Elsewhere in the Gilgamesh epic, as well as in other myths, the gods decide to punish humankind by sending a great flood. The god Enki spares a pious man by instructing him to build a large boat and bring his family and various animals on board. As the flood recedes, the man sends out a swallow and a raven to reconnoiter. When the land is found dry, the man offers a sacrifice to the gods. The Gilgamesh epic antedates Moses by roughly a thousand years.

11. **Cowries.** Cowrie shells, many from the Straits of Madagascar, were the first near-universal pre-money. In larger and smaller varieties, and in white or natural black, they have been found in excavations on all continents. As with the Mesopotamian disks, there is a possible sexual connection with cowries, again female: Sea, birth, mother-goddess, and the vulval look of these particular shells. See Marglin (1987), on "Yoni."

12. **Strong and threatening.** The Germans and Celts were neighbors in time and space. They shared a concentration of strife, war, and mythic destruction of the world. Said Caesar of the Celts: "Of gods they worship Mercury most of all. . . . They believe him the most influential for money-making and commerce" (*Gallic Wars,* 6.17).

13. **Homer and Hesiod.** The Heroics seem have anticipated the later Western ambivalence about the morality of wealth and property. MacIntrye (1984) notes that those who pursue a life course (like warrior) that makes them deserving of prosperity pursue at the same time "a course whose characteristic end is death" (p. 127).

14. **Role in society.** The key word is *themis* (later the name of the god of justice), which describes the divine agency from which the kings' judicial judgments flowed. Themis is judgment based on the *dike,* the custom of the people, the natural law foundation of Greek democracy (Maine, 1931).

15. **Apollo/Dionysius.** Nietzsche views Dionysius as the symbol for the plunging of the unfettered self into the ocean of life. He sees Apollo, on the other hand, as order and control, the principle of restraint that channels the exuberance of Dionysius into a beautiful result. Nietzsche did not assert that humankind must choose between the Dionysian and Apollonian ethics, nor did he subscribe to the view that Apollo/control must dominate Dionysius/passion. Rather, he believed that the fusion of the two would produce the most life-giving result, the *Übermensch* (Schmidt, 1987, pp. 378-379, 385). Baker (1947) similarly argued that such symbols "had as their theme the superiority of soul to body; [they reflected] the principle of *ekstasis* [stepping out]—the severance of soul from body in order to escape the terrible reincarnations of the wheel of birth and to achieve the divinity of a bodiless existence" (p. 6). Recognition of the polarity was not limited to Greece; in the Hindu world, Shiva was to Dionysius as Vishnu to Apollo (Parrinder, 1983, p. 222).

16. **Hermes/Hestia.** For a lengthy and thoughtful discussion of "the spirit of Hermes," see McClelland (1961). For a presentation of "Hestian feminism," see Thompson (1992). See also Shelmerdine (1995), the Homeric Hymn to Mercury and the Homeric Hymn to Hestia.

17. **Sacrifice of a bull.** The merger of the Minoan culture in Crete with the Mycenaean culture on the mainland produced a native Aegean culture in which the principal deity was the Mother of All Life, and her holy child was later viewed as the infant Zeus (Friess & Schneider, 1932, p. 214). Here animal sacrifice was common, and the bull was the sacred animal, noted (as always) for his strength, fertility, and sexual apparatus. The cults were connected with sacred stones, pillars, caves, and groves, all of which had sexual connotations.

The bull's vitality and sexuality formed the basis for Laum's theory on the origin of Western coins. Laum (1924, 1929, in Desmonde, 1976a, 1976b) finds the origin of coins in these ancient ceremonies. In his view, the sacrificial bull was the representation of the priest/king, and the distribution of its roast flesh was a communion ritual in which the king's mana was parceled out to the citizens in proportion to status and patronage. In time, he argues, medallions came to replace the morsels of roast bull, and those medallions evolved into coins. Because they signified the priest/king's favor, these medallions carried talismanic powers. Desmonde imposes a variety of psychoanalytic interpretations on these rituals.

18. **Chinese calligraphic system.** While Chinese script is not technically "calligraphic," the term seems adequate for present purposes. In any event, Jenner (1992, pp. 212-213) observes that the writing system, just as it contributed to China's precocious cultural advancement, also retarded its later economic development.

19. **Cosmic order.** This notion of cosmic order pervades Chinese thought. Another example is Chinese medicine, which is built on a system of specified "social" relations among body parts (Garrison, 1929, p. 73) and in which disease occurs when the relations are in disharmony. Oriental thought, probably more than occidental, is consistent with Wilson's (1998) goal of "consilience," or the unity of knowledge across disciplines.

20. **Early indigenous Americans.** The conventional wisdom is that, during the last stages of the last Ice Age, groups of Mongoloid people emigrated from China across a land bridge to the Yukon, thence, over thousands of years, to North, Central, and South America, as far south and east as Patagonia. More recent thinking is that settlement occurred much earlier, 30,000 to 50,000 years ago. Some researchers argue that certain similarities between South American Indians and Polynesian, Melanesian, and some Southeast Asian people are so strong that there must have been a substantial degree of transoceanic migration (Mason, 1957, pp. 21, 23). Still other authors argue for a spontaneous appearance of human beings on the various continents. Some of the scholars who disbelieve the land-bridge theory argue that it is Christianity's need to maintain the Garden of Eden story that accounts for the durability of the conventional explanation.

21. **Trading networks.** In addition to cowries, wampum was popular pre-money. Wampum is short for wampumpeag, the Algonquin name for the tubular beads the Indians made from various shells. Eventually the term generalized to all money (Quiggin, 1949, p. 305). The beads that bought Manhattan Island were probably shell beads.

22. **Slow and steady dancing.** Likewise, the ghost dance, a modern version of the ancient prophet dance intended to protect against natural cataclysm, involved a solemn shuffling side step. The Plains versions of both the sun dance and the ghost dance were more Dionysian. The Lakota, for example, in the sun dance, deprived themselves of food and water for days, and often inflicted great pain on themselves to foster visions; in nineteenth-century versions of the ghost dance, they worked themselves into trances and donned white "ghost" shirts to protect themselves against the soldiers' bullets. See Hultkrantz (1987a, 1987b), Gill (1987), and, especially, Walker (1917, pp. 143-147).

23. **Contribute what he could.** Consistent with that philosophy, most Indian communities were scrupulously egalitarian, and individual efforts to stand out met with firm disapproval. Exceptions were gaming and warfare. Gaming has a long history among the indigenous Americans, as among the Asians. In South America, betting seems to have been limited to races and games in which the result is clear and immediate (Cooper, 1949). In North America, gaming was more sophisticated. The Mississippians played a wide variety of games, and they gambled on the outcomes of all of them, apparently to increase the excitement. Later, the Oglala frequently played a particularly rough-and-ready version of lacrosse, and a game called "moccasins" in which the goal was to identify the moccasin under which a pebble was hidden, and the method

was to read the facial expressions on the one who hid it (Walker, 1982, pp. 66-67; see also Witkin, Dyk, Faterson, Goodenough, & Karp, 1962, and Wapner & Demick, 1991, on field dependence). In similar fashion, the Indians used war less for assertion and acquisition, more to satisfy a need for excitement (except for occasional "border skirmishes," about which they were deadly serious). In both gaming and fighting, victory brought prestige rather than wealth. Even among the particularly aggressive Plains Indians, a successful warrior "could still enhance his status by showing generosity to the poor, sharing his goods with relatives, engaging in lavish hospitality, and living cooperatively with others" (Flannery-Hertzfeld, 1994, p. 380).

24. **Old cities.** The cities generally had populations of a few thousand, except for Cuzco City, which held 100,000. City dwellers stored and traded maize, and sometimes called it money, although most commentators would quarrel with that usage. See, however, Taxay (1970, pp. 13-15) for an emphatic challenge to the conventional interpretation.

25. **Diametrically opposed.** For a scholarly argument supporting the diametric opposition of European and American Indian cultures, see Berkhofer (1979).

26. **Engage in trade.** Grierson (1903) describes "silent trade," in which, in the dead of night, pygmy hunters would hang a fresh carcass from a tree at the edge of a village, and, in the morning, the villagers would leave in its stead a suitable quantity of salt or other commodity. He notes that the pygmy blowguns assured fairness in the exchange.

27. **Free-flowing sexuality.** African sexuality and humor are also apparent in myth. According to one common myth, for example, the Supreme Creator originally made people without sex organs. They lived together happily for a long time but eventually became bored and asked the Supreme Creator to send other kinds of people. In return, he sent sex organs. At first, the sex organs behaved just like people, walking about by themselves. One day, when the people had separated themselves into two camps, the male sex organs attached themselves to the people in one camp, the female organs to people in the other. From that time on, there has been conflict and discord between the sexes (Willis, 1993, p. 93).

28. **Benevolent.** The lesser gods were not so benevolent, and they had to be propitiated through gifts (Parrinder, 1983, p. 60). Money was, and is, viewed as a particularly effective propitiation.

29. **Natural sanguinity.** Archaic African and American Indian cultures are similar in important respects, such as the use of ridicule (shaming) to control behavior, and the horizontal expansion of relationships, as contrasted to the vertical expansion seen in Asian and European cultures (DeLoria, 1944, *passim*; Maquet, 1972, pp. 59-60, 76-77). At the same time, Europeans and Asians fenced their lands, while Africans and American Indians kept the land open. Old laws and practices regarding fencing have taken on a new importance in contemporary treaty-rights litigation, for example, *Mille Lac Band of Ojibwe v. Minnesota,* 861 F. Supp. 784 (D. Minnesota 1994).

30. **The four strains.** I use the word "strain" instead of "race" because the latter has taken on excess baggage in recent years. For an early effort to "deconstruct" race, see Montagu (1960).

31. **Biological differentiation.** The contrary view is politically more popular but scientifically less satisfying: Why, other than for political reasons, would we think that biological differences among the races are limited to gross anatomical structures? The connection between body and soul is too intimate to be anything less than the joint product of cultural adaptation and biological inheritance.

32. **Substantial influence.** As early as 1975, Eysenck observed that "the fact that between 60% and 70% of the 'reliable' variation is genetically determined . . . means that extraversion, like most other traits, reflects genetical polymorphism and as such is exposed to the direction, stability or disruptive influence of natural selection" (Eaves & Eysenck, 1975, p. 195). Tellegen et al. (1988) and Lykken, Bouchard, McGue, and Tellegen (1993) similarly conclude that somewhat more than half of the variation in human characteristics is the result of heritable

neurophysiological differences ("nature") as distinguished from social and other environmental factors ("nurture").

33. **Of human life.** For a thoughtful anthropological discussion of cultural differences regarding money and property, see Parry and Bloch (1989).

CHAPTER 3

1. **Wealth.** To economists, money is an instrument of commerce, like coins or paper currency, while wealth is the total of what one owns, including but not limited to money. To people in general however, "money" also means "wealth," as in "My aunt has quite a bit of money," and wealth often implies riches, as "My uncle was a man of wealth." Sometimes even "money" implies a large amount, as in "After she came into money, she became intolerable." My compromise term for the economists' wealth is "money and property," though, for variety, I will occasionally use wealth or even money alone as a substitute for that phrase.

For a precis of the history of Western thinking about wealth, see Syntopicon (1990) and Davis (1987).

2. **Social or psychological conceptualization.** Wilson's (1998) point is that the new task for natural and social scientists alike, indeed, for scholars in all disciplines, is to try to unify knowledge through identification of a small number of fundamental elements. I would like to think that the present synthesis is a step in that direction.

3. **Capitalism versus socialism.** For a good history of capitalism and socialism, see Baran and Sweezy (1966). See also Ward (1888), Hayek (1954), Wuthnow (1989), Brandes (1976), Braudel (1985, 1994), Schumpeter (1954/1994), and Tawney (1920, 1926).

4. **Drivers.** Merrill and Reid (1981) seem to be the originators of this particularly comfortable nomenclature, which I adopt with appreciation—Drivers, Amiables, Expressives, and Analyticals (Analytics).

5. **Quaternary.** Some authors, like Pythagoras, Jung, and Schopenhauer, see the quaternary as fundamental to all of existence. For all practical purposes, some quaternaries are universal, like north/south/east/west and summer/winter/spring/fall. Others are culture linked, like Matthew/Mark/Luke/John, and, in the American Indian medicine wheel quaternary, red/white/yellow/black.

6. **Types.** The fourfold structure suggests "types," which are controversial in many quarters because they imply no variation among people of a given type and because they suggest that an individual of a type may validly be described as an instance of any other individual of that type. I will use the word "type" for convenience, but with the understanding that there is always variation associated with type: Everyone over 6'2" and male might be called a tall man, but some men are taller than others. At the same time, I would encourage using a primary type, a secondary type, and even an opposite countertype, or "shadow" (Jung, 1951/1971, pp. 144-146).

The quaternary also raises questions of categorical versus continuous measurement, which Kagan (1994, chap. 2) addresses in detail. This is an empirical question: The data themselves say whether they require categorical or continuous measurement. If the data are naturally arrayed along a continuum, they are continuous, and to treat them as categorical is to lose information (but perhaps to find convenience). If the data naturally cluster within cells such that there is no significant within-cell variance, they are categorical, and to treat them as continuous is to capitalize on measurement error. From a statistical point of view, continuous data are generally more convenient and always open to more powerful analyses. The question is still open as to which data are continuous, which categorical.

CHAPTER 4

1. **As civilizations advanced.** Newman (1983) contrasts the older practice of overemphasizing general trends and abstract principles regarding the evolution of cultures to the recent practice of overemphasizing detailed differences, and she tries, successfully, to find a middle road. My intent is to be similarly temperate, identifying abstract patterns not for all humankind but for each of the four principal cultures and acknowledging analogous patterns in subcultures within each of those. It goes without saying that there is an indeterminate (but considerable) amount of individual variation on each level.

2. **Natural law.** The most succinct presentation of natural law is the dictum "Do good and avoid evil," prescient of Freud's pleasure principle and Thorndike's law of effect (cf. *Summa Theologica*, 1964, I-II Q 94, A 2.). The devil is in the details: What exactly is good, and what is evil, can be devilishly hard to decipher. See Brown (1960, pp. 128-132) for elaboration.

3. **Toward good and away from evil.** Natural law operates in three arenas: the good of the individual, the good of the family, and the good of the community (Ryan, 1965, p. 28). The good of the individual requires us to do whatever is necessary to preserve life, for example, to avoid undue risk, to refrain from homicide or suicide, and, by extension, to spend what is required to promote individual health and welfare. The good of the family requires us to do whatever is necessary to preserve the essence of family, that is, to ward off threats to monogamy and to provide whatever else is necessary for the benefit of the family. The good of society requires us to do whatever is necessary to preserve social organization, for example, to protect health and promote welfare, to protect the weak from the strong, and to ward off threats to harmony. Thus natural law emphasizes the pursuit of good over the avoidance of evil, like Heroic and classical Greek philosophy, and in contrast to post-Enlightenment legalism.

4. **Nature versus nurture.** This ancient bifurcation is no less distracting in the study of law than in the study of personality. The reality is that behavior is the result of biopsychosocial forces, an interplay the intimacy of which we are just beginning to understand. Damasio (1994) presents the biopsychosocial point of view. See also Eysenck (1982) and Franklin (1987).

5. **Urukagina.** In Urukagina's decrees the word "freedom" occurs in writing for the first time, pictographed as "return to the mother." Freedom may thus be rooted in life in the mother's womb, before the fetters and demands of life outside; in the light of the similar connection between cowries, sea, and mother, freedom and money may have the same root.

6. **Protecting the poor.** The Sumerians and Babylonians by and large did not have much respect for the poor. Kramer (1963, p. 203) cites several aphorisms of the time: "When a poor man dies, do not try to revive him." "Wealth is hard to come by, but poverty is always with us." "The poor have no power." Many of the early laws were apparently intended to deal with those attitudes.

7. **Written legal code.** Archaeologists have uncovered thousands of clay-tablet contracts, promissory notes, deeds, wills, and court decisions, which together indicate a lively commercial trade during the period the Ur-Nammu Code was prepared (Kramer, 1956, p. 51). Money as exchange was already in high gear in those ancient days; presumably money as communication was not far behind.

8. **Sense of justice.** The values underlying the Code of Lipit-Ishtar, taken as a whole, sound remarkably like the values of Golden Age Greece, Golden Age Rome, and the United States of the 1940-1950s. Indeed, Kramer (1963, chap. 7, esp. pp. 264-265) argues that it was these values—justice, ambitiousness, competitiveness, etc.—that won for Sumer the achievements that have stood for 4,000 years. McClelland (1961) will show that it was the presence of these qualities that made civilizations wealthy, the absence that prevented or dissipated wealth.

9. **Mina.** The different coins were related by means of a clear formula: one shekel equaled one-half ounce avoirdupois; one mina, 60 shekels; one talent, 60 mina (Goodspeed, 1921, pp. 71-73, 77, 355).

10. **Well-defined conception.** The Code of Hammurabi contains provisions for what seems to be the first Q-TIP trust (qualified terminable interest property): The property a husband leaves his wife she can devise only to her children by him, not to other heirs, and not to her children by another husband.

11. **Religious ethics.** The religious nature of the Mosaic law made it the first to try to regulate daily life, as distinguished from occasional problems. In addition, Mosaic law is apodictic, a presentation of abstract principles, as distinguished from casuistic, a presentation in terms of the facts of a case: "When a man . . ." See Boecker (1980, pp. 54-55).

12. **Prohibited usury.** Strictly speaking, the Mosaic Code prohibited usury against other members of the Hebrew community: "If you lend money to *any of my people with you* who is poor, you shall not be to him as a creditor, and you shall not exact interest from him" (Exodus 22:25, emphasis added). This exclusion enabled the medieval Jews to become the bankers of Europe.

13. **Detailed guidelines.** The detail in some of these debates suggests a particularly analytic, even legalistic, mentality among some commentators, such as a debate about what rights the poor have to grain that falls into an anthole.

14. **Distinguished the Mosaic Code.** For a scholarly account of the laws of the Hebrew and surrounding cultures, see Smith (1931). For a discussion of consistency and conflict between biblical content and archaeological findings, see Wright (1965).

15. **Its predecessors.** For a scholarly account of the relations between the laws of Babylonia and the laws of the Hebrew people, see Johns (1914).

16. **Customary laws.** Allott (1960) observes that, at the prejurisprudential stage, customary laws around the world "tend to resemble each other more than any single Customary Law resembles a written system of law" (p. 62). Garrison (1929, chap. 1) makes the same point about "the identity of all forms of ancient and primitive medicine." Nevertheless, I would argue that the differentiation begins very early, as a function of the temperament of the culture.

17. **In this instance.** We concentrate on Athens, even though, in the earliest days, each city-state had its own laws. Family law was quite consistent across the ancient city-states, owing it its source in Heroic ideals. By Demosthenes' time (d. 322 B.C.), commercial law was similarly general.

18. **Mesopotamians.** For discussion of Greco-Roman private ownership versus Mesopotamian palace and temple economy, see Finley (1973).

19. **Range of laws.** Van D'Elden (1987, pp. 191-199, in Johnson, 1987) points out how natural fear combined with a drive toward "solidarity" eventually to produce the first loose life-insurance arrangements among the Roman legions during the Second Punic War. He also traces the first fraternal insurance organizations to the Middle Ages, and the first insurance contract to London's Peace Guild in 925 A.D. Weatherford (1997) cites other interesting "firsts."

20. *Mancipatio* **or the** *nexum.* Mancipatio and nexum involved components that date to antiquity. Both required five witnesses, upon whom the solemnity of the rite placed heavy obligations. Both required valuable consideration, and both limited the transaction to objects present. In earliest times, the transactions were restricted to that which could be held in one hand; later, when people wanted to buy and sell large items like houses, they substituted symbols for the objects themselves (e.g., a handful of soil).

21. **Nearly 1,000 years.** Other ancient Roman codes include the Gregorian Code (304 A.D.), the Hermogenian Code (365 A.D.), and the Theodosian Code (438 A.D.). For detail, see Pharr (1952). For classical expositions of Justinian laws, see Williams (1893), Ritterhausen (1840), and *Collections de Novelles de l'Empereur Justinien* (1912-1914).

22. **First known . . . Chinese legal code.** Hulsewe (1985, chap. 1) proposes that the first true legal codes appeared in some parts of the empire as early as the eighth century B.C. (about the time of Homer in the West), and throughout the empire in the middle of the fourth century B.C. (in Mencius' and Aristotle's time).

23. **Penal in nature.** For all its infamy, the penal system was unimportant in the lives of most Chinese because the system was difficult to administer, because it became corrupt and lost its credibility, and because Confucian values penetrate more deeply into daily life than the threat of punishment. Of greater concern was the civil system, which in the East was mediational rather than adversarial. In the mediation, a respected neutral party comes between the disputants and applies considerable Confucian social pressure in the pursuit of a settlement. To go to court, under Confucian values, was necessarily to lose face (Chen, 1973, pp. 4, 7-12). The 1990 film *The Story of Qiu Ju* illustrates mediation in contemporary China.

24. **Words for law.** Confucian *li* is like natural law—control via moral obligation. Legalist *fa* is like positive law—control via punishment and fear (Chen, 1811; Chen, 1973, pp. 28-29). See also Needham (1962, Vol. 2, pp. 530-532). Chen (1973) quotes from Han Shu's *Treatise on Punishments and the Law*: "[The sages] shaped the rules of proper behavior (li), created teachings, established laws (fa), and instituted punishments (hsing), always acting in accordance with the feelings of the people and patterning and modelling themselves on Heaven and Earth" (pp. 15-16).

25. **Suits of armor.** Paying fines with armor may also be a symbolic ritual in which he who receives the armor becomes stronger, and he who gives it up becomes more vulnerable. Armor, in the shape of a person, seems particularly easy to perceive as an extension of oneself.

26. **Han Code.** Chen (1973, p. 15, emphasis added) quotes a commentator who sees a natural law foundation in Chinese law: "Social righteousness has its origin in what is fitting for the many. What is fitting for the many is *what accords with the minds of men.* Herein is the essence of good government[, that law] . . . springs from the midst of men themselves, and by being brought back to man, it corrects itself" (from the *Huai-nan hung-lieh-chieh,* 100 B.C.). For further detail on money in ancient China, see Pan (1950).

27. **Bamboo bastinado.** Like so much else, the specifications for the bastinado were provided by central authority, for example, a five-foot bamboo rod, knots shaven off, one inch at the root, one half inch at the tip, applied to the bare buttocks in multiples of 100 strokes, up to 500. Noting that the victims often died before the specified number of strokes had been administered, later authorities reduced the number of strokes by half or even more. Even the lightened punishment often resulted in death or permanent disability (Hulsewe, 1955, pp. 128-129).

The shame component of Asian punishment should not be overlooked. At the time of the caning of an American teenager in Singapore for vandalism, an Asian student in the United States described to me his view of the horror of that punishment. With obvious anxiety, he described the humiliation that would come from being identified as a malefactor and publicly disrobed; he never even mentioned the physical pain or the possibility of disability.

28. **Sub-Saharan African law.** As a result of colonization, much of Africa today is covered by one body or another of formal European law. However, the farther one moves inland from the coastal cities, the more like one is to find effective and intact bodies of customary law.

29. **Individual ownership.** The right to alienate land is the difference between communal ownership (vested in the state or the clan or family) and individual ownership. Rattray (1929) observes: "The whole history of our own early laws seems to show a struggle to attain the right to alienate land. Every device and legal subtlety of the legal mind had to be brought to bear to destroy the barrier raised in the remote past, owing to deeply rooted and perhaps now forgotten causes which were in opposition to alienation" (p. 362).

30. **Matrimonial contract.** The customary law is somewhat lopsided. The husband can expel an adulterous wife, keep the consawment, and refuse to pay maintenance, but a wife can't expel an adulterous husband. However, if arbiters decide the marriage dissolution is the husband's

fault, the wife can demand her premarital property back, and the husband forfeits his consawment or marriage expenses (Sarbah, 1904, p. 52).

31. **Homicide, adultery.** Homicide is a broad concept in customary law. It includes not only murder and manslaughter but also adultery and defloration, for all are considered "taking of the person": adultery because it deprives the spouse of his or her exclusive sexual relationship with the participant, defloration because it "kills" virginity.

32. **Perceptual operations.** Jung further subdivided the operations into "perceiving" operations (sensing and intuiting) and "judging" operations (feeling and thinking). These are the P and J at the end of the well-known Myers-Briggs acronyms, for example, INTJ, ENSP.

CHAPTER 5

1. **Magical rites.** In much of the world, religion among the common folk in the countryside was far less formal than religion among the gentry in the cities, often concentrated in highly erotic rites intended to assure the fertility of the crops, the herds, and the peasants themselves.

2. **Aryan warriors.** Along with their chariots, the Aryans brought their castes, which still obtain in India: Brahman (priest or teacher), Kshatriya (warrior), Vaisya (tradesman), and Sudras (worker/serf), in descending order of social status (Reinach, 1930, pp. 53-54).

3. **Upanishads.** In the *Prasna Upanishad* and the *Taittirya Upanishad* appears the Vedic view of the four elements: earth, water, heat, and wind—plus space or "ether" (Radhakrishnan & Moore, 1957, pp. 50, 57).

4. **Abandonment of desire.** There is in Hinduism a "performance" music that promotes another kind of abandonment, to the ecstasy of divine love. The intensity increases through many stages until it culminates in twitching, weeping, shouting, dancing, and collapsing (Roche, 1987).

5. **Code of Manu.** Various authorities date the Code of Manu from the nineteenth-sixteenth centuries B.C. Del Mar (1885/1968, pp. 60, 139) estimates the thirteenth-twelfth century B.C., noting that the Code is a recompilation of a much older code, now lost. For a scholarly relating of the Code of Manu to economic theory, see Spengler (1980, chap. 3).

6. **Pursuit of knowledge.** Women, however, must have an interest in material things: "Men who seek their own welfare should always honor women on holidays and festivals with gifts of ornaments, clothes, and dainty foods" (Manu III, 59).

7. **Morally neutral.** Sri Aurobindo (Ghose), the twentieth-century mystic-philosopher, points out that although most people believe that spiritual life must be an ascetic life, from a broader vantage "a complete purity and self-mastery . . . would remain the same in poverty or in riches; for if it could be shaken or sullied by either, it would not be real or would not be complete" (Ghose, 1949, p. 945).

8. **Disdain wealth.** The Old Testament describes wealth as a reward for the disparagement of wealth! See Kings 3:10-13; Job 42:10-12; Proverbs 11:24-25. See Schmidt (1987, p. 43).

9. **In which they predominate.** In Japan the people practiced the Way of the Kami, or Shinto, a mysterious and supernatural religion that emphasized trying to understand the Kami's will for the people. Shinto and Buddhism have accommodated well, and most Japanese practice the two simultaneously (Naofusa, 1987).

10. **Money suddenly becomes corrupt.** Like the Hebrew Essenes, the Hindu Jains and Vaishnavas, and the Chinese Taoists, the Sufi Moslems emphasize control of the senses, renunciation of the world, and mystical union.

11. **Of the countryside.** For further reading on religious variety, see James (1902/1961), Smith (1958), and, for browsing, Eliade (1987).

CHAPTER 6

1. **Taoists . . . sought equilibrium.** The philosophical Taoism of the fourth and third centuries B.C. is distinguished from the religious Taoism of the second and third centuries A.D. by the relative absence of ritual. Both versions emphasized longevity, even immortality, and used mysticism and ecstasy to escape from civilization and the material world. In addition, Taoists condemn all discursive knowledge because it introduces multiplicity rather than unity. Lao-tzu says, "Femininity far surpasses the manly virtues" (quoted in Baldarin, 1987, p. 291).

2. **Practice of virtue.** Socrates apparently practiced what he preached. Xenophon (*Memorabilia* I:31) says he was "the most self-controlled of men in respect to his sexual and other appetites. . . . He had so trained himself to be moderate in his requirements that he was very easily satisfied with very slight possessions." Furthermore, Socrates "expressed surprise that a man who offered to teach goodness should demand to be paid for it."

3. **Property ownership.** Plato condemns purchase/sale as well as usury. He goes so far as to void any transaction that involves interest (*Laws* 742e, 849e, 915e).

4. **"That insatiable craving."** In his effort to eliminate craving, Plato even stripped competitiveness from social relations. The Heroics had described athletic contests as opportunities for individual achievement and acquisition, but Plato viewed them instead as opportunities to demonstrate excellence as such. Like dialogues and debates (in Plato's view), such activities should be contests without competitiveness. After reading his dialogues, it's difficult not to suspect in Plato a little repression of competitive inclinations.

5. **Substantial fees.** The young Socrates studied under Protagoras for a while, but could only afford the less expensive "short course" (Stumpf, 1971, p. 34). The existence of such a course suggests an early form of target marketing on the part of the pragmatic Protagoras.

6. **Money.** While Plato implied a "cartal" theory of money, in which money is independent of the material of which it is made, Aristotle preferred a "metallist" theory, in which money should be readily convertible into a particular commodity, preferably a metal, for example, gold (Schumpeter, 1954/1994, pp. 63, 288). For useful summaries of different economic theories of money, see Crump (1981, pp. 20-29) and Schumpeter (1954/1994, *passim*).

7. **Charging interest.** Aristotle describes a particularly noxious group of undesirables: "those who ply sordid trades, pimps and all such people, and *those who lend small sums at high rates*" (*Ethics* 1121b, emphasis added).

CHAPTER 7

1. **Collectivist ideals.** The reason Marxism and Christianity, so philosophically compatible (MacIntyre, 1984, p. 261), are such political enemies is Marx's view that human powers objectified become gods: "The more man places in God, the less he retains in himself" (Marx, 1844/1964, in MacIntyre, 1968, p. 49). Schumpeter himself (1942/1962, p. 5) noted a "religious quality" in Marxism, according to which, by virtue of the assumed moral superiority of the philosophy, there is no excuse for dissent. One also notes that such unconscious forces as the reaction formation have had enormous influence in the development of economic values and philosophies. For collectivist exhortations in an individualist culture, see West's *Shoes of the Fisherman* (1964) and Rolfe's *Hadrian VII* (1950).

2. **Communism of the early Church.** If Proudhon, the extremist, is right, that "property is theft," then communism, the antithesis of property, must be the cure. The essential characteristic of "crude communism" is that, in its reaction against property-as-oppression, it denies property ownership to everyone and in so doing robs them of some part of their identity, their "extended self" (Chapter 10). Through its ruthless denial not only of property but of humanity, communism, the antidote, becomes imperialism, the poison (MacIntyre, 1968, pp. 53-55).

3. **Christianized Aristotle.** There is a streak of utilitarianism that runs from Aristotle to Aquinas to Adam Smith and his successors. Like the early British economists, Aquinas supported individual ownership (for better maintenance and less haggling) and focused on the "common good," a concept approximately equal to "welfare economics." For elaboration, see Schumpeter (1954/1994, pp. 92, 97, 182). In addition, Thomas produced the same metallist theory that Aristotle had and Adam Smith would.

4. **Interest is sinful.** It was the Scholastics of the sixteenth and seventeenth centuries who found that interest was "the merchant's tool" and that to charge interest could sometimes be just.

5. **Doctrine of indulgences.** The Church's enthusiasm for indulgences is reflected in Friar John Tetzel's sales techniques, for example: "Priest! Noble! Merchant! Wife! Youth! Maiden! Do you not hear your parents and your other friends who are dead, and who cry from the bottom of the abyss: We are suffering horrible torments! A trifling alms would deliver us; you can give it, and you will not!" (Friar John Tetzel, "indulgence agent," quoted in Powell, 1962, p. 62).

6. **The sale of relics.** Powell (1962, p. 62) lists relics that have received "infallible approval" from various popes: Moses' staff, Noah's beard, Joseph's carpentry tools, and bread left over from the Last Supper.

7. **Reformed values.** In addition, John Wesley (1703-1791) preached a concise and consistent message: "Gain all you can, save all you can, give all you can," never exploiting, never dissipating, never yielding to self-gratification. His flock for the most part was enthusiastic about two of those principles (Powell, 1962, pp. 92-93).

8. **New European disposition.** The other major theme of the Enlightenment was the shift from "classical rationality," that is, the thinking of the Ancients and the Fathers, to "empirical rationality," that is, the views and methods of modern science (Popper, 1972, and Lonergan, 1958, in Lamb, 1992). Under empirical rationality, science was in, philosophy and (especially) theology were out. Empirical rationality would lead not only to astonishing scientific advance but also to an overemphasis on phenomena that are easier to observe and measure (behavior, matter) and a corresponding underemphasis on things more difficult (intuition, will, virtue).

CHAPTER 8

1. **Temperament.** Historically, "temperament" has implied more of a biological component than "personality," so the words were generally taken to describe different domains. On the basis of recent factor analytic studies, and because I assume that personality and temperament are biopsychosocial, I use the terms interchangeably, unless the context clearly calls for one or the other. See Angleitner and Ostendorf (1994).

2. **Neurophysiological, psychometric, and psychoanalytic research.** The psychoanalytic, legal, religious, and philosophical studies discussed here represent the *classical rationality,* the psychometric and neurophysiological studies the *empirical rationality.* The main advantages of the classical studies are that they have, to a substantial extent, stood the tests of time and place and that they can be as profound as human cognition is penetrating; the main disadvantage is that they are seldom submitted to, and often not supported by, external

verification, least of all empirical verification. The main advantages of the empirical rationality are that its methods and findings can be verified by independent research and that its measures are less likely to suffer from human idiosyncrasy and other frailties. Its main disadvantages are that it is likely to measure structures and processes that are of limited depth and importance. In particular, the psychometrics of personality and temperament generally use self-report questionnaires to collect data, and the neurophysiology of motivation and emotion, even assuming reliable measurement, has rarely been tested for generalizability.

The Quaternary reflects both the classical and empirical rationalities. In addition, through its attention to a variety of cultures and epistemologies, it seeks to reflect Lonergan's contemporary perspective, the *"transcultural" rationality.* See Lamb (1992).

3. **"Tomboyism."** The androgenized girls also showed a higher IQ than girls not exposed to androgen. But see Sloane (1993, pp. 174-184) for discussion regarding the IQ difference, the social meaning of tomboyism, and an environmental interpretation of these findings.

4. **Androgen.** Levy and Heller (1992) point out some developmental phenomena inconsistent with this traditional androgen-emphatic model and suggest a still unclear role for the female hormone, estrogen, particularly in prenatal development.

5. **Homogeneous categories.** More precisely, "factors" are weighted linear composites of variables that define space constructed on a matrix of product-moment correlations, usually of items. Because the mathematics are more complex than the definition, there is plenty of room for argument, for example, the Big Five versus Giant Three (see Basic Psychometric Dimensions of Personality later in this chapter).

6. **Our own questionnaire study.** Through the courtesy of DDB Needham Worldwide and Professor William Wells, University of Minnesota, we had available data from the 1992 and 1993 administrations of the Life Styles Survey, a 900-item, self-report, Likert-type inventory that addresses a wide range of topics dealing with consumer values, attitudes, and practices. The Life Styles Survey employs standing-panel quota samples representative of the U.S. adult population. Of the 2,500 females and 2,500 males surveyed by mail in the spring of each of the two years, usable responses were obtained from 1,725 males and 2,197 females in 1992, and 1,673 males and 2,017 females in 1993. The reliability and validity of Life Styles Survey data have been reported in, for example, O'Guinn and Wells (1989). Michael Swenson, a graduate student at the University of Minnesota, analyzed the data.

7. **Consensus.** For a superb early history of the structure of temperament with an emphasis on Introversion/Extraversion, see Eysenck (1953, esp. chaps. 4 and 5). It is worth noting that Eysenck found what appears to be Introversion/Extraversion in a second-order factor analysis of Guilford's primary mental abilities, thus introducing a healthy blurring of the cognitive and personality domains (pp. 181-183), of which subsequent researchers have lost sight.

8. **In the psychoanalytic arena.** For convenience, I use the term "psychoanalytic" to include what is generally called depth psychology and even psychoanalytically influenced clinical psychology, as well as psychoanalysis per se. My apologies to the memory of Dr. Freud, who asked even Jung not to use the term to describe anything but Freud's own line of thinking (Mussen & Rosenzweig, 1973, p. 191).

9. **Focus their energy inward.** Freud considered introversion incipient neuroticism: "[The introvert] must develop symptoms . . . if he does not find other outlets for his pent-up libido" (1920, quoted in Eysenck, 1953, p. 178). Jung disagreed: "It is a mistake to believe that introversion is more or less the same as neurosis. As concepts the two have not the slightest connection with one another" (1921, quoted in Eysenck, 1953, p. 179).

Krech et al. (1974, in Hall & Lindzey, 1957/1970, p. 327) distinguished between "deficiency" motives and "abundancy" motives. The deficiency motives have an introverted flavor, for example, need for succor (Amiable), need for security (Analytic); the abundancy motives have an extraverted flavor, for example, need to act on the surrounding environment.

10. **Epistemological foundation.** In the modern era, Kant and Wundt continued Galen's line of thinking, with a quaternary built on strong/weak and quick/slow responses to stimulation. In the contemporary era, Eysenck described a similar quaternary nearly fifty years ago (1953, pp. 367-369, 1982, p. 9), in his effort to synthesize even earlier work by Thurstone (1934), Rundquist and Sletto (1936), Darley and McNamara (1938), and Ferguson (1939). Eysenck found two factors, the first of which he interpreted as radicalism/conservativism, the second as practical/theoretical or, in James's terms, Toughminded/Tenderminded. Since then, at least three dozen variations have appeared, at least a few apparently independent of the psychometric tradition (e.g., Jung, 1923/1971).

In Eysenck's schema, as in Galen's before and Kagan's after, choleric was diagonally opposed to phlegmatic, and sanguine to melancholic. Timorously, mine makes choleric diagonally opposed to melancholic, and sanguine to phlegmatic, sharpening the dialectic.

More than the philosophical or psychological nomenclature, I lean toward Merrill and Reid's (1981) names for these constructs because these seem less cumbersome. Regardless of the nomenclature one uses, the important thing is to concentrate on the attributes themselves, rather than the labels.

11. **Fell into disrepute.** Conventional wisdom has it that work by Rostan's (1824) successors has been largely discredited—Viola (1909), Kretschmer (1921/1925), and Sheldon (1942, 1954). These three researchers all produced three-part frameworks that, to my reading, would have been quaternaries had the culture of the time permitted more explicit study of the female physique. In particular, Sheldon's visceratonia/endomorphy is characterized by a pronounced orality, cerebretonia/ectomorphy by a strong anality, but his somatotonia contains *both* "anti-oral" and "anti-anal" elements, suggesting a masking effect. I suspect that if Sheldon had dared to study women as thoroughly as he studied men, his Mesomorphs would have separated into masculine and feminine versions (competitive, aggressive, inclined toward paranoia versus restless, claustrophobic, inclined toward hysteria), thus completing the Quaternary. For further encouragement, see Eysenck (1953, chap. 9), Humphreys (1957), and Hall and Lindzey (1957/1970, chap. 9).

Sheldon received some posthumous notoriety in the 1990s, when the national media reported that a cache of his nude research photographs had been uncovered, in which some nationally recognized physiques figured prominently.

12. **Divergent cognitive associations.** The tendency of the nonthreatened organism to engage in divergent thinking and expansive behavior seems consistent with Jung's construct of the *wunderkind,* the unfettered and creative child, before socialization.

13. **Persistence.** Cloninger added "persistence" because his original set of three categories "did not consistently differentiate individuals with personality disorders or poor social adjustment from other well-adapted individuals with extreme personality profiles" and could not explain the paranoid and schizotypal personality disorders, among others (Cloninger, Svrakic, & Przybeck, 1993, p. 976).

14. **Five-factor interpretation.** Two of these five factors are considerably less reliable than the others, namely, emotional stability and intellect (a.k.a. open to experience). See Zuckerman (1994, p. 54).

15. **As a moderator framework.** Wernimont and Fitzpatrick (1972), Yamauchi and Templer (1982), and Furnham (1984) factor analyzed various aspects of the financial domain, obtaining factors that seem to emphasize what I have been calling the Analytic and Driver dimensions. Because financial behavior is a special case of general behavior, one should expect that an expanded collection of items suitably framed should produce basic financial factors analogous to the basic personality factors discussed here, that is, the Quaternary.

16. **Four psychosexual life stages.** One important difference between Freud's and Jung's systems is that Freud's sequential approach implies that succeeding stages are "better" or

"healthier" than preceding ones, while Jung's functions each have their healthy and unhealthy aspects. Quadrant theory is more Jungian in this respect.

It is worth noting that, expressed in Quaternary terms, Freud's system would array the anal and phallic "stages" at opposing ends of one continuum, the oral and genital stages at opposing ends of the other. If I am right that the four middle steps of Maslow's hierarchy correspond to the four quadrants, it is also interesting to observe that the two sequences—Freud's and Maslow's—reverse the first two steps or stages: Freud's oral-anal-phallic-genital versus Maslow's security (anal)—affection (oral)—esteem through strength—esteem through reputation.

It is also important to note that stage theories have been developed with emphasis on male psychosexual development and in a European American cultural context. Stages more broadly derived may be the same or, more likely, different. Brody (1985) and Franz and White (1985) provide discussions of female development.

17. **"Sense of Inferiority."** Adler viewed maturity as the capacity to go beyond one's own interests to those of other people, that is, altruism; hence he viewed the lust for power over other people as a central characteristic of the immature personality. Adler's system was more social and less biological than Freud's, hence more appealing to the American temperament. As we shall see in Chapter 8, his "sense of inferiority" is an intimate part of the Driver/Amiable dimension. Adler at various times described the primary motive also as the "will to power" and "striving for perfection."

18. **Quaternaries of their own.** Horney, Maslow, and Peck, psychoanalysts all, each proposed a version of the Quaternary. Horney's (1937) comprised "compliant people," who need affection, approval, and a strong partner on whom they can depend; "detached people," who need to restrict life, to keep it under control; "aggressive people," who need power, achievement, and people whom they can exploit; and (untitled) assertive people, who need people who will admire them.

Abraham Maslow (1954) proposed a hierarchy of six needs, the middle four of which are the most descriptively useful and correspond to the Quaternary: "esteem through reputation," or a need for recognition, prestige, status, dominance, attention, and appreciation; "esteem through strength," or a need for achievement, adequacy, mastery, and competence; "belonging," or a need for affiliation with friends, love, family, and a place in a group; and "security," or a need for protection such as afforded by conservative practices. His remaining needs are, at the bottom of the hierarchy, physiological needs (water, food, sex), and, at the top, need for self-actualization, the rare and transient perfection of the human personality (Hall & Lindzey, 1957/1970, p. 327; Maslow, 1954).

Finally, M. Scott Peck, in his singularly successful *The Road Less Traveled* (1978), described a "risk of love" for each of the four types: "The risk of independence," or the risk that if we break out of other people's expectations of us, we may be hurt; paradoxically, an opportunity to discover and value ourselves. He describes this as the risk that dependent (Amiable) people need to take. "The risk of loss," or the risk that if we expose ourselves to life and love and loss, we might be hurt; paradoxically, an opportunity to live a full and vital life. This is the need that avoidant (Analytic) people need to take. "The risk of confrontation," or the risk that if we challenge another person's behavior or values, we may be hurt; paradoxically, an opportunity to grow in humility. This is the risk that competitive people (Drivers) need to take. "The risk of commitment," or the risk that if we engage and stay engaged with another person, we may be hurt; paradoxically, an opportunity to grow in intimacy. This is the risk that impetuous (Expressive) people need to take. Viewed in Freudian terms, the risk of independence seems to be the "oral" risk; that is, the risk that the oral personality needs to take if he or she is to achieve mature relationships. Similarly, the risk of loss is the "anal" risk, the risk of confrontation the "phallic" risk, and the risk of commitment the "genital" risk.

Among Murray's "complexes" are these four, each coupled here with a pair of corresponding needs, each combination clearly connected with one of our four temperaments (Murray, 1938, p. 363, cited in Hall & Lindzey, 1957/1970, pp. 162-163, 187-188, 1940, pp. 152-153):

1. Oral succorance—passive and dependent tendencies, manifested in passive oral activities (e.g., thumb-sucking), compulsive eating and drinking, inhibited aggressive needs; coupled with need affiliation and need succorance; that is, *Affiliativeness.*

2. Oral aggression—aggressiveness, manifested in aggressive oral activities (e.g., gnawing a T-bone steak), general aggressiveness; coupled with need achievement and need dominance; that is, *Acquisitiveness.*

3. Anal retention—prudishness, resistance to other people's suggestions, need for order, cleanliness, and retention of possessions; and Freud's "parsimony, cleanliness, and obstinacy"; need order, need infavoidance; that is, *Concentration.*

4. Anal rejection—need for disorder, autonomy, aggression, anal sexuality; need exhibition, need autonomy; that is, *Divergence.*

19. **Thematic Apperception Test.** The Thematic Apperception Test (TAT) comprises a series of pictures presented on cards. Respondents are asked to tell stories about the pictures, in their own words, with testing conditions designed to elicit emotional, semiconscious material. The stories the respondents tell are studied against standard protocols for signs of various needs. The number and choice of pictures depends on the needs of interest. For more detail, see Murray (1956), McClelland, Atkinson, Clark, and Lowell (1953), and Atkinson (1958).

20. **Needs.** Some of Murray's needs, sorted by Jungian function, are as follows: "sensing," or need achievement, need dominance, need rejection, need aggression, need sentience, and need counteraction; "feeling," or need affiliation, need nurturance, need succorance, need abasement, and need deference; "intuition," or need exhibition, need autonomy, and need defendance; and "thinking," or need infavoidance (avoid embarrassment), need order, and need understanding.

21. **Myers-Briggs Type Indicator.** The Myers-Briggs Type Indicator (MBTI) measures sixteen types. The MBTI set consists of the four basic types × introversion/extraversion × judging/perceiving. It does not attempt to measure semiconscious phenomena.

The MBTI supplanted the Jungian Type Indicator by adding the judging/perceiving dimension (Myers & McCaulley, 1988). Similar though less widely used instruments are described in Keirsey and Bates (1984), Kroeger and Thuesen (1988), Merrill and Reid (1981), and Alessandra and O'Connor (1990). The Center for Applications of Psychological Type (Gainesville, Florida) is a clearinghouse for information about these instruments, especially the MBTI.

Myers's insistence on categorical sorting in the face of a mainstream tradition of continuous scoring is one of the reasons the MBTI has not received the attention from academic psychologists that it probably deserves. Though the 1985 *MBTI Manual,* with its limited provision for optional continuous scoring, received substantial praise from the *Mental Measurements Yearbook,* the accepted authority in test reviewing, the MBTI's supporting data would have been much more persuasively presented in a formal construct validity framework.

22. **Financial temperament.** Gurney (1988) was among the first, if not the first, researchers to address a "money personality."

23. **Loss of regard.** Fenichel (1935/1938) connects fear of loss of regard with the castration anxiety, fear of weaning, and fear of bodily loss through defecation. From these, along with physical pleasure, he arrives at the motivation to hold back and accumulate.

24. **Bean-counters.** One wonders if "bean-counting" is yet another veiled fecal reference in the Analytic context.

25. **Righteousness.** In fact, I would add that there seem to be both masculine and feminine representations of this righteousness: the overordered *mind* of which Jones speaks, bent on bringing all the world into its way of thinking (e.g., the Cultural Revolution; Nazism), and what

might be viewed as an "overordered soul," equally bent on imposing its feelings and emotional values upon the rest of the world (e.g., the political correctness movement).

26. **African capitalism.** Iliffe (1983, p. 86) describes an African capitalism distinctive for its close proximity to adversarial socialism. To the extent that socialism represents Anima (see Table 8.1f), our notion of a tenderminded capitalism is consistent with this analysis.

27. **Envy or jealousy.** Sexual jealousy also seems related to individualism/collectivism and jealousy/envy in general. Individualists by and large insist on exclusive access to their sexual partner; collectivists seem more willing to share.

28. **Into a tigress.** Merrill and Reid (1981, pp. 73-79) describe a similar dynamic. At low levels of stress, they say, the person "digs in his heels," intensifies his characteristic way of doing things. Under high stress, however, the person briefly takes on the characteristics of his opposing temperament. For example, the Driver under low stress becomes more of a Driver, the Amiable more of an Amiable, and so on. Upon hearing of the loss of his fortune, for example, the Driver might become emotionally dependent (cf. Animus), might even break down and cry, and, in the stress of divorce court, the Amiable might become a temporary tigress. McClelland (1961) attempts to administer the TAT in a way that elicits the otherwise repressed responses. In the same vein, Binstock and Ely (1971) have called attention to the "power of powerlessness," and MacIntyre (1984, p. 261) has noted "a certain radical individualism" underlying Marxist collectivism.

CHAPTER 9

1. **Very same biopsychosocial forces.** Weber (e.g., 1922/1978) emphasized the influence of cultural factors on economic success, and McClelland (e.g., 1961) pointed out how individual psychological factors affect the culture. I am trying to introduce biological factors as well, and to shift the focus more (but surely not exclusively) in the direction of the individual contribution to the definition of the culture and to levels of economic achievement and patterns of economic ebb and flow. For an early illustration of this line of thinking, see Schachter and Singer (1962).

2. **Triune brain.** Cloninger and Gilligan (1987), on the basis of a review of ethological studies, suggest "that the phylogeny of temperament began with a behavioral inhibition (harm avoidance) system in all animals, next added an activation (novelty-seeking) system in more advanced animals, and then added subsystems for behavioral maintenance (reward dependence) in reptiles and later phyla" (p. 457). This phylogeny corresponds roughly with MacLean's triune brain.

3. **"Explosion of meaning."** Csikszentmihalyi and Rochberg-Halton (1981, p. 176ff.) remind us of Dewey's dynamic description of the formation of meaning. They propose a three-stage process that seems consistent with Edelman's and Bruner's: Our perception of the aesthetic qualities of a thing stirs up an "inner commotion" (Dewey's term), which sets the stage for further understanding; focusing attention on the thing establishes a psychic closeness with the thing, which is pleasant and therefore recurring; the closeness motivates us toward closer understanding of how the thing fits into our life and world.

4. **Edelman asserts.** For skeptical reactions to Edelman's theories, see Barlow (1988) and Crick (1989). For Edelman's views on the psychology of the unconscious, see Edelman (1990) and Winson (1985).

5. **Speech and meaning.** Bruner points out that his conception of meaning is supported not only by Edelman's (1987, 1990, 1992) neuroscience but Reynolds's (1980) anthropology and Lewin's (1989) and Humphrey's (1986) primatology.

6. **Moral dimension.** The connections between life/death and good/bad in the biological survival sense and between good/bad and good/evil in the moral sense invite rapprochement between biology and philosophy/theology and add a moral dimension to many money issues, which I believe is the fundamental reason behind the intensity of conflict over money.

7. **Lose track of the difference.** In Csikszentmihalyi's (1990) words:

> [Flow] is what the sailor holding a tight course feels when the wind whips through her hair, when the boat lunges through the waves like a colt—sails, hull, wind, and sea humming a harmony that vibrates in the sailor's veins. It is what a painter feels when the colors on the canvas begin to set up a magnetic tension with each other, and a new *thing,* a living form, takes shape in front of the astonished creator. (p. 3)

8. **Particular classes of possessions.** For related discussion on the use of symbolic interactionism see Engestrom and Middleton (1996).

9. **Group dynamics.** Gifts are an important way to extending self. For thoughtful discussions on gifts and gifting on the individual and family level, see Kohut (1987), Crump (1981, pp. 70-71), and Zelizer (1994, chap. 3). Boulding (1971-1985, p. 27ff.) leads us to think about the meaning of group transactions ("gift information") such as welfare payments and loans to developing countries. Such group gifts can be interpreted like individual gifts, vehicles that communicate feelings of competence, neediness, freedom, and security, as well as the repressed feelings associated with each. Thus the people of the donor country say, at least sometimes, "We are stronger than you; we despise your weakness—and our weak underside envies your getting this for nothing." And the recipients reply, "We are weak, we loathe you for your gift—and we shall eventually overcome you."

For further discussion of the meanings of gifts, see Kohut (1987), Mauss (1966), Schwartz (1967), and Gregory (1982). For a superb annotated bibliography on "gifted money," see Zelizer (1994, pp. 237-249).

CHAPTER 10

1. **Conflicts.** For refreshing views on cultural differences as the root of global conflicts, see Hsu (1981) and, especially, Huntington (1996).

2. **EVLN.** In the EVLN model, Exit corresponds to Driver ("I'd end the relationship."), Voice to Expressive ("I'd confront my boyfriend."), Loyalty to Amiable ("I'd stick by him."), and Neglect to Analytic ("I'd back off and let our relationship drift."). The quotations are from Bryson (1991, p. 202, Table 8.4). We have already seen in Chapter 8 that the circumplex model is a special case of the Quaternary.

3. **Need affiliation.** Atkinson, McClelland, and associates (e.g., Atkinson, 1964; McClelland, 1961) also developed a scoring system for a third motive, which they called "need power" and which in turn arose as the researchers contemplated a similar measure of "need security." Research on need security apparently did not proceed. Need power has received much less study than need affiliation and, especially, need achievement. In general, need power is defined as a "concern over controlling the means of influencing the behavior of another person" (Atkinson, 1964, p. 227). Need power is high in people who are argumentative and who like to try to convince other people to think or do something, reminiscent of the charisma of the Expressive. Completion of this work would have matched the Quaternary: need achievement, need affiliation, need power (Expressive charisma), and need security (Analytic).

4. **Classification of "personality disorders."** The *DSM-IV* (p. 845ff.) describes culture-specific syndromes that seem consistent with the Quaternary: melancholic preoccupation with death ("ghost sickness") among many American Indian tribes, excited outbursts and

concentration difficulties (*"boufee delirante," "zar"*) among many African peoples, and cognitive-processing difficulties (*"hwa-byung," "shenjing shuairuo," "taijim kyofusho"*) among many Asian peoples. Curious, too, in the light of the shadow, are certain disorders that seem just the opposite of the characteristic behaviors of the cultures: bursts of extreme excitement (*"pibloktoq"*) among Eskimo (Indian) people, and frenzy (*"latah"*) among Asian people.

5. **Save for retirement.** Peterson (1993, 1996) argues that saving for retirement is central to any workable solution to the U.S. Social Security troubles, but he points out that few Americans, surely including the enormous middle class, set aside enough to keep themselves even relatively independent. Mr. Peterson's analysis appears to have provided the economic foundation for Mr. Perot's presidential campaign.

Quadrant theory can help us understand the psychological side of the retirement savings problem and the proposed solutions, for example, the envy and jealousy behind tax policies that encourage consumer spending and discourage saving and investing for retirement, and public reactions to proposals for limiting or extending entitlement benefits. It cannot substitute for public or congressional will.

6. **Economic decline.** McClelland (1961, p. 47) emphasizes child-raising standards (see Winterbottom, 1958). He theorizes that given a warm and supporting mother and a distant father, rigorous standards produce need achievement, which produces economic success, which in turn leads to less rigorous child-raising in subsequent generations, which leads to economic decline. The rigorous standards are those that Weber observed in Calvin's teachings, as we discussed in Chapter 7.

7. **Also in Africa.** Landes (1998) surveys the fortuity and ingenuity that led to the patterns of wealth and poverty that characterize the various nations of the modern world. Landis turns to culture to explain economic success and failure; McClelland (1961) turns to social psychology to explain culture. We add neurophysiology to the mix.

8. **Jeopardize both systems.** Naisbitt (1996) describes eight features of traditional Asian culture that he sees shifting in a Westerly direction. My colleague Chin-Chuan Lee is at work on an analysis of the turnover of Hong Kong from Britain to the People's Republic of China.

9. **Fictional literature.** Popular and serious fictional literature can be used to "flesh out" hypothetical constructions. Anderson (1997) describes the use of fictional television characters for such purposes.

References

Abraham, Karl. (1976). The spending of money in anxiety states. In Ernest Borneman (Ed.), *The psychoanalysis of money* (pp. 299-302). New York: Urizen. (Original work published 1917)

Adams, J. S. (1994). The meaning of housing in America. *Annals of the Association of American Geographers, 74*, 515-526.

Adler, A. (1956). *The individual psychology of Alfred Adler.* New York: Harper and Row.

Albright, W. F. (1961). The role of the Canaanites in the history of civilization. In G. Ernest Wright (Ed.), *The Bible and the ancient Near East.* New York: Doubleday Anchor.

Alessandra, T., & O'Connor, M. J. (1990). *People smart.* La Jolla, CA: Keynote.

Allott, Albert. (1960). *Essays in African law.* London: Butterworth.

American Psychiatric Association. (1994). *Diagnostic and statistical manual of mental disorders* (4th ed.). Washington, DC: Author.

American Psychological Association. (1966). *Standards for educational and psychological tests and manuals.* Washington, DC: Author.

Anastasi, T. (1992). *Personality selling.* New York: Sterling.

Anderson, Cheri L. (1997). *Fictional narratives in research.* Ph.D. thesis, University of Minnesota.

Anderson, Norman. (1976). *Law reform in the Muslim world.* London: Althore.

Angell, Norman. (1929). *The story of money.* New York: Frederick A. Stokes.

Angleitner, Alois, & Ostendorf, Fritz. (1994). Temperament and the Big Five factor of personality. In Charles F. Halverson, Jr., Geldolph A. Kohnstamm, & Roy Martin (Eds.), *The developing structure of temperament and personality from infancy to adulthood* (pp. 69-90). Hillsdale, NJ: Lawrence Erlbaum.

Ansbacher, H. L. (1971). Adler, Alfred. In *Encyclopedia Britannica* (Vol. 1, pp. 148-149). Chicago: William Benton.

Ante-Nicean fathers (American ed., 10 vols.). (1908-1911). New York: Scribner.

Aristophanes. (1938). *Ecclesiazusae* [The company of women] (W. J. Oates & E. O'Neill, Jr., Eds. and Trans.). New York: Random House.

Aristotle. (1921). Politica (Benjamin Jowett, Trans.). In W. D. Ross (Ed.), *The works of Aristotle.* New York: Oxford University Press.

Aristotle. (1985). *Nichomachean ethics* (Terence Irwin, Trans.). Indianapolis, IN: Hacke.

Atkinson, John W. (1958). *Motives in fantasy, action, and society.* New York: Van Nostrand.

Atkinson, John W. (1964). *Introduction to motivation.* New York: Van Nostrand.

Attneave, Carolyn. (1982). Indian families. In M. McGoldrick, J. K. Pearce, & J. Giordanno, *Ethnicity and family therapy.* New York: Guilford.

Babe, Robert E. (1995). *Communication and the transformation of economics.* Boulder, CO: Westview (HarperCollins).

245

Badian, Ernest. (1996). Sergius Catalina, Lucius. In Simon Hornblower & Anthony Spewforth (Eds.), *Oxford classical dictionary* (3rd ed.). Oxford, UK: Oxford University Press.

Bakan, D. (1966). *The duality of human existence: An essay on psychology and religion.* Skokie, IL: Rand-McNally.

Baker, Hershel. (1947). *The image of man.* New York: Harper and Row.

Baker, Wayne. (1987). What is money? A social structural perspective. In M. S. Mizruchi & M. Schwartz (Eds.), *Intercorporate relations: The structural analysis of business.* Cambridge, UK: Cambridge University Press.

Baker, Wayne E., & Jimerson, Jason B. (1992). The sociology of money. *American Behavioral Scientist, 35*(6), 678-693. [Special issue: The Meanings of Money, Kenneth O. Doyle, Ed.]

Baldarin, Farzeen. (1987). Taoism: An overview. In Mircea Eliade (Ed.), *The encyclopedia of religion* (Vol. 14, pp. 288-306). New York: Macmillan.

Baran, Paul, & Sweezy, Paul. (1966). *Monopoly capital.* London: Penguin.

Barlow, H. B. (1988). Neuroscience: A new era? *Nature, 18,* 331.

Bartlett, Sir Frederick C. (1932). *Remembering.* Cambridge, UK: Cambridge University Press.

Baumgarth, William P., & Regan, Richard J. (Eds.). (1988). *St. Thomas Aquinas/On law, morality, and politics.* Indianapolis, IN: Hackett.

Beebe, John. (Ed.). (1983). *Money, food, drink, and fashion and analytic training.* Fellbach, Germany: Bonz.

Belk, Russell W. (1988). Possessions and the extended self. *Journal of Consumer Research, 15,* 139-168.

Belk, Russell W. (1989). Extended self and extending paradigmatic perspective. *Journal of Consumer Research, 16,* 129-132.

Belk, Russell W., Bahn, Kenneth D., & Mayer, Robert N. (1982). Developmental recognition of consumption symbolism. *Journal of Consumer Research, 9,* 4-17.

Benedict, Ruth. (1934). *Patterns of culture.* New York: New American Library (Houghton Mifflin).

Berg, Adriane. (1988). *How to stop fighting about money and make some.* New York: Avon.

Berkhofer, Robert F., Jr. (1979). *The white man's Indian.* New York: Random House.

Bernard, Malcolm. (1996). *Fashion as communication.* London: Routledge.

Biblioteca de autores cristianos. (1944-). Madrid: La Editorial Catolica.

Biebuyck, Daniel P. (1987). African religious drama. In Mircea Eliade (Ed.), *The encyclopedia of religion* (Vol. 4, pp. 462-465). New York: Macmillan.

Bilalama. (1969). Laws of Bilalama (Albrecht Goetz, Trans.). In James B. Pritchard (Ed.), *Ancient Near Eastern texts relating to the Old Testament* (3rd ed.). Princeton, NJ: Princeton University Press.

Binstock, Robert H., & Ely, Katherine (Comps.). (1971). *The politics of the powerless.* Cambridge, MA: Winthrop.

Bloch, Maurice, & Parry, Jonathan. (Eds.). (1982). *Death and regeneration of life.* Cambridge, UK: Cambridge University Press.

Blood, Robert O., & Wolfe, Donald M. (1960). *Husbands and wives.* Glencoe, IL: Free Press.

Blumstein, Phillip, & Schwartz, Pepper. (1983). *American couples: Money, sex, work.* New York: Morrow.

Boas, Franz. (1970). *The social organization and secret societies of the Kwaikutl Indians.* New York: Johnson Reprint. (Original work published 1895)

Boecker, Hans J. (1980). *Land and the administration of justice in the Old Testament and ancient Near East.* London: Society for Promoting Christian Knowledge.

Borneman, Ernest. (Ed.). (1976). *The psychoanalysis of money.* New York: Urizen.

Boulding, Kenneth E. (1971-1985). Notes on a theory of philanthropy. In Kenneth E. Boulding, *Collected papers* (Vol. 2). Boulder, CO: Associated University Press.

Bradley, Denis J. M. (1997). *Aquinas on the two-fold human goal: Reason and human happiness in Aquinas' moral science.* Washington, DC: Catholic University of America Press.

Branden, Nathaniel. (1966). Alienation. In Ayn Rand, *Capitalism.* New York: New American Library (Signet). (Originally published in *The Objectivist Newsletter,* July/August/September, 1965)

Brandes, Stuart D. (1976). *American welfare capitalism.* Chicago: University of Chicago Press.

Braudel, Fernand. (1985). *Civilization and capitalism, 15th-18th century.* New York: Perennial Library.

Braudel, Fernand. (1994). *A history of civilizations.* New York: Lane.

Breger, Louis. (1974). *From instinct to identity: The development of personality.* Englewood Cliffs, NJ: Prentice Hall.

Bridges, P. K. (1978). The biological basis of personality. In F. Brambilla, P. K. Bridges, E. Endroczi, & G. Heuser, *Perspectives in endocrine psychobiology* (pp. 479-503). London: Wiley.

Brinkerhoff, David B., & White, Lynn K. (1985). *Sociology.* St. Paul, MN: West.

Brock, S. A. (1994). *Using type in selling.* Palo Alto, CA: Consulting Psychologists Press.

Brody, Leslie R. (1985). Gender differences in emotional development. In Abigail J. Stewart & M. Brinton Lykes (Eds.), *Gender and personality* (pp. 14-61). Durham, NC: Duke University Press.

Brown, Brendan F. (Ed.). (1960). *The natural law reader.* New York: Oceana.

Brown, Norman O. (1959). *Life against death.* Middletown, CT: Wesleyan University Press.

Bruner, Jerome. (1990). *Acts of meaning.* Cambridge, MA: Harvard University Press.

Bryson, Jeff B. (1991). Modes of responses to jealousy-evoking situations. In Peter Salovey (Ed.), *Psychology of jealousy and envy* (pp. 178-207). New York: Guilford.

Buber, Martin. (1966). *I and thou.* (Ronald Gregor Smith, Trans., 2nd ed.). Edinburgh: T & T Clark. (Original work published 1958)

Burggraf, Shirley P. (1997). *The feminine economy and Economic man.* Reading, MA: Addison-Wesley.

Buchan, James. (1997). *Frozen desire: The meaning of money.* New York: Farrar Straus Giroux.

Buhler, G. (1886). *Sacred books of the East* (Vol. 15). Oxford, UK: Clarendon.

Burstein, M. L. (1963). *Money.* Cambridge, MA: Schenkman.

Butcher, James N. (1990). *Development and use of the MMPI-2 content scales.* Minneapolis: University of Minnesota Press.

Calvin, John (Jean). (1936). *Institutes of the Christian religion* (John Allen, Trans., 7th American ed.). Philadelphia: Presbyterian Board of Christian Education.

Calvin, Jean. (1989). *Calvin's institutes* (Hugh T. Kerr, Ed.). Louisville, KY: Westminster/John Knox.

Campbell, D. T., & Fiske, D. W. (1959). Convergent and discriminant validity by the multitrait multimethod matrix. *Psychological Bulletin, 56,* 81-105.

Campbell, Joseph. (Ed.). (1971). *The portable Jung* (R. F. C. Hull. Trans.). New York: Viking.

Cancian, Frank. (1965). *Economics and prestige in a Maya community.* Stanford, CA: Stanford University Press.

Cann, R. L., Stoneking, M., & Wilson, A. C. (1987). Mitochondrial DNA and human evolution. *Nature, 325,* 31-36.

Carlson, Richard. (1997). *Don't worry, make money.* New York: Hyperion.

Casson, Lionel, & Price, Martin. (1981). *Coins, culture, and history in the ancient world.* Detroit, MI: Wayne State University.

Cathcart, J., & Alessandra, T. (1985). *Relationship strategies.* Chicago: Nightingale-Conant.

Cather, Willa. (1941). Paul's case. In M. Edmund Speare (Ed.), *The pocket book of short stories* (pp. 211-253). New York: Pocket Books. (Also published in *The Troll Garden,* New York: McClure, Philips, & Co., 1905, and *Youth and Brightness,* New York: Knopf, 1920)

Cattell, Raymond B. (1948). Concepts and methods in the measurement of group syntality. *Psychological Review, 55,* 48-63.

Cattell, Raymond B. (1957). *Personality and motivation structure and measurement.* Yonkerson-Hudson, NY: World Book.

Catechism of the Catholic Church. (1994). Libreria Editrice Vaticana. Chicago: Loyola University Press.

Chekhov, Anton. (1941). The darling. In M. Edmund Speare (Ed.), *The pocket book of short stories* (p. 246). New York: Pocket Books. (Also published in Thomas Seltzer, Ed., *The best Russian short stories,* New York: Modern Library, 1925)

Chen, Huan-Chang. (1811). *The economic principles of Confucius and his school.* New York: Columbia University Press.

Chen, Philip M. (1973). *Law and justice: The legal systems in China 2400 B.C. to 1960 A.D.* New York: Dunellen.

Choisy, Eugene. (1902). *L'Etat Chritien Calviniste a Geneve au temps de Theodore de Beze.* Geneva: C. Eggimann.

Cloninger, C. R. (1991). Brain networks underlying personality development. In B. J. Carroll & J. E. Barrett (Eds.), *Psychopathology and the brain* (pp. 183-208). New York: Raven.

Cloninger, C. R., & Gilligan, S. B. (1987). Neurogenetic mechanisms of learning: A phylogenetic perspective. *Journal of Psychiatric Research, 21,* 457-472.

Cloninger, C. Robert. (1986). A unified biosocial theory and its role in the development of anxiety states. *Psychiatric Development, 3,* 167-226.

Cloninger, C. Robert. (1987). A systematic method for clinical description and classification of personality variants. *Archives of General Psychiatry, 44,* 573-588.

Cloninger, C. Robert, Svrakic, Dregan M., & Przybeck, Thomas. (1993). A psychobiological model of temperament and character. *Archives of General Psychiatry, 50,* 975-990.

Cohen, Jerome A., Edwards, R. R., & Chen, F. C. (1980). *Essays on China's legal tradition.* Princeton, NJ: Princeton University Press.

Cohen, Joel B. (1989). An over-extended self? *Journal of Consumer Research, 16,* 125-128.

Coleman, James S. (1990). *Foundations of social theory.* Cambridge, MA: Harvard University Press.

Coleman, James S., & Fararo, Thomas J. (1992). *Rational choice theory: Advocacy and critique.* Newbury Park, CA: Sage.

Collections de Novelles de l'Empereur Justinien. s. n. (1912-1914). Paris: Sirey.

Collinson, Patrick. (1990). The late medieval Church and its Reformation. In John McManners (Ed.), *The Oxford illustrated history of Christianity* (pp. 233-266). Oxford, UK: Clarendon.

Colquhoun, Patrick Macchombaich. (1851). *Summary of the Roman civil law* (Vols. I-IV). London: V & R Stevens and Sons.

Coole, Arthur Braden. (1936). *Coins in China's history.* Tientsin, China: Student Work Department of the Tientsin win Academy.

Confucius. (1963). *The great learning* (Wing-tsit Chan, Trans.). Princeton, NJ: Princeton University Press.

Confucius. (1979). *The analects* (D. C. Lau, Trans.). New York: Penguin.

Cooper, C. (1976). The house as symbol of the self. In J. Lang et al. (Eds.), *Designing for human behavior: Architecture and the behavioral sciences.* Stroudsburg, PA: Dowden, Hutchinson, and Ross.

Cooper, John M. (1949). Games and gambling. In Julian H. Steward (Ed.), *Handbook of South American Indians* (Vol. 5, Bulletin 143, pp. 503-534). Washington, DC: Smithsonian Bureau of American Ethnology.

Costa, P. T., & McCrae, R. R. (1988). Personality in adulthood: A 6-year longitudinal study of self-reports and spouse ratings on the NEO Personality Inventory. *Journal of Personality and Social Psychology, 54,* 853-863.

Costa, P. T., Jr., & McCrae, R. R. (1992). Four ways five factors are basic. *Personality and Individual Differences, 13,* 653-656.

Crick, Francis. (1989). Neural Edelmanism. *Trends in Neurosciences, 12,* 240-248.

Cronbach, Lee J. (1957). The two disciplines of scientific psychology, *American Psychologist, 12,* 671-684.

Cronbach, Lee J. (1975). Beyond the two disciplines of scientific psychology, *American Psychologist, 30,* 116-127.

Cronbach, L. J., & Meehl, P. E. (1955). Construct validity in psychological tests. *Psychological Bulletin, 52,* 281-302.

Crump, Thomas. (1981). *The phenomenon of money.* London: Routledge & Kegan Paul.

Crump, Thomas. (1992). Money as a ritual system. *American Behavioral Scientist, 35*(6), 669-677. [Special issue: The Meanings of Money, Kenneth O. Doyle, Ed.]

Csikszentmihalyi, Mihalyi. (1970). Sociological implications in the thought of Teilhard de Chardin. *Zygon, 5*(2), 130-147.

Csikszentmihalyi, Mihalyi. (1990). *Flow.* New York: Harper.

Csikszentmihalyi, Mihalyi. (1996). *Creativity: Flow and the psychology of discovery and invention.* New York: HarperCollins.

Csikszentmihalyi, Mihalyi. (1997). *Finding flow: The psychology of engagement with everyday life.* New York: Basic Books.

Csikszentmihalyi, Mihalyi, & Rochberg-Halton, Eugene. (1981). *The meaning of things.* Cambridge, UK: Cambridge University Press.

Culin, Stewart. (1992). *Games of the North American Indians.* Lincoln: University of Nebraska Press. (Original work published 1907)

Damasio, A. (1994). *Descartes' error.* New York: Putnam.

Dandekar, R. N. (1987). Vedanta [End of the Veda]. In Mircea Eliade (Ed.), *The encyclopedia of religion* (Vol. 15, pp. 207-214). New York: Macmillan.

Darley, J. G., & McNamara, W. J. (1938). A factor analysis of test-retest performance on attitude and adjustment tests. *Journal of Educational Psychology, 29,* 652-664.

Davidson, Richard J., & Sutton, Steven K. (1995). Affective neuroscience: The emergence of a discipline. *Current Opinion in Neurobiology, 5,* 217-224.

Davis, Joel J. (1997). *Advertising research.* Upper Saddle River, NJ: Prentice Hall.

Davis, Winston. (1987). Wealth. In Mircea Eliade (Ed.), *The encyclopedia of religion.* New York: Macmillan.

Davitt, Thomas E. (1968). The basic values in law. In *Transactions of the American Philosophical Society* (Vol. 58, p. 5). Philadelphia: American Philosophical Society.

Deiner, Ed. (1994). Assessing subjective well-being: Problems and opportunities. *Social Indicators Research, 31*(2), 103-157.

Del Mar, Alexander. (1968). *A history of money in ancient countries.* New York: Burt Franklin. (Original work published 1885)

DeLoria, Ella. (1944). *Speaking of Indians.* New York: Friendship Press.

Derryberry, Douglas, & Tucker, Don M. (1992). Neural mechanisms of emotions. *Journal of Consulting and Clinical Psychology, 60*(3), 329-338.

Desmonde, William H. (1976a). The origin of money in animal sacrifice. In Ernest Borneman (Ed.), *The psychoanalysis of money* (pp. 113-133). New York: Urizen.

Desmonde, William H. (1976b). On the anal origin of money in Animal Sacrifice. In Ernest Borneman (Ed.), *The psychoanalysis of money* (pp. 107-111). New York: Urizen.

Diamond, Solomon. (1957). *Personality and temperament.* New York: Harper.

Dichter, Ernest. (1964). *Handbook of consumer motivations.* New York: McGraw-Hill.

Dichter, Ernest. (1971). *Motivating human behavior.* New York: McGraw-Hill.

DiGaetani, John. (1994). *Money: Lure, lore, and literature.* Westport, CT: Greenwood.

Dittmar, Helga. (1992). *The social psychology of material possessions.* New York: St. Martin's.

Dominguez, Joe, & Robin, Vicki. (1992). *Your money or your life.* New York: Penguin.

Donne, John. (1971). Meditation XVII, Devotions upon emergent occasions. In A. J. Smith (Ed.), *The complete English poems of John Donne* (p. 100). New York: St. Martin's. (Original work published 1624)

Douglas, Mary. (1970). *Natural symbols.* New York: Random House.

Douglas, Mary, & Isherwood, Brian. (1979). *The world of goods.* New York: Basic Books.

Dowey, Edward A. (1971). Calvin. In *Encyclopedia Britannica* (Vol. 4, pp. 671-674). Chicago: William Benton.

Doyle, Kenneth O. (1972). *Interaction: Readings in human psychology.* Lexington, MA: D. C. Heath.

Doyle, Kenneth O. (1991). *Construction of the money orientation measure (MOM).* Presented at the conference Money: Lure, Lore, and Liquidity, Hofstra University, Hempstead, NY.

Doyle, Kenneth O. (1991-1998). *Wealth accumulation and management.* New York: American Institute of Certified Public Accountants.

Doyle, Kenneth O. (1992a). Long-term health care, voluntary self-impoverishment, and family stress. *American Behavioral Scientist, 35*(6), 803-808. [Special issue: The Meanings of Money, Kenneth O. Doyle, Ed.]

Doyle, Kenneth O. (1992b). Money and the behavioral sciences. *American Behavioral Scientist, 35*(6), 641-657. [Special issue: The Meanings of Money, Kenneth O. Doyle, Ed.]

Doyle, Kenneth O. (1992c). The symbolic meaning of house and home: An exploration in the psychology of goods. *American Behavioral Scientist, 35*(6), 790-802. [Special issue: The Meanings of Money, Kenneth O. Doyle, Ed.]

Doyle, Kenneth O. (1992d). Toward a psychology of money. *American Behavioral Scientist, 35*(6), 708-724. [Special issue: The Meanings of Money, Kenneth O. Doyle, Ed.]

Doyle, Kenneth O., & Houk, Larry K. (1990). *The spend down solution.* St. Paul, MN: Knightsbridge St. John.

Doyle, Kenneth O., Hanchek, Ann, & McGrew, Julie. (1994). Communication in the language of flowers. *Horticulture Technology, 4*(3), 211-216.

Driver, G. R., & Miles, J. C. (1956). *The Babylonian laws.* Oxford, UK: Clarendon.

DuBois, Philip H. (1970). *A history of psychological testing.* Boston: Allyn & Bacon.

Duesenberry, J. S. (1949). *Income, saving, and the theory of consumer behavior.* Cambridge, MA: Harvard University Press.

Dye, David H. (1984). *Southeastern ceremonial complex.* Lincoln: University of Nebraska Press.

Dye, David H., & Cox, Cherlyn A. (1990). *Towns and temples along the Mississippi.* Birmingham: University of Alabama Press.

Eaves, L. J., & Eysenck, H. J. (1975). The nature of extraversion: A genetical analysis. *Journal of Personality and Social Psychology, 32,* 102-112.

Edelman, G. (1992). *Bright air, brilliant fire.* New York: Basic Books.

Edelman, Gerald M. (1987). *Neural Darwinism: The theory of neuronal group selection.* New York: Basic Books.

Edelman, Gerald M. (1990). *The remembered present: A biological theory of consciousness.* New York: Basic Books.

Edwards, C. (1934). *The world's earliest laws.* London: Watts.

Ehrlich, Paul R., & Ehrlich, Anne H. (1974). *The end of affluence.* New York: Ballantine.

Einzig, Paul. (1966). *Primitive money* (2nd ed.). Oxford: Pergamon. (Original work published 1949)

Eliade, Mircea. (Ed.). (1987). *The encyclopedia of religion.* New York: Macmillan.

Emmons, Robert A. (1986). Personal strivings: An approach to personality and subjective well-being. *Journal of Personality and Social Psychology, 51*(5), 1058-1068.

Engestrom, Yrjo, & Middleton, David. (1996). *Cognition and communication at work.* New York: Cambridge University Press.

Epstein, Seymour. (1994). Integration of the cognitive and the psychodynamic unconscious. *American Psychologist, 49*(8), 709-724.

Erasmus, Desiderius. (1941). *Praise of folly* (Hoyt Hopewell Hudson, Trans.). Princeton, NJ: Princeton University Press.

Erhardt, A. A., & Baker, S. W. (1973). *Hormonal aberrations and their implications for the understanding of normal sex differentiation.* Paper presented at the meetings of the Society for Research in Child Development, Philadelphia.

Erhardt, A. A., & Money, John. (1967). Progestin-induced hermaphroditism: IQ and psychosexual identity in a study of 10 girls. *Journal of Sex Research, 3,* 83-100.

Erikson, E. (1959). *Identity and the life cycle.* New York: International Universities Press.

Erikson, Erik. (1950). *Childhood and society.* New York: Norton.

Evans, Joseph W., & Ward, Leo R. (Eds. and Trans.). (1976). *The social and political philosophy of Jacques Maritain: Selected readings.* Notre Dame, IN: University of Notre Dame Press. (Original work published as *Du Regime Temporel et de la Liberte,* Paris: Desclee de Brouwer, 1933)

Eysenck, Hans J. (1944). General social attitudes. *Journal of Social Psychology, 19,* 207-227.

Eysenck, Hans J. (1957). *The psychology of politics.* London: Routledge and Kegan Paul.

Eysenck, Hans J. (1953). *The structure of human personality.* New York: Wiley.

Eysenck, Hans J. (1982). *Personality, genetics, and behavior.* New York: Praeger.

Eysenck, Hans J. (1991). Dimensions of personality: Sixteen, 5, or 3?—Criteria for a taxonomic paradigm. *Personality and Individual Differences, 12,* 773-790.

Eysenck, Hans J. (1994). The Big Five or Giant Three: Criteria for a paradigm. In Charles F. Halverson, Jr., Geldolph A. Kohnstamm, & Roy Martin (Eds.), *The developing structure of temperament and personality from infancy to adulthood* (pp. 37-51). Hillsdale, NJ: Lawrence Erlbaum.

Eysenck, Hans J., & Eysenck, S. B. G. (1964). *Manual of the Eysenck Personality Inventory.* London: University of London Press.

Faber, Ronald F. (1992). Money changes everything: Compulsive buying from a biopsychosocial perspective. *American Behavioral Scientist, 35*(6), 809-819. [Special issue: The Meanings of Money, Kenneth O. Doyle, Ed.]

Fairbank, John King. (1992). *China.* Cambridge, MA: Harvard University Press (Belknap).

Fang, I-wing. (1997). *A history of mass communication.* Boston: Focal.

Feldman, F. L. (1976). *The family in today's money world.* New York: Family Service Association of America.

Felton-Collins, Victoria. (1990). *Couples and money.* New York: Bantam.

Fenichel, Otto. (1938). The drive to amass wealth. *Psychoanalytic Quarterly, 7,* 69-95. (Originally read before the Psychoanalytic Society of Czechoslovakia, Prague, January 5, 1935, David Brunswick, Trans.)

Ferenczi, Sandor. (1976). The ontogenesis of the interest in money. In Ernest Borneman (Ed.), *The psychoanalysis of money* (pp. 81-90). New York: Urizen. (Original work published 1914 in *Internationale Zeitschrift für aerztliche Psychoanalyze, 2,* 506-513)

Ferguson, L. W. (1939). Primary social attitudes. *Journal of Psychology, 8,* 217-223.

Festinger, Leon. (1942). Wish, expectation and group standards as factors influencing level of aspiration. *Journal of Abnormal and Social Psychology, 37.*

Finley, Moses I. (1973). *The ancient economy.* Berkeley: University of California Press.

Finley, Moses I. (1981). *Economy and society in ancient Greece* (B. D. Shaw & R. P. Saller, Eds.). New York: Penguin.

Finn, Daniel Rush. (1992). The meanings of money: A view from economics. *American Behavioral Scientist, 35*(6), 658-668. [Special issue: The Meanings of Money, Kenneth O. Doyle, Ed.]

Fiske, Susan T., & Taylor, Shelly. (1991). *Social cognition.* New York: McGraw-Hill.

Flannery-Hertzfeld, Regina. (1994). North American Plains Indians. In *Encyclopedia Britannica,* (Vol. 13, pp. 379-383). Chicago: Encyclopedia Britannica.

Forward, Susan, & Buck, Craig. (1994). *Money demons.* New York: Bantam.

Franklin, Jon. (1987). *Molecules of the mind.* New York: Atheneum.

Franz, Carol E., & White, Kathleen M. (1985). Individuation and attachment in personality development: Extending Erikson's theory. In Abigail J. Stewart & M. Brinton Lykes (Eds.), *Gender and personality* (pp. 136-168). Durham, NC: Duke University Press.

Freedman, David Noel. (1961). Old Testament chronology. In G. Ernest Wright (Ed.), *The Bible and the ancient Near East.* New York: Doubleday Anchor.

Freud, Sigmund. (1920). *General introduction to psychoanalysis.* New York: Liveright.

Freud, Sigmund. (1961). *Civilization and its discontents.* New York: Norton. (Original work published 1930)

Freud, Sigmund. (1965). *The interpretation of dreams.* New York: Avon. (Original work published 1900)

Freud, Sigmund. (1976). Character and anal eroticism. In Ernest Borneman (Ed.), *The psychoanalysis of money* (pp. 73-90). New York: Urizen. (Original work published 1905)

Friday, Nancy. (1983). *Jealousy.* Toronto: Bantam.

Friedman, Milton. (1957). *A theory of the consumption function.* Princeton, NJ: National Bureau of Economic Research, Princeton University.

Friess, Horace L., & Schneider, Herbert W. (1932). *Religions in various cultures.* New York: Henry Holt.

Fromm, Erich. (1947). *Man for himself.* New York: Holt, Rinehart & Winston.

Fromm, Erich. (1955). *The sane society.* New York: Rinehart.

Fromm, Erich. (1956). *The art of loving.* New York: Harper.

Fromm, Erich. (1959). *Sigmund Freud's mission.* New York: Harper.

Fromm, Erich. (1976). *To have or to be?* New York: Penguin.

Fuller, Morris. (1890). *Our title deeds.* London: Griffith, Farran, Okeden, and Welsh.

Furnham, Adrian. (1984). Many sides of the coin—The psychology of money usage. *Personality and Individual Differences, 5,* 501-509.

Furnham, Adrian, & Lewis, Alan. (1986). *The economic mind.* New York: St. Martin's.

Galbraith, John Kenneth. (1958). *The affluent society.* Boston: Houghton Mifflin.

Galbraith, John Kenneth. (1975). *Money.* Boston: Houghton Mifflin.

Galbraith, John Kenneth. (1992). *The culture of contentment.* Boston: Houghton Mifflin.

Garman, E. Thomas. (1997). *Consumer economic issues in America.* (4th ed.). Houston, TX: Dame.

Garman, E. Thomas, & Forgue, R. E. (1997). *Personal finance* (5th ed.). Boston: Houghton Mifflin..

Garrison, Fielding H. (1929). *An introduction to the history of medicine* (4th ed.). Philadelphia: Saunders.

Geertz, Clifford. (Ed.). (1971). *Myth, symbol and culture.* New York: Norton.

Geertz, Clifford. (1973). *The interpretation of cultures: Selected essays.* New York: Basic Books.

Gehman, Richard J. (1989). *African traditional religion in biblical perspective.* Kijabe, Kenya: Kesho.

Ghose, Sri Aurobindo. (1949). *The life divine.* New York: Greystone.

Gibbons, A. (1991). Looking for the father of us all. *Science, 251,* 378-380.

Giddens, Anthony. (1990). *The consequences of modernity.* Stanford, CA: Stanford University Press.

Gilder, George. (1981). *Wealth and poverty.* New York: Basic Books.

Gill, Sam D. (1987). North American shamanism. In Mircea Eliade (Ed.), *The encyclopedia of religion* (Vol. 13, pp. 216-219). New York: Macmillan.

Glathe, Harry. (1939). *The origin and development of Chinese money.* Shanghai: Chinese Journal Publishing Co.

Goldberg, Herb, & Lewis, Robert T. (1978). *Money madness.* New York: Morrow.

Goldberg, Lewis R. (1990). An alternative "description of personality": The Big Five factor structure. *Journal of Personality and Social Psychology, 59,* 1216-1229.

Goldberg, Lewis R., & Rosolack, Tina K. (1994). The Big Five factor structure as an empirical framework: An empirical comparison with Eysenck's P-E-N model. In Charles F. Halverson, Jr., Geldolph A. Kohnstamm, & Roy Martin (Eds.), *The developing structure of temperament and personality from infancy to adulthood* (pp. 7-35). Hillsdale, NJ: Lawrence Erlbaum.

Golden, Marissa Martina. (1992). Exit, voice, loyalty, and neglect: Bureaucratic responses to presidential control during the Reagan administration. *Journal of Public Administration, 2,* 29-62.

Gonzalez, Justo L. (1990). *Faith and wealth.* San Francisco: Harper and Row.

Goodspeed, George Steven. (1921). *A history of the Babylonians and Assyrians.* New York: Scribner.

Goody, J., & Tambiah, S. J. (1973). *Bridewealth and dowry.* Cambridge, UK: Cambridge University Press.

Gossage, Howard Luck. (1967). The gilded bough: Magic and advertising. In F. Matson & A. Montague (Eds.), *The human dialogue.* New York: Free Press.

Gough, H. G. (1957). *California Psychological Inventory: Manual.* Palo Alto, CA: Consulting Psychologists Press.

Gray, J. A. (1982). *The neuropsychology of anxiety.* New York: Oxford University Press.

Gray, John. (1993). *Men are from Mars, women are from Venus.* New York: HarperCollins.

Green, Edwin. (1989). *Banking: An illustrated history.* Oxford, UK: Phaidon.

Green, Robert G., Harris, Robert N., Jr., Forte, James A., & Robinson, Margaret. (1991). Evaluating FACES III and the circumplex model: 2440 families. *Family Process, 30*(1), 55-73.

Gregory, C. (1982). *Gifts and commodities.* London: Academic Press.

Gregory, C. A. (1997). *Savage money.* Amsterdam: Harwood.

Grierson, P. J. H. (1903). *The silent trade: A contribution to the early history of human intercourse.* Edinburgh: W. Green.

Griffith, R. T. H. (1920-1926). *The hymns of the Rigveda* (2 vols., 3rd ed.). Banaras, India: E. J. Lazarus.

Groseclose, Elgin E. (1934). *Money: The human conflict.* Norman: University of Oklahoma Press.

Grueber, Erwin. (1886). *The Roman law of damage to property.* Oxford, UK: Clarendon.

Gurney, Kathleen. (1988). *Your money personality.* New York: Doubleday.

Habermas, Jürgen. (1989). *The theory of communicative action* (Vol. 2). Boston: Beacon.

Hall, Calvin S., & Lindzey, Gardner. (1970). *Theories of personality* (2nd ed.). New York: Wiley. (Original work published 1957)

Hall, Edward T. (1959). *The silent language.* Garden City, NY: Doubleday.

Halpern, Diane F. (1992). *Sex differences in cognitive abilities.* Hillsdale, NJ: Lawrence Erlbaum.

Halverson, Charles F., Jr., Kohnstamm, Geldolph A., & Martin, Roy. (1994). Current conceptions of the structure of adult personality. In Charles F. Halverson, Jr., Geldolph A. Kohnstamm, & Roy Martin (Eds.), *The developing structure of temperament and personality from infancy to adulthood* (pp. 1-5). Hillsdale, NJ: Lawrence Erlbaum.

Hamilton, Edith. (1983). *The Greek way.* New York: Norton. (Original work published 1930)

Hammurabi. (1904). *The Code of Hammurabi* (Robert Francis Harper, Ed. and Trans.). Chicago: University of Chicago Press.

Han Fei Tzu. (1959). *Complete works* (W. K. Liao, Trans.). London: Arthur Probsthain.

Harris, Marvin. (1974). *Cows, pigs, wars, and witches: The riddles of culture.* New York: Random House.

Harris, Marvin. (1977). *Cannibals and kings.* New York: Random House.

Harrison, A. F., & Bramson, R. M. (1982). *Styles of thinking.* New York: Anchor.

Harrison, A. R. W. (1971). *Law of Athens.* Oxford, UK: Clarendon.

Hathaway, S. R., & McKinley, J. C. (1951). *Minnesota Multiphasic Personality Inventory manual.* New York: Psychological Corporation.

Hawkes, Jacquetta. (1973). *The first great civilizations.* New York: Knopf.

Hawtrey, Sir Ralph. (1925). *The economic problem.* London: Longmans & Green.

Hayek, Friedrich R. von. (Ed.). (1954). *Capitalism and the historians.* Chicago: University of Chicago Press.

Heesterman, J. C. (1993). *The broken world of sacrifice.* Chicago: University of Chicago.

Heesterman, Jan C. (1987). Vedism and Brahmanism. In Mircea Eliade (Ed.), *The encyclopedia of religion* (Vol. 15, pp. 217-242). New York: Macmillan.

Heidel, Alexander. (1946). *The Gilgamesh epic and Old Testament parallels.* Chicago: University of Chicago Press.

Heilbroner, Robert L. (1985). *The nature and logic of capitalism.* New York, Norton.

Henke, P. G. (1990). Potentiation of inputs from the posterolateral amygdala to the dentate gyrus and resistance of stress ulcer formation in rats. *Physiology and Behavior, 47,* 659-664.

Hepburn, Alonzo B. (1903). *A history of coinage and currency in the United States.* New York: Macmillan.

Herrnstein, Richard J. (1990). Rational choice theory: Necessary but not sufficient. *American Psychologist, 45,* 356-367.

Herrnstein, Richard J., & Murray, Charles. (1994). *The bell curve.* New York: Free Press.

Hillel. (1918). Tract Shabbath. In *Babylonian Talmud* (Vol. 1). Boston: Talmud Society.

Hiltebeitel, Alf. (1987). Gambling. In Mircea Eliade (Ed.), *The encyclopedia of religion* (Vol. 5, pp. 468-474). New York: Macmillan.

Hoebel, E. A. (1954). *The law of primitive man.* Cambridge, MA: Harvard University Press.

Holm, Bill. (1990). *Coming home crazy.* Minneapolis, MN: Milkweed Editions.

Holzman, P. S. (1954). The relation of assimilation tendencies in visual, auditory, and kinesthetic time-error to cognitive attitudes of leveling and sharpening. *Journal of Personality, 22,* 375-394.

Horney, Karen. (1937). *The neurotic personality of our time.* New York: Norton.

Horney, Karen. (1967). *Feminine psychology.* New York: Norton.

Hsu, Francis. (1981). *Americans and Chinese: Passage to differences* (3rd ed.). Honolulu: University of Hawaii.

Hulsewe, A. F. P. (1955). *Remnants of Han law.* Leiden, The Netherlands: Brill.

Hulsewe, A. F. P. (1985). *Remnants of Ch'in law.* Leiden, The Netherlands: Brill.

Hultkrantz, Abe. (1987a). Ghost dance. In Mircea Eliade (Ed.), *The encyclopedia of religion* (Vol. 5, pp. 544-547). New York: Macmillan.

Hultkrantz, Abe. (1987b). North American religions. In Mircea Eliade (Ed.), *The encyclopedia of religion* (Vol. 10, pp. 526-535). New York: Macmillan.

Hume, R. E. (1931). *The thirteen principal Upanishads* (2nd ed.). London: Oxford University Press.

Humphrey, Caroline, & Hugh-Jones, Stephen. (1992). *Barter, exchange, and value: An anthropological approach.* Cambridge, UK: Cambridge University Press.

Humphrey, Nicolas. (1986). *The inner eye.* Boston: Faber and Faber.

Humphreys, Lloyd G. (1957). Characteristics of type concepts with special reference to Sheldon's typology. *Psychological Bulletin, 54,* 218-228.

Huntington, Samuel P. (1996). *The clash of civilizations.* New York: Touchstone (Simon & Schuster).

Iliffe, John. (1983). *The emergence of African capitalism.* Minneapolis: University of Minnesota Press.

Inglis, Fred. (1972). *The imagery of power: A critique of advertising.* London: Heinemann.

Jackson, Kevin. (1995). *The Oxford book of money.* Oxford, UK: Oxford University Press.

James, William. (1890). *Principles of psychology* (2 vols.). New York: Henry Holt.

James, William. (1961). *The varieties of religious experience.* New York: Collier-Macmillan. (Original work published 1902)

Jenner, W. J. F. (1992). *The tyranny of history.* London: Penguin.

Jensen, Arthur R. (1969). How much can we boost IQ and scholastic achievement? *Harvard Educational Review, 39,* 1-123.

Johns, C. H. W. (1914). *The relations between the laws of Babylonia and the laws of the Hebrew people.* London: Oxford University Press.

Johnson, Harold J. (Ed.). (1987). *The medieval tradition of the natural law.* Kalamazoo, MI: Medieval Institute.

Jones, William. (Trans.). (1994). *The great Qing code.* Oxford, UK: Clarendon.

Jost, Madeline. (1996). Hermes. In Simon Hornblower & Anthony Spewforth (Eds.), *Oxford classical dictionary* (3rd ed., pp. 690-691). Oxford, UK: Oxford University Press.

Jung, C. (1923). *Psychological types.* New York: Harcourt Brace.

Jung, Carl G. (1971). Psychological types. In Joseph Campbell (Ed.), *The portable Jung* (R. F. C. Hull, Trans.). New York: Viking. (Original work published 1923)

Jung, Carl G. (1971). Aion: Phenomenology of the self. In Joseph Campbell (Ed.), *The portable Jung* (R. F. C. Hull, Trans.). New York: Viking. (Original work published 1951)

Justinian. (1932). Novella. In *The civil law* (S. P. Scott, Trans.). New York: AMS Press. (Reprinted from an original in the Biddle Law Library, University of Pennsylvania)

Justinian. (1973). *Corpus juris civilis* [The civil law] (S. P. Scott, Trans.). New York: AMS Press.

Justinian. (1987). *Institutes* (Peter Birks & Grant McLeod, Trans.). Ithaca, NY: Cornell University Press.

Kagan, Jerome. (1994). *Galen's prophecy.* New York: Basic Books.

Kahneman, D., Knetch, J., & Thaler, R. (1986). Fairness as a constraint on profit seeking: Entitlements in the market. *American Economic Review, 76,* 728-741.

Kahneman, D., Slovic, P., & Tversky, A. (Eds.). (1982). *Judgment under uncertainty: Heuristics and biases.* Cambridge, UK: Cambridge University Press.

Kant, Immanuel. (1974). *Anthropology from a pragmatic point of view.* The Hague: Nijhoff. (Original work published 1798)

Katona, George. (1951). *Psychological analysis of economic behavior.* New York: McGraw-Hill.

Katona, George. (1964). *The mass consumption society.* New York: McGraw-Hill.

Katona, George. (1980). *Essays on behavioral economics.* Ann Arbor: Survey Research Center, University of Michigan.

Katz, Don. (1993, June). Men, women, and money. *Worth,* pp. 55-61.

Kaye, Yvonne. (1991). Credit, cash and co-dependency. Deerfield Beach, FL: Health Communications.

Kefir, N., & Corsini, R. J. (1974). Dispositional sets: A contribution to typology. *Journal of Individual Psychology, 30,* 163-178.

Keirsey, David, & Bates, Marilyn. (1984). *Please understand me: Character and temperament types.* Del Mar, CA: Prometheus Nemesis.

Keynes, John Maynard. (1936). *The general theory of employment, interest and money.* London: Macmillan.

Khan, Mehr Muhammad Nawaz. (1989). *Islamic and other economic systems.* Lahore, Pakistan: Islamic Book Service.

Kirchoff, Paul. (1946). The social and political organization of the Andean peoples. In Julian H. Steward (Ed.), *Handbook of South American Indians* (Vol. 5, pp. 293-311). Washington, DC: Smithsonian Institution.

Klein, Melanie. (1957). *Envy and gratitude.* New York: Basic Books.

Knox, John Jay. (1969). *A history of banking in the United States.* New York: Kelley.

Kochman, Thomas. (1981). *Black and white: Styles in conflict.* Chicago: University of Chicago Press.

Kohlberg, Lawrence. (1984). *The psychology of moral development.* San Francisco: Harper and Row.

Kohut, Heinz. (1987). *The Kohut seminars on self psychology and psychotherapy with adolescents and young adults* (Miriam Elson, Ed.). New York: Norton.

The Koran (N. J. Dawood, Trans.). (1993). London: Penguin.

Korchin, S. J. (1976). *Modern clinical psychology.* New York: Basic Books.

Kramer, Samuel Noah. (1956). *From the tablets of Sumer.* Indian Hills, CO: Falcon's Wing.

Kramer, Samuel Noah. (1959). *History begins at Sumer.* New York: Doubleday.

Kramer, Samuel Noah. (1963). *The Sumerians.* Chicago: University of Chicago Press.

Krech, D., Crutchfield, R. S., & Livson, N. (1974). *Elements of psychology.* (3rd ed.). New York: Knopf.

Kretschmer, Ernst. (1925). *Physique and character* (W. J. H. Spratt, Trans.). New York: Harcourt. (Original work published in German in 1921)

Kroeger, Otto, & Thuesen, Janet M. (1988). *Type talk: The sixteen personality types that determine how we live, love, and work.* New York: Dell.

Krueger, D. W. (1986). *Money: The last taboo.* New York: Brunner/Mazel.

Kuhn, T. (1962). *The structure of scientific revolutions.* Chicago: University of Chicago Press.

Lamb, Matthew L. (1992). Theology and money: Rationality, religion, and economics. *American Behavioral Scientist, 35*(6), 735-755. [Special issue: The Meanings of Money, Kenneth O. Doyle, Ed.]

Lambert, W. G. (Ed. and Trans.). (1960). *Babylonian wisdom literature.* New York: Oxford University Press.

Landes, David S. (1998). *The wealth and poverty of nations.* New York: Norton.

Langdon, Stephen Herbert. (1931). Epic of Gilgamesh. In *Mythology of all races: Vol. V. Semitic* (pp. 234-269). Boston: Archaeological Institute of America and Marshall Jones.

Lao Tzu. (1989). *The tao te ching* (Ellen M. Chen, Trans.). New York: Paragon House.

Lasche, Christopher. (1978). *The culture of narcissism.* New York: Norton.

Laum, Bernard. (1924). *Heiliges Geld.* Tubingen, Germany: J. C. B. Mohr.

Laum, Bernard. (1929). *Uber das Wesen des Munzgeldes.* Halle, Germany: A. Reichmann.

Lauterbach, A. T. (1954). *Man, motives, and money.* Ithaca, NY: Cornell University Press.

Lawler, E. E. (1971). *Pay and organizational effectiveness.* New York: McGraw-Hill.

Lawler, Edward E. (1990). *Strategic pay.* San Francisco: Jossey-Bass.

LeDoux, Joseph E. (1994, June). Emotions, memory, and the brain. *Scientific American,* pp. 50-57.

LeDoux, Joseph E. (1995). Emotion: Clues from the brain. *Annual Review of Psychology, 46,* 209-235.

Lee, Chin-Chuan. (1998). Power, self-censorship, and political transition in Hong Kong. *Harvard International Journal of Press/Politics, 3*(2), 53-73.

Lee, Chin-Chuan. (in press). *Money, power, and media: Communication patterns in cultural China.* Evanston, IL: Northwestern University Press.

Lee, Richard B., & DeVore, Irven. (1968). *Symposium on man the hunter.* Chicago, IL: University of Chicago Press.

Leibenstein, Harvey. (1976). *Beyond Economic man: A new foundation for microeconomics.* Cambridge, MA: Harvard University Press.

Leiss, William, Kline, Stephen, & Jhally, Sut. (1986). *Social communication in advertising.* Toronto: Methuen.

Levy, J., & Heller, W. (1992). Gender differentiation in human neuropsychological function. In A. Gerall, H. Moltz, & I. Ward, *Handbook of behavioral neurobiology: Vol. 11. Sexual differentiation* (pp. 245-274). New York: Plenum.

Lewin, Robert. (1989). *Human evolution: An illustrative introduction* (2nd ed.). Boston: Blackwell Scientific.

Lewis, Alan, Webley, Paul, & Furnham, Adrian. (1995). *The new economic mind: The social psychology of economic behavior.* New York: Harvester Wheatsheaf.

Lindgren, Henry Clay. (1980). *Great expectations: The psychology of money.* Los Altos, CA: William Kaufmann.

Lockhart, Russell A. (1983). Coins and psychological change. In John Beebe (Ed.), *Money, food, drink, and fashion and analytic training.* Fellbach, Germany: Bonz.

Loeb Classical Library. (1912-). *Greek and Latin authors.* Cambridge, MA: Harvard University Press.

Loevinger, Jane. (1976). *Ego development.* San Francisco: Jossey-Bass.

Lonergan, Bernard. (1958). *Insight.* New York: Philosophical Library.

Lonergan, Bernard. (1988). *Collection: Papers by B. Lonergan* (F. E. Crowe, Ed.). Toronto: University of Toronto Press.

Looft, W. R. (1971). The psychology of more. *American Psychologist, 26,* 561-565.

Lowie, Robert H. (1946a). Property among the tropical forest and marginal tribes. In Julian H. Steward (Ed.), *Handbook of South American Indians* (Vol. 1, pp. 351-367). Washington, DC: Smithsonian Institution.

Lowie, Robert H. (1946b). Social and political organization of the tropical forest and marginal tribes. In Julian H. Steward (Ed.), *Handbook of South American Indians* (Vol. 1, pp. 313-350). Washington, DC: Smithsonian Institution.

Luther, Martin. (1931). Long sermon on usury. In *Works of Martin Luther.* Philadelphia: Holman Co. and Castle. (Original work published 1519-1520)

Luther, Martin. (1931). Sermon on Trade and Usury. (1524). In *Works of Martin Luther.* Philadelphia: Holman Co. and Castle. (Original work published 1524)

Lykken, D. T., & Tellegen, A. (1996). Happiness is a stochastic phenomenon. *Psychological Science, 7,* 186-199.

Lykken, D. T., Bouchard, T. J., McGue, M., & Tellegen, A. (1993). Heritability of interests: A twin study. *Journal of Applied Psychology, 78*(4), 649-661.

Lykken, D. T., McGue, M., Tellegen, A., & Bouchard, T. J. (1992). Emergenesis: Genetic traits that may not run in families. *American Psychologist, 47,* 1565-1577.

MacArthur, R. H., & Wilson, E. O. (1967). *The theory of island biogeography.* Princeton, NJ: Princeton University Press.

Macdonnel, A. A. (1922). *Hymns from the Rigveda.* London: Oxford University Press.

Machiavelli, Niccolò. (1952). *The prince* (Luigi Ricci, Trans.). New York: New American Library.

MacIntyre, Alisdair. (1968). *Marxism and Christianity.* Notre Dame, IN: Notre Dame University Press.

MacIntyre, Alisdair. (1984). *After virtue: A study in moral theory* (2nd. ed.). Notre Dame, IN: Notre Dame University Press.

MacLean, P. D. (1990). *The triune brain in evolution: Role in paleocerebral functions.* New York: Plenum.

MacPherson, C. B. (1962). *The political theory of possessive individualism: Hobbes to Locke.* Oxford, UK: Oxford University Press.

Madanes, Cloe. (1994). *The secret meaning of money.* San Francisco: Jossey-Bass.

Maine, Henry S. (1931). *Ancient law.* London: Oxford University Press.

Maquet, Jacques. (1972). *Civilizations of black Africa* (J. Mayfield, Trans.). New York: Oxford University Press.

Marglin, Frederique Apffel. (1987). Yoni. In Mircea Eliade (Ed.), *The encyclopedia of religion* (Vol. 15, pp. 530-535). New York: Macmillan.

Marshall, Alfred. (1930). *Principles of economics* (8th ed., pp. 88-90). London: Macmillan.

Martin, H. H., & Martin, C. J. (1982). *Martin Operating Styles Inventory.* El Cajon, CA: Organization Improvement.

Marty, Martin. (1971). Lutheranism. *Encyclopedia Britannica* (Vol. 14, pp. 443-448). Chicago: William Benton.

Marx, Karl. (1964). The power of money in a bourgeois society. In *The economic and philosophic manuscripts of 1844.* New York: International Publishers. (Original work published 1844)

Maslow, Abraham. (1954). *Motivation and personality.* New York: Harper.

Mason, J. Alden. (1957). *The ancient civilizations of Peru* (Rev. ed.). New York: Penguin.

Mauss, Marcel. (1966). *The gift: Forms and functions of exchange in archaic societies* (I. Cunnison, Trans.). London: Cohen & West.

McAllester, David P. (1980). *Hogans: Navajo houses and house songs.* Middletown, CT: Wesleyan University Press.

McAllester, David P. (1987). Music and religion in the Americas. In Mircea Eliade (Ed.), *The encyclopedia of religion* (Vol. 10, pp. 178-182). New York: Macmillan.

McCaulley, M. H. (1981). Jung's theory of psychological types and the Myers-Briggs Type Indicator. In P. McReynolds (Ed.), *Advances in psychological assessment* (Vol. 5, pp. 294-352). San Francisco: Jossey-Bass.

McClelland, David C., Atkinson, John W., Clark, R. A., & Lowell, E. L. (1953). *The achievement motive.* New York: Appleton-Century-Crofts.

McClelland, David. (1961). *The achieving society.* Princeton, NJ: Van Nostrand.

McCracken, G. (1990). *Culture and consumption.* Indianapolis: Indiana University Press.

McNeill, William H. (1979). *A world history* (3rd ed.). New York: Oxford University Press.

Mead, George Herbert. (1934). *Mind, self, and society from the standpoint of a social behaviorist.* Chicago: University of Chicago Press.

Mead, Margaret. (1937). *Cooperation and competition among primitive peoples.* New York and London: McGraw-Hill.

Mellan, Olivia. (1994). *Money harmony.* New York: Walker.

Mencius. (1963). *The book of Mencius* (Wing-tsit Chan, Trans.). Princeton, NJ: Princeton University Press.

Merrill, D., & Reid, R. (1981). *Personal styles and effective performance.* Radnor, PA: Chilton.

Metraux, Alfred. (1946). Religion and shamanism. In Julian H. Steward (Ed.), *Handbook of South American Indians* (Vol. 5, pp. 559-599). Washington, DC: Smithsonian Institution.

Mikalson, John D. (1996). Hestia. In Simon Hornblower & Anthony Spewforth (Eds.), *Oxford classical dictionary* (3rd ed.). Oxford, UK: Oxford University Press.

Millman, Marcia. (1991). *Warm hearts and cold cash: The intimate dynamics of families and money.* New York: Free Press.

Mills, A. D., & Faure, J. M. (1991). Diversion selection for duration of chronic immobility and social reinstatement behavior in Japanese quail *(Coturnix japonica)* chicks. *Journal of Comparative Psychology, 105,* 25-38.

Mitchell, Wesley C. (1914). Human behavior and economics. *Quarterly Journal of Economics, 29,* 1.

Mithen, Steven. (1996). *The prehistory of the mind.* London: Thames and Hudson.

Money, J. (1978). Phylogeny and ontogeny in gender identity differentiation. In F. Brambilla, P. K. Bridges, E. Endroczi, & G. Heuser, *Perspectives in endocrine psychobiology* (pp. 467-478). New York: Wiley.

Money, J., & Erhardt, A. A. (1972). *Man and woman, boy and girl.* Baltimore: Johns Hopkins University Press.

Montagu, M. F. A. (1960). *An introduction to physical anthropology* (3rd ed.). Springfield, IL: Charles C Thomas.

Morris, C. (1942). *Paths of life.* New York: Harper.

Mo Tzu. (1963). *Basic writings* (Burton Watson, Trans.). New York: Columbia University Press.

Murray, H. A. (1936). Techniques for a systematic investigation of fantasy. *Journal of Psychology, 3,* 115-143.

Murray, H. A. (1938). *Explorations in personality.* Oxford, UK: Oxford University Press.

Murray, Henry A. (1940). What should psychologists do about psychoanalysis? *Journal of Abnormal Psychology, 35,* 150-175.

Murray, Henry A. (1956). *Thematic Apperception Test and manual.* New York: Psychological Corporation.

Mussen, Paul, & Rosenzweig, Mark. (1973). *Psychology.* Lexington, MA: D. C. Heath.

Myers, Irene B. (1980). *Gifts differing.* Palo Alto, CA: Consulting Psychologists Press.

Myers, Irene B., & McCaulley, M. H. (1988). *Manual: A guide to the development and use of the Myers-Briggs Type Indicator.* Palo Alto, CA: Consulting Psychologists Press.

Naisbitt, John. (1996). *Megatrends Asia.* New York: Touchstone.

Nance, Wayne E., & Charlesworth, Edmund A. (1993). *Mind over money.* Nashville, TN: Nelson.

Naofusa, Hirai. (1987). Shinto. In Mircea Eliade (Ed.), *The encyclopedia of religion* (Vol. 13, pp. 280-294). New York: Macmillan.

Needham, Joseph. (1962). *Science and civilization in China.* New York: Cambridge University Press.

Needleman, Jacob. (1991). *Money and the meaning of life.* New York: Doubleday.

The New English Bible. (1970). Oxford and Cambridge, UK: Oxford University Press and Cambridge University Press.

Neusner, Jacob. (1988). *The way of the Torah.* Englewood Cliffs, NJ: Prentice Hall.

Nicene and post-Nicene fathers (American Ed., two series, 10 vols. each). (1886-1901). New York: Christian Literature.

Nietzsche, F. (1989). *Beyond good and evil* (W. Kaufmann, Trans.). New York: Random House. (Original work published 1886)

Nietzsche, F. (1974). *Genealogy of morals and peoples and countries.* New York: Gordon. (Original work published 1887)

Newman, Katherine S. (1983). *Law and economic organization.* New York: Cambridge University Press.

Noelle-Neumann, Elizabeth. (1984). *The spiral of silence.* Chicago: University of Chicago Press.

O'Guinn, T. C., & Faber, R. J. (1989). Compulsive buying: A phenomenological exploration. *Journal of Consumer Research, 16,* 147-157.

O'Guinn, T., & Wells, W. (1989). Subjective discretionary income. *Marketing Research, 1,* 32-41.

Olson, David H. (1986). Circumplex model VII: Validation studies and FACES III. *Family Process, 25,* 337-351.

Olson, David H. (1991). Three-dimensional (3-D) circumplex model and revised scoring of FACES III. *Family Process, 30*(1), 74-79.

Olson, E. B., & Morgan, W. P. (1982). Rat brain monoamine levels related to behavioral assessment. *Life Sciences, 30,* 2095-2100.

Opsahl, R. L., & Dunnette, M. D. (1966). The role of financial compensation in industrial motivation. *Psychological Bulletin, 66,* 94-118.

Packard, Vance. (1957). *The hidden persuaders.* New York: McKay.

Palmer, Vernon W. (1970). *The Roman Dutch and Sesotho law of delict.* Leiden: A. W. Sijthoff.

Pan, Ku. (1950). *Food and money in ancient China.* Princeton, NJ: Princeton University Press.

Parrinder, Geoffrey. (Ed.). (1971). *World religions.* New York: Facts on File.

Parrinder, Geoffrey. (Ed.). (1983). *World religions: From ancient history to the present.* New York: Newnes.

Parry, Jonathan, & Bloch, Maurice. (1989). *Money and the morality of exchange.* Cambridge, UK: Cambridge University Press.

Parsons, T., & Smelser, N. J. (1956). *Economy and society.* New York: Free Press.

Patrologiae cursus completus . . . series latina (J. P. Migne, Ed.). (1844). Paris: Garnier.

Peck, M. Scott. (1978). *The road less traveled.* New York: Simon & Schuster.

Penwill, D. J. (1951). *Kamba customary law.* Kampala, Kenya: East Africa Literature Bureau.

Peterson, Peter G. (1993). *Facing up: How to rescue the economy from crushing debt and restore the American dream.* New York: Simon & Schuster.

Peterson, Peter G. (1996). *Will America grow up before it grows old?* New York: Random House.

Pharr, Clyde. (1952). *The Theodosian code.* Princeton, NJ: Princeton University Press.

Piaget, Jean. (1952). *The origins of intelligence in children.* New York: International Universities Press.

Piergiovanni, Vito. (1993). *The growth of the bank.* Berlin: Duncker and Humblot.

Plato. (1941). *Republic* (Francis M. Cornfeld, Trans.). London: Oxford University Press.

Plato. (1942). *Apology* (B. Jowett, Trans.). Princeton, NJ: Van Nostrand.

Poduska, Bernard. (1985). Financial counseling using principles of Adlerian psychology. *Journal of Individual Psychology, 41*(2), 136-146.

Poduska, Bernard. (1993). *For love and money.* Pacific Grove, CA: Brooks/Cole.

Polanyi, Karl. (1957). The economy as an instituted process. In Karl Polanyi, Conrad M. Arenberg, & Harry W. Pearson (Eds.), *Trade and market in the early empires* (pp. 264-266). Glencoe, IL: Free Press.

Popper, K. (1972). *Objective knowledge: An evolutionary approach.* Oxford, UK: Oxford University Press.

Porteus, John. (1969). *Coins in history.* London: Weidenfeld & Nicholson.

Powell, Luther P. (1962). *Money and the Church.* New York: National Board of the YMCA.

Powers, William K. (1987). Native American religious dramas. In Mircea Eliade (Ed.), *The encyclopedia of religion* (Vol. 4, pp. 465-467). New York: Macmillan.

Prelec, Drazen, & Herrnstein, Richard J. (1991). In R. J. Zeckhauser (Ed.), *Strategy and choice.* Cambridge, MA: MIT Press.

Prelinger, Ernst. (1955). Extensions and structure of the self. *Journal of Psychology, 47,* 13-23.

Pythagoras. (1732). *Golden verses* (Nickolas Rowe, Trans.). London: Printed for J. Tonson, and sold by W. Feales.

Quiggin, Alison H. (1949). *A survey of primitive money.* London: Methuen.

Rachlin, Howard, & Laibson, David I. (Eds.). (1997). *The matching law: [Herrnstein's] papers in psychology and economics.* New York and Cambridge, MA: Russell Sage Foundation and Harvard University Press.

Radhakrishnan, S. (Ed. and Trans.). (1957). The Bhagavadgita. In S. Radhakrishnan & C. A. Moore, *The Bhagavadgita* (pp. 101-163). New York: Harper and Bros. (Original work published 1948)

Radhakrishnan, Sarvepalli, & Moore, Charles A. (1957). *A source book in Indian philosophy,.* Princeton, NJ: Princeton University Press.

Ramsay, William. (1967). Catalina L. Sergius. In William Smith (Ed.), *Dictionary of Greek and Roman biography and mythology* (Vol. 1). New York: AMS Press.

Rand, Ayn. (1963). *The fountainhead.* New York: New American Library. (Original work published 1943)

Rand, Ayn. (1957). *Atlas shrugged.* New York: Random House.

Rand, Ayn. (1966). *Capitalism.* New York: New American Library (Signet).

Rapoport, A. (1969). *House form and culture.* Englewood Cliffs, NJ: Prentice Hall.

Ratchford, B. T. (1987, August/September). New insights about the FCB grid. *Journal of Advertising Research,* pp. 24-38.

Rattray, R. S. (1929). *Ashanti law and constitution.* Oxford, UK: Clarendon.

Reinach, Solomon. (1930). *Orpheus: A history of religions* (Florence Simmonds, Trans.). New York: Horace Liveright.

Reinisch, J., & Sanders, S. (1992). Prenatal hormonal contributions to sex differences in human cognitive and personality development. In A. Gerall, H. Moltz, & I. Ward, *Handbook of behavioral neurobiology: Vol. 11. Sexual differentiation* (pp. 221-243). New York: Plenum.

Reinisch, June Machover, Rosenblum, Leonard A., & Sanders, Stephanie A. (1987). *Masculinity/femininity.* New York: Oxford University Press.

Reynolds, Vernon. (1980). *The biology of human action* (2nd ed.). San Francisco: Freeman.

Ritterhausen, Konrad. (1840). *Expositio methodica novellarum imperatoris Justiniani.* Florence: Apud Josephum Celli.

Roback, Abraham. (1931). *The psychology of character* (2nd ed.). New York: Harcourt Brace.

Roche, David. (1987). Music and religion in India. In Mircea Eliade (Ed.), *The encyclopedia of religion* (Vol. 10, pp. 185-191). New York: Macmillan.

Rolfe, Frederick. (1950). *Hadrian VII.* London: Chatto and Windus. (pseud. Frederick Baron Corvo)

Rosenblatt, Paul C., Walsh, Patricia R., & Jackson, Douglas A. (1976). *Grief and mourning in cross-cultural perspective.* New Haven, CT: Human Relations Area Files.

Rostan, L. (1824). *Cours elementaire d'hygiene* (2nd ed.). Paris: Bechnet Jeune.

Rubinow, D. R., & Schmidt, P. J. (1996). Androgen, brain, and behavior. *American Journal of Psychiatry, 153*(8), 974-984.

Rundquist, E. A., & Sletto, R. F. (1936). *Personality in the Depression.* Minneapolis: University of Minnesota Press.

Rupp, Ernest Gordon. (1971). Luther, Martin. In *Encyclopedia Britannica* (Vol. 14, pp. 436-443). Chicago: William Benton.

Rusbult, Caryl, Johnson, Dennis J., & Morrow, Gregory D. (1986). Determinants and consequences of exit, voice, loyalty, and neglect: Responses to dissatisfaction in adult romantic involvements. *Human Relations, 39*(1), 45-63.

Rushton, J. P., Fulker, D. W., Neale, M. C., Nias, D. K. B., & Eysenck, H. J. (1986). Altruism and aggression: To what extent are individual differences inherited? *Journal of Personality and Social Psychology, 50,* 1192-1198.

Rushton, J. Philippe. (1995). *Race, evolution, and behavior.* New Brunswick, NJ: Transaction Publishing.

Rustow, Alexander. (1980). *Freedom and domination.* Princeton, NJ: Princeton University Press.

Ryan, Columba. (1965). The traditional concept of the natural law: An interpretation. In Illtud Evans (Ed.), *Light on the natural law.* Baltimore: Halicon.

Sahlins, Marshall. (1972). *Stone Age economics.* New York: Aldine.

Salovey, Peter. (1991). *The psychology of jealousy and envy.* New York: Guilford.

Sanford, R. N. (1937). The effects of abstinence from food upon imaginal processes: A preliminary experiment. *Journal of Psychology, 2,* 129-136.

Sarbah, J. M. (1904). *Fanti customary laws* (2nd ed.). London: Clowes.

Scarre, Chris. (Ed.). (1993). *Timelines of the ancient world.* Washington, DC: Smithsonian Institution.

Schachter, S., & Singer, J. E. (1962). Cognitive, social, and physiological determinants of emotional state. *Psychological Review, 69,* 377-399.

Schmidt, T. E. (1987). *Hostility to wealth in the synoptic gospels.* Sheffield, UK: Sheffield Academic Press.

Schopenhauer, A. (1974). *On the fourfold root of the principle of sufficient reason* (E. F. J. Payne, Trans.). LaSalle, IL: Open Court.

Schumpeter, Joseph A. (1951). *Imperialism and social classes* (Heinz Norden, Trans., & Paul M. Sweezy, Ed.). New York: Augustus Kelley.

Schumpeter, Joseph A. (1962). *Capitalism, socialism and democracy.* New York: Harper and Row. (Original work published 1942)

Schumpeter, Joseph A. (1994). *History of economic analysis* (8th ed.). New York: Oxford University Press. (Original work published 1954)

Schwartz, B. (1967). The social psychology of the gift. *American Journal of Sociology, 73*(1), 1-11.

Scitovsky, Tibor. (1976). *The joyless economy.* New York: Oxford University Press.

Scitovsky, Tibor. (1986). How to bring joy into economics. In Tibor Scitovsky, *Human desire and economic satisfaction* (pp. 183-203). New York: New York University Press.

Scitovsky, Tibor. (1992). *The joyless economy: The psychology of human satisfaction* (Rev. ed.). New York: Oxford University Press.

Shah, D. V., Domke, D., & Wackman, D. B. (1996). To thine own self be true. *Communication Research, 23*(5), 509-560.

Sheldon, William H. (1942). *Varieties of temperament.* New York: Harper.

Sheldon, William H. (1954). *Atlas of men: A guide for somatotyping the adult male at all ages.* New York: Harper.

Shell, Marc. (1982). *Money, language, and thought.* Berkeley: University of California Press.

Shelmerdine, Susan G. (1995). *The Homeric hymns.* Newburyport, MA: Focus Information Group.

Short, R. V., & Balaban, E. (1994). *The differences between the sexes.* Cambridge, UK: Cambridge University Press.

Siegel, R. E. (1968). *Galen's system of physiology and medicine.* Farmington, CT: Karger.

Simmel, Georg. (1971). *On individuality and social forms* (Donald N. Levine, Ed.). Chicago: University of Chicago Press.

Simmel, Georg. (1978). *The philosophy of money* (Tom Bottomore & David Frisby, Trans.). London: Routledge & Kegan Paul. (Original work published 1900)

Simpson, W. K. (1972). *Literature of ancient Egypt.* New Haven, CT: Yale University Press.

Sizemore, Russell F., & Swearer, Donald K. (1990). *Ethics, wealth, and salvation.* Columbia: South Carolina University Press.

Sloan, W. David, & Stovall, James G. (1993). *The media in America: A history* (2nd ed.). Scottsdale, AZ: Publishing Horizons.

Sloane, Ethel. (1993). *Biology of women* (3rd ed.). Albany, NY: Delmar.

Smith, Adam. (1976). *Theory of moral sentiments.* Oxford, UK: Clarendon. (Original work published 1753)

Smith, Adam. (1953). *An inquiry into the nature and causes of the wealth of nations.* Chicago: Henry Regnery. (Original work published 1776)

Smith, Huston. (1958). *The religions of man.* New York: Harper and Row.

Smith, J. Powis. (1931). *The origin and history of Hebrew law.* Chicago: University of Chicago Press.

Sohm, Rudolph. (1907). *The institutes: A textbook of the history and system of Roman private law* (3rd ed.). Oxford, UK: Clarendon.

Spengler, Joseph J. (1980). *Origins of economic thought and justice.* Carbondale: Southern Illinois University Press.

Steele, Francis. (1948). The Code of Lipit-Ishtar. *American Journal of Archaeology, 52*(3), 425-450.

Steinbeck, John. (1939). *The grapes of wrath.* New York: Viking.

Steward, Julian H. (1949). South American cultures: An interpretative summary. In Julian H. Steward (Ed.), *The comparative ethnology of South American Indians* (Vol. 5, Bulletin 143, pp. 669-772). Washington, DC: Smithsonian Bureau of American Ethnology.

Stewart, Alexander. (1887). *On temperaments.* London: Crosby Lockwood.

Stringer, C. B., & Andrews, P. (1988). Genetic and fossil evidence for the origin of modern humans. *Science, 239,* 1263-1268.

Stumpf, Samuel E. (1971). *Philosophy.* New York: McGraw-Hill.

Sullivan, Harry Stack. (1953). *The interpersonal theory of psychiatry.* New York: Norton.

Summa Theologica. (1964). New York: McGraw-Hill.

Syntopicon. (1990). Wealth. In *Great books of the Western world* (2nd ed., pp. 1038-1070). Chicago: Encyclopedia Britannica.

Tannen, Deborah. (1989). *Talking voices: Repetition, dialogue and imagery in conversational discourse.* Cambridge, UK: Cambridge University Press.

Tannen, Deborah. (1990). *You just don't understand.* New York: Ballantine.

Tawney, R. H. (1920). *The acquisitive society.* New York: Harcourt Brace.

Tawney, R. H. (1926). *Religion and the rise of capitalism.* New York: Harcourt Brace.

Taxay, Don. (1970). *Money of the American Indians.* Flushing, NY: Nummus.

Teilhard de Chardin, Pierre. (1959). *The phenomenon of man.* London: Collins.

Teilhard de Chardin, Pierre. (1964). *The future of man.* New York: Harper and Row.

Tellegen, A. (1982). *Brief manual for the Multidimensional Personality Questionnaire.* Unpublished document, University of Minnesota, Department of Psychology.

Tellegen, A. (1985). Structures of mood and personality and their relevance to assessing anxiety, with an emphasis on self-report. In A. H. Tuma & J. D. Maser (Eds.), *Anxiety and the anxiety disorder.* Hillsdale, NJ: Lawrence Erlbaum.

Tellegen, Auke, Lykken, David T., Bouchard, Thomas J., Jr., Wilcox, Kimberly J., Segal, Nancy L., & Rich, Stephen. (1988). Personality similarity in twins reared apart and together. *Journal of Personality and Social Psychology, 54*(6), 1031-1039.

Thierry, Henk. (1984). Systems of remuneration. In P. J. D. Drenth, H. Thierry, P. J. Willems, & C. J. de Wolfe (Eds.), *Handbook of work and organizational psychology.* Chichester, UK: Wiley.

Thierry, Henk. (1992). Payment: Which meanings are rewarding? *American Behavioral Scientist, 35*(6), 694-707. [Special issue: The Meanings of Money, Kenneth O. Doyle, Ed.]

Thomas, Alexander, & Chess, Stella. (1977). *Temperament and development*. New York: Brunner/Mazel.

Thompson, J. A. K. (1955). *Aristotle: Ethics*. Harmondsworth, UK: Penguin.

Thompson, Patricia J. (1992). *Bringing feminism home*. Charlottetown: Home Economics Publishing Collective, University of Prince Edward Island.

Thorlief, Boman. (1960). *Hebrew thought compared with Greek*. Philadelphia: Westminster.

Thurstone, L. L. (1934). Vectors of the mind. *Psychological Review, 41*, 1-32.

Ure, Percy N. (1951). *Justinian and his times*. Baltimore: Penguin.

van Arsdale, M. (1982). *A guide to family financial counseling*. Homewood, IL: Dow Jones-Irwin.

van den Haag, Ernest. (Ed.). (1979). *Capitalism: Sources of hostility*. New Rochelle, NY: Epoch Books for the Heritage Foundation.

Veblen, Thorstein. (1976). The preconceptions of the classical economists. In Max Lerner (Ed.), *The portable Veblen*. New York: Viking. (Original work published in *The place of science in modern civilization*, 1896)

Veblen, Thorstein. (1976). *Theory of the leisure class*. New York: Macmillan. (Original work published 1899)

Vigilant, L., Stoneking, M., Harpending, H., Hawkes, K., & Wilson, A. C. (1991). African populations and the evolution of human mitochondrial DNA. *Science, 253*, 1503-1507.

Viola, G. (1909). *Le legge de correlazione morfologia dei tippi individuali*. Padua, Italy: Prosperini.

Waldmar, Carl. (1994). *Word dance: The language of Native American culture*. New York: Facts on File.

Walker, Barbara G. (1983). *Women's encyclopedia of myths and secrets*. San Francisco: Harper and Row.

Walker, James R. (1917). *The sun dance and other ceremonies of the Oglala division of the Teton Dakota*. New York: Trustees of the American Museum of Natural History.

Walker, James R. (1982). *Lakota society/James R. Walker*. Lincoln: University of Nebraska Press, Oglala Social Customs in Lakota Society.

Walzer, Michael. (1983). *Spheres of justice*. New York: Basic Books.

Wapner Seymour, & Demick, Jack. (1991). *Field dependence-independence: Cognitive style across the life span*. Hillsdale, NJ: Lawrence Erlbaum.

Ward, C. Osborne. (1888). *The ancient lowly: A history of the ancient working people from the earliest known period to the adoption of Christianity by Constantine* (8th ed.). Chicago: Charles H. Kerr.

Weatherford, Jack C. (1997). *The history of money*. New York: Crown.

Weber, Max. (1964). *The sociology of religion* (Ephraim Fishoff, Trans.). Boston: Beacon.

Weber, Max. (1976). *The Protestant ethic and the spirit of capitalism* (T. Parsons, Trans., 2nd ed.). New York: Scribner. (Original work published 1934)

Weber, Max. (1978). *Economy and society*. Berkeley: University of California Press. (Original work published 1922)

Weinstein, Grace. (1986). *Men, women and money*. Chicago: New American Library.

Wells, William, & Prensky, David. (1996). *Consumer behavior*. New York: Wiley.

Wells, William D. (1995). *Recent developments in interactive advertising*. Presented at the Marketing Technologies Symposium, University of Illinois, Urbana-Champaign.

Wernimont, P. F., & Fitzpatrick, S. (1972). The meaning of money. *Journal of Applied Psychology, 56*, 218-226.

West, Morris. (1964). *Shoes of the fisherman*. New York: Dell.

White, R. W. (1960). Competence and the psychosexual stages of development. In M. R. Jones (Ed.), *Nebraska Symposium on Motivation*. Lincoln: University of Nebraska Press.

Whitling, Beatrice B. (Ed.). (1967). *Six cultures: Studies of child rearing.* New York: Wiley.

Wilkins, A. S. (Ed.). (1961). *Orations of Cicero against Catilina.* London: Macmillan.

Williams, B. A. (1988). Reinforcement, choice, and response strength. In R. C. Atkinson, R. J. Herrnstein, G. Lindzey, & R. D. Luce (Eds.), *Steven's handbook of experimental psychology* (Vol. 2, pp. 167-244). New York: Wiley.

Williams, James. (1893). The institutes of Justinian illustrated in English. (2nd ed.). London: s.n.

Williams, Jonathan. (1998). *Money: A history.* New York: St. Martin's.

Williams, Xandria. (1996). *The four temperaments: How to achieve love, health, and happiness by understanding yourself and the people around you.* New York: St. Martin's.

Willis, Roy. (Ed.). (1993). *World mythology.* New York: Henry Holt.

Wilson Learning Corporation. (1984). *Counsellor selling.* Eden Prairie, MN: Author.

Wilson, A. C., & Cann, R. L. (1992). The recent African genesis of humans. *Scientific American, 266,* 68-73.

Wilson, Edward O. (1992). *The diversity of life.* Cambridge, MA: Harvard University Press.

Wilson, Edward O. (1998). *Consilience: The unity of knowledge.* New York: Knopf.

Winson, Jonathan. (1985). *Brain and psyche: The biology of the unconscious.* Garden City, NY: Anchor/Doubleday.

Winterbottom, Marian R. (1958). The relation of need for achievement to learning experiences in independence and mastery. In J. W. Atkinson (Ed.), *Motives in fantasy, action, and society* (pp. 453-478). Princeton, NJ: Van Nostrand.

Wiseman, Thomas. (1974). *The money motive.* London: Hutchinson.

Witkin, H. A., Dyk, R. B., Faterson, H. F., Goodenough, D. R., & Karp, S. A. (1962). *Psychological differentiation.* New York: Wiley.

Wittgenstein, Ludwig. (1953). *Philosophical investigations* (G. E. M. Anscombe, Trans.). London: Oxford University Press.

Worth, S., & Adair, J. (1972). *Through Navajo eyes.* Bloomington: Indiana University Press.

Wright, G. Ernest. (Ed.). (1965). *The Bible and the ancient Near East.* New York: Anchor.

Wuthnow, Robert. (1989). *Communities of discourse: Ideology and social structure in the Reformation, the Enlightenment, and European socialism.* Cambridge, MA: Harvard University Press.

Wuthnow, Robert. (1994). *God and mammon in America.* New York: Free Press.

Yamauchi, K., & Templer, D. (1982). The development of a money attitude scale. *Journal of Personality and Assessment, 46,* 522-528.

Yaron, Reuven. (1969). *The laws of Eshnunna.* Jerusalem: Hebrew University Press.

Zahan, Dominique. (1987). West African religions. In Mircea Eliade (Ed.), *The encyclopedia of religion* (Vol. 15, pp. 371-377). New York: Macmillan.

Zeckhauser, R. J. (Ed.). (1991). *Strategy and choice.* Cambridge, MA: MIT Press.

Zelizer, Viviana. (1989). The social meaning of money: Special monies. *American Journal of Sociology, 95,* 342-377.

Zelizer, Viviana A. (1994). *The social meaning of money.* New York: Basic Books.

Zuckerman, Marvin. (1994). An alternative five-factor model for personality. In Charles F. Halverson, Jr., Geldolph A. Kohnstamm, & Roy Martin (Eds.), *The developing structure of temperament and personality from infancy to adulthood* (pp. 53-68). Hillsdale, NJ: Lawrence Erlbaum.

Appendix

Good Books on the Social Meanings
of Money and Property

This appendix presents an annotated list of interesting books not cited in the body of the present work. Each includes substantial sections on psychology and money, some considerably more penetrating than others. This is not intended to be a comprehensive review—my apologies to anyone whose good work I neglect. It's worth mentioning the obvious, that the older the book, the less likely its financial advice may be useful (or legal) today.

Goldberg, Herb, and Lewis, Robert T. (1978). *Money madness*. New York: Morrow.
   Popular essays on how the ways people use money leads to stress in many parts of their lives. The authors propose that money can mean power, affection, control, or freedom, and they propose various forms of "madness" under each meaning.

Lindgren, Henry Clay. (1980). *Great expectations: The psychology of money.* Los Altos, CA: William Kaufmann.
   Professor Lindgren presents an early survey of psychological thought about the place of money in American society and the social meaning it carries. His discussion ranges from classical origins to contemporary attitudes about wealth and poverty.

Krueger, David W. (Ed.). (1986). *The last taboo.* New York: Brunner/Mazel.
   This is a thoughtful collection of psychoanalytic essays on money and, especially, on the place of money is psychotherapy. Seven or eight of the 24 chapters are of interest to the general reader.

Berg, Adriane. (1988). *How to stop fighting about money and make some.* New York: Avon.
   A lawyer with a clear interest in depth psychology and a lot of practical experience working with families gives sound legal advice in the context of personal motivation and interpersonal conflict.

Weinstein, Grace. (1986). *Men, women and money.* Chicago: New American Library.

One of the earliest, and still one of the best, semipopular books on the subject of money and property in male-female relationships. The authors wrap commonsense financial advice in streetwise psychology.

Gurney, Kathleen. (1988). *Your money personality.* New York: Doubleday.

Through statistical analysis of questionnaire data, Dr. Gurney identifies nine "money personalities," describes them in detail, and shows how to maximize their strengths and minimize their weaknesses for the purpose of becoming "a winner in the money game."

Felton-Collins, Victoria. (1990). *Couples and money.* New York: Bantam.

Both a psychologist and a financial planner, Dr. Felton-Collins uses the quaternary—"Drivers," "Relaters," "Freewheelers," and "Hedgers"—as the basis for identifying money motives and messages. With particular attention to the influence of past experiences on male-female relationships, she writes lightly but with insight about how couples can understand each other better and form a partnership with regard to both money and love.

Kaye, Yvonne. (1991). *Credit, cash and co-dependency.* Deerfield Beach, FL: Health Communications.

A psychotherapist who specializes in codependency offers sound advice, accessibly presented, about serious financial problems associated with that disorder, with special emphasis on money as anesthetic and money as escape.

Needleman, Jacob. (1991). *Money and the meaning of life.* New York: Doubleday.

This philosophy professor's curious—and important—thesis is that money is not as important to us as it should be! His point is that if we were to pay more real attention to its meaning, money could provide a means for revitalizing the soul through increased self-knowledge.

Millman, Marcia. (1991). *Warm hearts and cold cash: The intimate dynamics of families and money.* New York: Free Press.

In this collection of particularly thoughtful essays on the social-psychological dynamics of money in family relationships, Professor Millman examines how people bring the principles and practices of the marketplace into their relationships. Through engaging case studies, she shows "how much of our emotional capital is tied up in accounts with parents, children, spouses, and siblings."

Dominguez, Joe, and Robin, Vicki. (1992). *Your money or your life.* New York: Penguin.

This book is a rare combination of sound financial advice and inspiration for the simple life. The focus of its psychology is the reassessment of what really constitutes happiness; the focus of its financial advice is life simplification.

Both authors left high-stress careers to found the New Road Map Foundation (Seattle).

Nance, Wayne E., and Charlesworth, Edmund A. (1993). *Mind over money.* Nashville, TN: Nelson.

A registered investment adviser (Nance) and clinical psychologist (Charlesworth) join forces to produce a book that concentrates on standard financial topics, with chapters alerting us to a variety of "dysfunctions" that can steal our peace of mind as well as interfere with our planning.

Mellan, Olivia. (1994). *Money harmony.* New York: Walker.

A psychotherapist and business consultant, Ms. Mellan offers a practical guide to resolving financial conflicts. She describes and explains nine "money types," showing the strengths and weaknesses of each. Following a useful discussion of men versus women with regard to money meanings, she presents structured exercises that couples can follow toward conflict resolution and the enhancement of intimacy.

Forward, Susan, and Buck, Craig. (1994). *Money demons.* New York: Bantam.

Sensible counsel in popular form, some of it very insightful. This book is aimed at women but useful for people of either sex who are struggling with gambling and other efforts at sabotaging oneself and one's relationships.

Madanes, Cloe. (1994). *The secret meaning of money.* San Francisco: Jossey-Bass.

Codirector of the Family Therapy Institute in Washington, Dr. Madanes shows how the meanings of money crop up in all areas and at all stages of family life, and she illustrates standard family therapy approaches to the solution of problems and the improvement of relationships. Easy reading, with much wisdom.

Carlson, Richard. (1997). *Don't worry, make money.* New York: Hyperion.

Author of *Don't sweat the small stuff,* Dr. Carlson offers a potpourri of a hundred modest ideas for improving your financial condition that center in worrying less and building better personal and business relationships.

Buchan, James. (1997). *Frozen desire: The meaning of money.* New York: Farrar Straus Giroux.

A journalist and novelist, Mr. Buchan converts an enormous investment in reading and personal experience into a true "psychology of money," the thesis of which is that the function of money, because it symbolizes different things to different people, is to elicit and communicate "incarnate desire." He supports his thesis with a series of critical studies of people and events down the ages and around the world, and representative of what he calls the Age of Money. (For a preview, see *Granta, 49,* Fall 1994, 91-102.)

Name Index

271

Subject Index

Acquisitiveness 22-24, 116-17
  European archetype, 22
  run amok, 214
Adultery, as homicide, 235
  money as, 5
  as theft, 69
Affiliativeness, 32-34, 116-17, 130
  American Indian archetype, 32
  run amok, 214
African Customary Law, 67ff
  emphasis on dignity, 70
  vs. Chinese, 74, 117
Alimony:
  in Mesopotamian law, 54
Almsgiving:
  in Augustine, 107
  in Buddhism, 84
  in Calvin, 112
  in Islam, 84
  Weber's paradox, 84
American Indian customary law, 71ff
  emphasis on harmony, 72
  vs. European, 71
Amiable Type, illustration of, 199-200
Amiable/Driver dimension, 139-40
  as "Level II" factor, 147
  in Needham data, 143
  neurophysiological support for, 139-40
  proposed neural substrate for, 139
  psychoanalytic support for, 162
  psychometric support for, 141-43.
    See also Affiliativeness/Acquisitiveness;
    Amiable Type; Driver Type
Amputation, money as substitute for, 54
Amygdala, 189-190
Anality, and hoarding, 12

Analytic type, illustration of, 196-97
Analytic/Expressive Dimension, as "Level II
  factor," 147
  in Needham data, 143
  neurophysiological support for, 138-39
  proposed neural substrate for, 138
  psychoanalytic support for, 158-59, 161-
  62
  psychometric support for, 147. *See also*
    Analytic Type, Expressive Type,
    Concentration/Expansiveness
Androgen, 128-29, 238
  effects on psychological experience, 128
  and tough-/ tendermindedness, 128
Anima. *See* Animus/Anima
Animus/Anima, 130-32. *See also*
  Tough-/Tendermindedness
Anthropologie (Kant), 126
Apollo. *See* Apollo/Dionysius
Apollo/Dionysius, 27, 228
  in Benedict, 33
  compared to Shiva/Vishnu, 33, 228
Appetite, "Irascible" vs. "Concupiscient"
  (Aquinas), 108. *See also* Dialectics
Archetypal values, 21
Ascending brain connections, 175
Astrologers, medieval, 126
Attitudes, biological basis of, xi
"Autobiographies," 191

"Badge of Efficiency," property as (Veblen),
  11
Badges of competence, 6
Bank, 3
Barter, 225

About the Author

Kenneth O. Doyle studied the classical curriculum at Salvatorian Seminary (St. Nazianz, Wisconsin), Salvatorian Novitiate (Colfax, Iowa) and Mount St. Paul College (Waukesha, Wisconsin); philosophy at the Pontifical Gregorian University (Rome) and Marquette University (Milwaukee); and psychology at the University of Minnesota (Twin Cities), where he is Associate Professor in the School of Journalism and Mass Communication and Codirector of the Mass Communication Research Division. For twelve years he was a practicing financial planner and investment adviser representative, with licenses in general securities, life and health insurance, and real estate. He is editor of *The Meanings of Money* (Sage, 1992) and author of *Wealth Accumulation and Management* and a variety of other books and articles. His web address is www.KenDoyle.umn.edu